The Poetry of SEAMUS HEANEY

A CRITICAL STUDY

NEIL CORCORAN

ff

faber and faber

For my mother, Angela Corcoran

First published in 1998
by Faber and Faber Limited
3 Queen Square London WC1N 3AU

Photoset by Wilmaset, Birkenhead, Merseyside
Printed in England by CPI Antony Rowe, Chippenham, Wiltshire

A CIP record for this book
is available from the British Library

ISBN 0-571-17747-6

Contents

Preface

The original edition of this book, published in 1986, has stayed in print over the years and has started to look a little dusty, finishing, as it does, with *Station Island* (1984). I am glad to have had the opportunity to bring it up to date by discussing the later volumes and the critical prose, and also by taking stock in footnotes of significant responses to Heaney in the intervening period, including some to what I said myself in the first edition. In addition to these expansions, I have revised the earlier chapters extensively, sometimes only stylistically, but elsewhere more substantively too. Occasionally, I find an original reading redundant or wrongly focused (an extended critique of 'A Lough Neagh Sequence', for instance) and I jettison it; more usually I find some readings insufficiently detailed, and I add to them (the discussion of 'Broagh' in the chapter on *Wintering Out*, for instance, the bog poems of *North*, and 'Triptych' and 'The Strand at Lough Beg' in *Field Work*). The book was originally published as part of a series whose remit included an introductory biographical chapter. At the time, it would have been extremely difficult to have made such a chapter out of the available data on Heaney's life; so I solicited his help and eventually wrote the chapter using, and directly quoting, material acquired during a weekend of interviews with him in Dublin in 1985. This has been much cited in subsequent critical discussion; and I therefore reprint it, with minor revisions and additions, as an appendix to this book.

When Michael Allen kindly reprints the final chapter of the first edition in his *New Casebook* on Heaney, a volume which collects some of the large amount of critical work produced in the last ten or twelve years, he observes that it 'illustrates how powerful the poet's collaborative presence can be, especially when it is reinforcing in the critic the kind of New Critical attitudes and techniques to which Heaney's own mind is attuned'.[1] This is ambivalently poised between compliment to, and derogation of, the critic, since it notably does not say that the poet's powerful presence makes for powerful criticism; and I take the point, of course, that 'collaborative presence' includes such things as taking a critical tune from the poet's interviews and critical essays. This critical method and style were intended to accord with the introductory nature of the series to which the book was a contribution; and it still seems to me in practice very difficult to consider a living writer as purely a textual function in the way some kinds of criticism would prescribe. Perhaps the 'death of the author' can be securely proclaimed, in individual cases, only after biological death; certainly even the most deconstructive criticism of contemporaries tends to consider the evidence of interviews, broadcasts, journalism, readings, and so on in ways that purity of deconstructive motive would seem to preclude.

However, as Allen himself admits, there is New Criticism and New Criticism; and I hope that my own version of it in the first edition both allowed scope for utterly non-collaborative, independent opinion and judgement, and registered an informed knowledge of historical and political contexts in ways that some 'New Criticism' was, and is, actively inimical to. If there was a degree of (perhaps culpable) unselfconsciousness in my critical attitudes and method in the first version of this book, however, I became more conscious subsequently; and in a study of post-war poetry published in 1993, I evolved a formula for defining the

---

1 Michael Allen, 'Introduction', in *Seamus Heaney* (Macmillan *New Casebooks*, 1997), 8.

combination of formalism and historicism which is, I think, the kind of criticism I write there and, I hope, write in the new chapters here; and also, in my view, wrote, at least in nascent form, in the first edition of this book. I say that 'Good poems are always both symptomatic and exemplary: if they enable us to test the conditions of the historical influences or events which produced them, they also offer paradigms of how the inchoate in a culture may be made to cohere, ratifyingly, in language and form. Bound by their historical moment, they are also our access to their moment'.[2]

The present critical age demands that we be self-conscious in this way about our critical activity, and rightly so in many ways. Yet this placing of critical and theoretical activity at the centre of contemporary preoccupation can lead to the opposite of colla-boration; that is, condescension. Some contemporary literary criticism takes a *de-haut-en-bas* attitude to the work it discusses, in a discourse of unmasking, exposing, deconstructing which can leave the work, in the terms I offer above, all symptom and no example, fix the critic in a characteristic attitude of ironic disapproval or even contestation, and ignore the poem's nature as a formal entity. While this sometimes makes for illuminating criticism, I favour a method in which the poem itself offers some resistance to discursive critical appropriation, in which the serene unflappability of procedure, method and ideology sur-prises or shocks itself occasionally by formal recognitions; recognitions, furthermore, which have a congruence with pleasure rather than investigation. There are otherwise intelli-gent readings of Heaney which seem to me vitiated by precisely the lack of such surprise. David Lloyd, for instance, in a widely reprinted article entitled 'Pap for the Dispossessed: Seamus Heaney and the Poetics of Identity', has very arresting things to say about the ways in which Heaney's use of myth and his inheritance of various forms of romanticism render his work 'profoundly symptomatic of the continuing meshing of Irish

2 Neil Corcoran, *English Poetry Since 1940* (Longman, 1993), xv.

cultural nationalism with the imperial ideology which frames it'.[3] The analysis is a compelling one and is in tune with post-colonial readings of other writers who appear, after such unmasking, trapped in a similar double bind, in which nationalism repeats or mirrors the binary discourse of the power it has supplanted, or wishes to supplant. Lloyd's eschewing of formalist analysis, however, does not prevent him from a sudden brusque description of Heaney as 'a minor Irish poet'; whereas – although one takes the *épater le bourgeois* motive of the tactic – the whole tenor of the piece is to make such literary-qualitative judgements nugatory. There are other essays which 'unmask' Heaney in different ways, notably by feminist critics; and some of these, in my view, are much more securely anchored in formal as well as ideological distinctions. The essays of Patricia Coughlan and Elizabeth Butler Cullingford, which I cite occasionally in what follows, are salient cases in point.

If I dwell here on some of the more negative criticism Heaney has attracted,[4] it is partly because to a critic inclined more positively this work offers stimulating challenge and goad. It is also, however, because it constitutes some of the most intelligent and stimulating criticism Heaney has received. This is possibly because a negative, or relatively negative response to a greatly admired and successful figure is likely to profit from the

3 Lloyd's article, first published in *Boundary* in 1985, forms part of his book *Anomalous States: Irish Writing and the Post-Colonial Moment* (Lilliput, 1993). It is reprinted in Michael Allen's *New Casebook* on Heaney (Macmillan, 1997).

4 And there is more; notably Desmond Fennell's 'Whatever You Say, Say Nothing: Why Seamus Heaney is No. 1', *Stand*, vol. 32 no. 4 (Autumn 1991), 38–65, an intensely controversial piece in its day and subsequently much derided for its apparently strongly republican *parti-pris*. I have to say that this seems less apparent to me than it does to some critics and that the essay, while vitiated by illogic and over-assurance, occasionally makes a point worth mature consideration: for instance, its charge that Heaney drastically misreads Simone Weil in *The Redress of Poetry*, and that the concept of 'redress' is not unlike that of prayer in monastic Catholicism; which renders it, of course, mystically unsusceptible to proof.

corrective drive to account for and articulate itself; but it is also because to read a lot of Heaney criticism is to discover more than one's fair share of repetition and derivativeness. In the text and footnotes of what follows I gratefully acknowledge what seems to me the finest critical writing on this poet; but, despite his being one of the most written-about contemporary writers, this book, I hope, offers some original and provocative readings and re-readings.

In the first edition I acknowledged the assistance of John Byrne, Gillian Corcoran, Paul Driver and Seamus Heaney himself. I gratefully do so again now, and add the names of Patrick Crotty, Jerzy Jarniewicz, Antoinette Quinn and Neil Rhodes.

Neil Corcoran
St Andrews
September 1997

Roots and Reading:
Death of a Naturalist (1966)
and *Door into the Dark* (1969)

I began as a poet when my roots were
crossed with my reading.
Seamus Heaney, *Preoccupations*

Seamus Heaney's first two books derive their primary material from his own origins, his rural childhood and young manhood in Co. Derry; and, although this world maintains a presence in every one of Heaney's subsequent volumes, *Death of a Naturalist* and *Door into the Dark* explore and exhaust a particular way of treating it. *Door into the Dark*, however, is also a transitional book which, if it contains poems that would not have been out of place in the first book, also points forward to *Wintering Out*. It seems appropriate, then, to consider both volumes together under the general rubric of the 'early work', but to hold them apart too, initially, in an attempt to describe the individual character of each.

Death of a Naturalist

What its original reviewers singled out for praise in Heaney's first volume is still its most obvious feature. The observed and recollected facts of his early rural experience are conveyed in a language of great sensuous richness and directness. Digging potatoes and turf, picking blackberries, churning butter and ploughing are all rendered in poems which, like the synaesthetic blur of the bluebottles in the poem 'Death of a Naturalist' itself, weave 'a strong gauze of sound' around their occasions. The most obvious characteristics of this sound are its onomatopoeia and its alliterative effects. The onomatopoeia – 'the squelch and slap / Of soggy peat' in 'Digging', 'the plash and gurgle of the sour-breathed milk, / the pat and slap of small spades on wet lumps' in 'Churning Day' – is the element in Heaney's work which most readily lends itself to parody: Philip Hobsbaum has described it as 'Heaneyspeak ... the snap-crackle-and-pop of diction.[1] It can also, however, produce such extraordinary effects as the 'bass chorus' of the frogs in 'Death of a Naturalist':

> Right down the dam gross-bellied frogs were cocked
> On sods; their loose necks pulsed like sails. Some hopped:
> The slap and plop were obscene threats. Some sat
> Poised like mud grenades, their blunt heads farting.

The sheer noise Heaney manages to make out of English vowels there is remarkable – a dissonant cacophony that forces the mouth to work overtime if the reader speaks the lines aloud. Some of the alliterative effects of the poems are equally striking: the clamour and clang of the opening line of 'Churning Day', for instance – 'A thick crust, coarse-grained as limestone rough-cast' or, in 'Blackberry-Picking', 'We hoarded the fresh berries in the byre. / But when the bath was filled we found a fur ...', the second line of which imitates the alliterative line of Anglo-Saxon poetry, with its four main stresses, three carrying the heavy alliteration, and the 'f' sound also originating in the 'fresh' of the previous line, whose second half similarly alliterates on 'b'.

Such effects came naturally enough to Heaney, no doubt, as the result of his interest in Anglo-Saxon poetry and in Hopkins; but, sanctioned by Ted Hughes's absorption of similar early influences, they seemed to ally him, in 1966, with a reaction against some of the decorums of recent English poetry. Almost expecting the epithet 'earthy' (one early reviewer spoke of the 'soil-reek of Ireland'), his poems seemed designed to go where

1 Philip Hobsbaum, 'Craft and Technique in *Wintering Out*', in Tony Curtis (ed.), *The Art of Seamus Heaney* (Seren, 1982; 3rd ed., 1994), 35–43.

A. Alvarez said English poetry should in his combative and influential introduction to *The New Poetry*, the Penguin anthology of 1962, 'beyond the gentility principle'. That anthology singled out Ted Hughes for praise; and some of Hughes's stylistic devices are obviously a direct, indeed an overwhelming, influence, on some of the poems of *Death of a Naturalist*: on the technique of eliding title into first line in 'The Diviner' and 'Trout'; on the military and phallic metaphors in 'Trout' itself and in 'Cow in Calf'; and on the similar metaphors and insistent anthropomorphisms in 'Turkeys Observed' ('He lorded it on the claw-flecked mud / With a grey flick of his Confucian eye'). These poems have their eyes so eagerly trained on *The Hawk in the Rain* and *Lupercal*, Hughes's first two books, that, even allowing for the element of comedy that undoubtedly inheres in them too, they tend towards pastiche.

Something more subtle and complex has been learnt from Hughes in 'Digging', however, where the shape and movement of his well-known poem 'The Thought-Fox' seems to have been deeply assimilated and absorbed. Although the ostensible subject matter of the poems is quite different, both situate their poets behind a window, pen in hand, in the act of composition. The Hughes poem is more specifically preoccupied with its own making, as it intently conjures up the notion and image of 'fox' which – a 'thought' made word – is also the conjuration of the poem itself. 'The Thought-Fox' conveys an impression of utter concentration, as what is recollected from experience stirs again in the 'darkness' of creative imagination, and issues eventually in the words which recreate that life on the page:

> Till, with a sudden sharp hot stink of fox
> It enters the dark hole of the head.
> The window is starless still; the clock ticks,
> The page is printed.

Heaney's poem is less intent on its own process and more concerned, ultimately, to enforce a moral and propose an aesthetic, but its progress is very similar to Hughes's. The sight of his father digging below the window conjures a memory of him digging potatoes 'twenty years away' and, beyond that, of his grandfather digging turf; and just as the fox enters 'the dark hole of the head' in 'The Thought-Fox', these associated memories merge in Heaney's head, and emerge as words on the page:

> The cold smell of potato mould, the squelch and slap
> Of soggy peat, the curt cuts of an edge
> Through living roots awaken in my head.
> But I've no spade to follow men like them.
>
> Between my finger and my thumb
> The squat pen rests.
> I'll dig with it.

The analogy between pen and spade is, of course, the major point of the poem, and it is characteristically Heaney's own, as I shall show; but the shape of 'Digging', and its self-consciousness about the relationship between exterior and interior, experience and language, nature and mind, show him inheriting something much richer and more sustaining in early Hughes than those elements of style which involve a degree of pastiche. The way in which Heaney makes the inherited shape his own in 'Digging' is an early indication of his true strength: he is not subdued to, but liberated by, the achievement of his earliest exemplar.

Although it is possible to detect a variety of relatively unabsorbed influences on Heaney's first poems – Robert Frost, Robert Graves and Norman MacCaig, for instance – a similar liberation may be discovered in what *Death of a Naturalist* absorbs from Patrick Kavanagh and from Wordsworth. The risky unpredictability and individuality of Kavanagh's work make him inimitable in any formal sense, even if 'At a Potato Digging' may have been sanctioned by *The Great Hunger* (1942), Kavanagh's long poem on the metaphorical 'hunger' (for a more fulfilling existence) of Patrick Maguire, a Co.

4

Monaghan farmer, which opens by watching 'the potato-gatherers like mechanized scarecrows move / Along the sidefall of the hill'; Heaney's opens in a later, actually 'mechanized' agricultural world in which a 'mechanical digger wrecks the drill' of potatoes. Kavanagh's assumption, however, that such Irish rural experience – which is the experience of labour, of work – was a proper subject for poetry in English was genuinely liberating for Heaney. He makes the point powerfully himself when he says, 'I have no need to write a poem to Patrick Kavanagh: I wrote *Death of a Naturalist*'.[2]

If Kavanagh is in these ways an ambience for early Heaney, some of the central poems in the book have deeply absorbed a more specifically describable Wordsworthian example. 'Death of a Naturalist' itself, 'The Barn' and 'Blackberry-Picking' are, as it were, written in the margin of such passages as the boat-stealing episode in Book I of *The Prelude* and the separate poem 'Nutting', which was originally intended for that long poem. These are poems in which an enlargement of consciousness is enacted in an interchange between mind and nature. In the passage from *The Prelude*, the stealing of the boat – 'an act of stealth / And troubled pleasure' – is repaid with the child's terror of a huge cliff which, 'As if with voluntary power instinct', seems to stride after him, leaving its aftertaste in his imagination when

> ... huge and mighty forms, that do not live
> Like living men, moved slowly through my mind
> By day, and were the trouble of my dreams.

In 'Nutting', the child's act of hostility towards nature – the wanton destruction of a hazel copse – is succeeded by guilt and remorse:

2 Quoted in Douglas Dunn (ed.), *Two Decades of Irish Writing* (Carcanet, 1975), 35. The fact that Heaney writes on Kavanagh in both *Preoccupations* and *The Government of the Tongue* indicates his sense of the poet's abiding relevance to his own work.

> unless I now
> Confound my present feelings with the past,
> Even then, when from the bower I turned away
> Exulting, rich beyond the wealth of kings,
> I felt a sense of pain when I beheld
> The silent trees and the intruding sky.

These moments in Wordsworth are part of the process of Nature's education of the poet, moments in which the child's knowledge of reality is extended. In Heaney, 'The Barn' enforces a similar knowledge when it moves, towards its close, 'Over the rafters of sleep', into a nightmarishly specific instance of 'huge and mighty forms': 'I lay face-down to shun the fear above. / The two-lugged sacks moved in like great blind rats.' Both 'Death of a Naturalist' and 'Blackberry-Picking' come to an end with explicit statements of the new knowledge acquired during the incidents they describe. At the end of 'Death of a Naturalist', after seeing the 'angry frogs' which might develop from the apparently delightful classroom frogspawn, and hearing their bass chorus, 'I sickened, turned and ran. The great slime kings / Were gathered there for vengeance and I knew / That if I dipped my hand the spawn would clutch it.' The reaction is exactly that of the child in *The Prelude* – 'With trembling hands I turned'; and Heaney's 'I knew' is the terrified knowledge of the threat implicit in apparently benign natural forms. The guilty fantasy of the frogs' 'vengeance' for his act of seizing frogspawn is prefigured by Wordsworth's fantasy of being hounded by the cliff. Both are instances in which fear provokes a newly disillusioned epistemological development.

At the end of 'Blackberry-Picking', the knowledge comes not in fantasy but in the actual necessity enforced when the picked blackberries ferment: 'I always felt like crying. It wasn't fair / That all the lovely canfuls smelt of rot. / Each year I hoped they'd keep, knew they would not.' 'It wasn't fair' is the child's querulous, petulant recognition of inevitability, the stamped foot with which he responds to a world which will never meet his desires; and this knowledge, as the poem's metaphorical language intimates, is also heavy with the knowledge of sexuality. The first blackberry's 'flesh was sweet', leaving 'lust for / Picking', and the children's palms end up 'sticky as Bluebeard's' (the murderer of numerous wives in Perrault's famous tale). The sexual metaphor is also present in 'Nutting', where the hazel copse is 'A virgin scene' in which the child 'with wise restraint, / Voluptuous, fearless of a rival, eyed / The banquet' before shattering it with 'merciless ravage', a kind of rape leaving the copse 'Deformed and sullied'. In both Wordsworth and Heaney, the sexual implication is developed naturally out of the anecdote: 'Nutting' and 'Blackberry-Picking' are poems about the end of innocence.

The 'death of a naturalist' is also, however, the birth of a poet; and what seems now of most interest in this first book of Heaney's is the relationship in it between his early experience and his early experience of writing poetry. The trying-on of different styles and manners, the rhyming of his own experiences with poems by Hughes, Kavanagh and Wordsworth, with the aim of discovering the kind of poet he might himself become, appears a matter of eager enjoyment in *Death of a Naturalist*, of relish, rather than the 'anxiety' customarily ascribed, after Harold Bloom, to the relationship between poets and their precursors.[3] This exuberant performance of the present moment of the poem is the essential signature of the book, and this frequently protects it from the emotion common in poems which recollect childhood experience, nostalgia. The poems appear so heartened by the fact that the early experience has provided their own inspiration that the pastness or lostness of the experience itself is dissolved in the joy of creativity.

This joy, however, derives also from Heaney's view of his own poetry as, in certain respects, continuous with the rural

3 See Harold Bloom, *The Anxiety of Influence* (Oxford University Press, 1973). This is not necessarily to deny the validity of Bloom's theory in relation to other poetry, including later work by Heaney himself.

experience it describes: hence those poems in which he dis-
covers, in the place of his origin, analogies for the art of poetry,
'The Diviner' and 'Digging' itself. When he discusses 'The
Diviner' in 'Feeling into Words' in *Preoccupations*, Heaney
points up the analogy quite straightforwardly, telling us that
the Renaissance poet Philip Sidney in his *Apologie for Poetry*
notes that 'Among the Romans a Poet was called *Vates*, which
is as much as a Diviner'.[4] Both poet and diviner seem, to
Heaney, to have 'a gift for mediating between the latent re-
source and the community that wants it current and released'.
The point of the analogy, therefore, is to promote the notion of
the poet as intimately involved with his own community,
serving it with words and forms as the diviner serves it with
vital water. The poem itself, however, discovers its central
metaphor not in the primary world of the diviner, or in the
secondary world of the poet, but in a tertiary realm, that of
radio: 'The rod jerked down with precise convulsions, / Spring
water suddenly broadcasting / Through a green aerial its secret
stations.' The metaphor is entirely apt in the way it imagines
both poet and diviner seizing out of the air an otherwise
invisible, or inaudible, reality. It is also apt in that it reminds
us how a culture has developed from, and is still rooted in, an
agriculture, since to 'broadcast' was originally to cast seed
widely over the land; and it may also wittily alert us to the fact
that, if the modern poet is an ancient 'diviner', he may well
also be a 'broadcaster' in the contemporary sense, particularly
if he wants to keep in touch with a community. The careful
aptness of the metaphor, alert to etymology, is in keeping with

4 This is a prime instance in Heaney's early work of the way generative literary
learning is secreted in the poem itself, but readily declared in the criticism and,
sometimes, the interviews. This kind of coaching and coaxing of his readers is
one of the reasons why Heaney's own eloquent interpretations of his earlier
poems have been so successful in setting a critical agenda for their subsequent
discussion. In the later poetry, the relationship between poetry and criticism is
very different, as I shall show, and the poems are sometimes much more likely to
include 'scholarly' references as part of their own behaviour and performance.

the poem's own care to give the diviner his due, however, and not merely to appropriate him as an analogy. There is no forcing of similitude, and nothing in the poem asserts it; it is insinuated, not insisted.

I am not at all sure that the same can be said for the better-known 'Digging'. The basic metaphor – the pen as spade – informs a great deal of Heaney's subsequent work, when it is translated out of its specifically agricultural application into a view of poetry as archaeology, the poem as an act of cultural and historical retrieval. 'Digging' confesses the discontinuity before it asserts a willed continuity:

> But I've no spade to follow men like them.
>
> Between my finger and my thumb
> The squat pen rests.
> I'll dig with it.

In 'Feeling into Words', Heaney writes of this poem as if it is an illustration of the 'proverbial' wisdom of a saying remembered from his childhood: 'the pen's lighter than the spade'. In fact, however, this is the wisdom of an agricultural labourer who knows the heaviness of the spade, and knows that there is something easier as a way of life; the word 'lighter' in the proverb opens a huge gap between the worlds of manual work and education. That gap is narrowed in 'Digging' to the single blank line before its final stanza; and the analogy, far from acknowledging the pen's lightness, in fact wants it 'squat' and heavy again. The strain of over-determination in this shows up in the opening lines, where the pen is not only a spade but a gun, which seems at least one analogy too many for a short poem; and it shows too in the false note of the backslapping exclamation, 'By God, the old man could handle a spade', which may register genuine filial pride, and pride in an ancestry of agricultural labourers, but which nevertheless sounds uneasily over-assertive. The depth of the poem's desire to close the gap between education and origin is, however, genuinely moving too, and the result of, and witness to a great affection. This is a poem which would do almost anything to avoid the ethical sense of its poet's physical attitude as he 'look[s] down' at a father 'under' him; would do almost anything, that is, to avoid condescension.

Nevertheless, if the poem is over-assertive in the enforcing of its moral, and in the proposing of a first aesthetic – thereby betraying, despite itself, an insecurity – it is also an extremely important poem in the Heaney *oeuvre*, in that it opens up, as soon as the work itself opens up, an issue which remains at the root of a large number of subsequent poems: the proper relationship between this poet and his own first community. As 'Digging' indicates, this is primarily, in *Death of a Naturalist*, the relationship with his immediate family – father and grandfather in 'Digging', his father alone in a number of other poems, his younger brother in 'Mid-Term Break', his mother glimpsed in 'Churning Day', his father's uncle in 'Ancestral Photograph'. These are all affectionate family memories, registering intimacy, warmth, tenderly respectful recall. 'Follower', however, allows an emotion of distress to cloud these primary affiliations and allegiances when its conclusion reverses the paternal and filial roles:

> I wanted to grow up and plough,
> To close one eye, stiffen my arm.
> All I ever did was follow
> In his broad shadow round the farm.
>
> I was a nuisance, tripping, falling,
> Yapping always. But today
> It is my father who keeps stumbling
> Behind me, and will not go away.

When the artist Noel Connor accompanied this poem with a drawing for the collaboration *Gravities*, he drew a large dark bird, its wings spread in flight, dimly visible behind a spider's web opening and spreading towards the viewer; and this quasi-Joycean imagery appropriately counterpoints the poem's own sense of being constricted by one's entanglement in family and origin.[5] The word 'stumbling' makes the emotion of the poem a cruel irritation with, precisely, the weakness of age; and this may be a measure of how the figure of the father in 'Follower' represents, in addition to the actual biological father, that network of loyalties and attachments which can be as much confinement as consolation in any origin. 'Follower' is the clearest instance in *Death of a Naturalist* of what Heaney describes, in 'From Monaghan to the Grand Canal', in *Preoccupations*, as 'the penalty of consciousness, the unease generated when a milieu becomes material', where he is, significantly, discussing the work of Patrick Kavanagh.

In the volume's final poem, 'Personal Helicon', there are signs that this kind of self-consciousness will eventually become a more openly declared element in the work. The poem owes something to the 'greenhouse' poems of the American poet, Theodore Roethke (on whom Heaney writes in *Preoccupations*), which similarly elaborate a psychology from a symbolically suggestive childhood world of vegetal process. In 'Personal Helicon', rather than providing analogies for poetry, as in 'The Diviner' and 'Digging', that world is itself turned into a little myth of poetic inspiration. The wells of Heaney's childhood become the springs of the Muses' mountain of Helicon, which were sources of inspiration for anyone who drank there. In the personal myth of the poem, Helicon is crossed with Narcissus, who fell in love with his own reflection; and the image of inspiration derived from the childhood world is one of circularity and reflexivity: the wells 'had echoes, gave back your own call / With a clean new music in it', where the echo gives you back your call but also transforms it into something different from itself. Both novelty and music, this is therefore a kind of ur-poem; and when the ending of 'Personal Helicon' articulates an aim for the poet's own work – 'I rhyme / To see

5 See Seamus Heaney and Noel Connor, *Gravities: A Collection of Poems and Drawings* (Charlotte Press, 1979), 14–15.

myself, to set the darkness echoing' – it is to emphasize the possibly narcissistic self-entrancement of poetry. If 'Digging' and 'The Diviner' humbly make the poet the inheritor of rural traditions of labour and service, 'Personal Helicon' more egotistically suggests that the importance of the poem lies in its ability to reveal the poet to himself, restoring in language what has been lost in reality. Established in *Death of a Naturalist*, these are the poles of social responsibility and self-exploration between which all of Heaney's subsequent work has oscillated.

Door into the Dark

1 Sexuality

The title of Heaney's second collection obviously links the book to the final lines of *Death of a Naturalist*, implying a renewed attempt, in poetry, 'to see myself, to set the darkness echoing'; and this kind of linkage between Heaney's various books, where the final poem of one volume suggests something of what may be expected in the next, persists as a principle of organization throughout his career to date, as many commentators have pointed out. This manifestly promotes a sense of anticipation, but it also suggests a Yeatsian conception of a developing and integrated *oeuvre*, a sure-footedness willing to programme self-development, reaching for, or daring what 'The Errand' in *The Spirit Level* will call 'the next move in the game'. The word 'dark' does indeed echo throughout the second book, and the darkness of the self suggested by 'Personal Helicon' is only one of the 'darks' to which the book's door gives access. The others are those of artistic creation itself and, increasingly towards the book's close, of the Irish landscape and its history.

When he discusses his title in 'Feeling into Words', Heaney says that he intended it to 'gesture towards' the idea of poetry as 'a point of entry into the buried life of the feelings or as a point of exit for it. Words themselves are doors; Janus is to a certain extent their deity, looking back to a ramification of roots and associations and forward to a clarification of sense and meaning.' This has its consonance with T. S. Eliot's concept of the 'dark embryo' within the poet 'which gradually takes on the form and speech of a poem';[6] and *Door into the Dark* does have its actual embryos and foetuses – in 'Mother', 'Cana Revisited' and 'Elegy for a Still-Born Child'. It is possible too to think of it as a book in which a new, finer and more subtle kind of Heaney poem seems to be embryonically present, but not yet quite born. If Heaney has himself defined one way in which Janus is its appropriate god, I would suggest another: some of its poems, particularly the analogical poems, 'The Forge' and 'Thatcher', look back to one of the major kinds in *Death of a Naturalist*, whereas others, and in particular the concluding 'Bogland', are the origin, the nurturing 'wet centre', of a subsequent manner and procedure and, in particular, of the major sequence of 'bog poems' initiated by 'The Tollund Man' in *Wintering Out*.

There is a rather too self-consciously knowing element about those poems in *Door into the Dark* which most obviously look backwards.[7] 'The Forge', which gives the volume its title, is a sonnet which uses another rural craft, the blacksmith's, as a further analogy for poetry. For all the precision of evocation in some of its details – that 'unpredictable fantail of sparks', for instance – it seems over-insistent and *voulu*. The real occupation tends to disappear behind its metaphorical significance. The

6 See T. S. Eliot, 'Critical Note', in *The Collected Poems of Harold Monro*, ed. Alida Monro (Cobden-Sanderson, 1933), xiii–xvi. This is quoted in C. K. Stead's *The New Poetic: Yeats to Eliot* (1964) in a chapter entitled 'Eliot's "Dark Embryo"' which, as I suggest in Chapter 9, influenced Heaney's view of Eliot and of poetry in general.

7 Henry Hart, in *Seamus Heaney: Poet of Contrary Progressions* (Syracuse University Press, 1992), offers an enthusiastic reading of *Door into the Dark*, in which he discovers in it a deployment of the 'traditional meditational techniques' of Catholic doctrine and practice. This seems to me not proven; but it makes, nevertheless, for an interesting account of the poems which sets Heaney's Catholicism firmly in congruence with his poetic practice.

'forge' of the title seems, even initially, less an actual forge than 'the quick forge and working-house of thought' – the imagination, that is – in Shakespeare's *Henry V*; and there is hyperbolic strain in the religious metaphor which makes the anvil 'an altar / Where he expends himself in shape and music'. The over-determination also shows in that rather facile opposition between the 'immoveable' value presumed to inhere in the blacksmith's trade, and the vulgarly 'flashing' traffic of the industrialized world beyond the door-jamb, and in that sudden view of the man himself, 'leather-aproned, hairs in his nose', and grunting, which seems mere caricature. The excitement of self-discovery evident in the earlier exercises in analogy has congealed here into something too studied and mannered; 'The Forge', unlike 'The Diviner', has too much the look of a poem that is looked at. Which is why the less artificial 'Thatcher', which keeps its eye firmly on its object, is more successful in releasing, uninsistently, another analogy – the thatcher's 'Midas touch' – which, in its celebration of economy, scrupulousness, a disciplined parsimony, anticipates the characteristic strengths of *Wintering Out* and *North*: the later manner is being advocated in a poem which belongs, generically, to the earlier.

If rhyming 'to see myself' is, in some sense, a programme for *Door into the Dark*, this does not, however, imply any confessional directness. The 'buried life of the feelings', and particularly of sexual feeling, is certainly present in the book, giving it its fecund, slippery, slightly voyeuristic character, with instances of, and images deriving from, seed, intercourse, generation, pregnancy, and marriage. Such 'feelings', however, are not confessionally declared, but diverted through metaphor, symbol, allegory, anecdote and dramatic monologue. In the monologues 'The Wife's Tale' and 'Undine', for instance, views of the mutuality and inter-dependence of men and women are exposed. In the realistic monologue of 'The Wife's Tale' the tone is not always very assured. When Heaney speaks as a woman in these poems of *Door into the Dark*, it still seems very much his own

voice doing the talking, and Randall Jarrell's comment on
Robert Lowell's 'The Mills of the Kavanaughs' seems apposite:
'You feel, "Yes, Robert Lowell would act like this if he were a
girl"; but whoever saw a girl like Robert Lowell?'[8] The wife in
'The Wife's Tale' would talk like this – 'But I ran my hand in the
half-filled bags / Hooked to the slots. It was hard as shot, /
Innumerable and cool' – if she were Seamus Heaney; and she
would talk like this – 'And that was it. I'd come and he had
shown me / So I belonged no further to the work' – if she were
Seamus Heaney imitating Robert Frost. That sudden veering of
this presumably Irish wife's voice into the north of Boston
accents of one of Frost's women is perhaps the technical sign
of the poem's failure of empathy. For all that the men are
'grateful' in the poem's Breughel-like closing line, there is
something too authoritatively directing in the husband, and
too humbly subservient in her, for the monologue to ring true
as her account of the relationship.

The monologue-allegory of 'Undine' is more protected from
such a lapse. The 'undine' of Heaney's title is a female water-
spirit who, by marrying a mortal and bearing him a child, might
receive a soul – might, in other words, become human. In
Heaney's account of the poem in 'Feeling into Words', he
makes it 'a myth about agriculture, about the way water is
tamed and humanized when streams become irrigation canals,
when water becomes involved with seed'; but the monologue of
the undine is of course the voice of a woman responding sexually
to a man, describing an encounter which reaches its climax and
resolution in an evocation of sexual interdependence:

> I swallowed his trench
>
> Gratefully, dispersing myself for love
> Down in his roots, climbing his brassy grain –
> But once he knew my welcome, I alone
> Could give him subtle increase and reflection.

8 Randall Jarrell, *Poetry and the Age* (1955; Faber and Faber edn., 1973), 230.

He explored me so completely, each limb
Lost its cold freedom. Human, warmed to him.

The poem has, like 'The Wife's Tale', its element of male pre-
sumption: that 'Gratefully' is placed so prominently as to make
it seem altogether too deferential.[9] Nevertheless, this mono-
logue does also articulate the woman's own proper pride,
making her gratitude commensurate with his dependence on
her – for the 'increase' of, presumably, sexual tumescence, his
own sense of himself, and the possibility of a child, with its
more than merely narcissistic 'reflection' of him. As the mono-
logue of a water-spirit, 'Undine' may be understood as the
well's answer to the 'big-eyed Narcissus' who stares into it in
'Personal Helicon'.

In the volume as a whole, however, these satisfactions of
mutuality are complemented by the darker sexuality of 'A Lough
Neagh Sequence'. The poem gives Heaney his first opportunity
for an organized form more ample than the individual lyric, an
attempt renewed frequently, in different ways, in his later work.
It has a strange and compelling subject: the extraordinary life-
cycle of the eels and the work-cycle of the fishermen on Lough
Neagh in Northern Ireland. As the cycle of the poem itself moves
through proverb, legend, realism and 'visionary' transmutation,
the eel-fishing becomes, in part, a kind of objective correlative
for the compulsions of human sexuality. The sequence manages
to conjure 'eelness' – as Heaney has said Hughes's 'The

9 Patricia Coughlan, in 'Bog Queens: The Representation of Women in the
Poetry of John Montague and Seamus Heaney', in *Gender in Irish Writing*, ed.
Toni O'Brien Johnson and David Cairns (Open University Press, 1991),
observes of my comment here that I 'severely understate the case'. She views
'Undine' and 'Rite of Spring' as 'classic fantasies of male sexual irresistibility'.
In my account here I read 'Undine' as something else too; but Coughlan's essay
is a telling account of how, in some of Heaney's work, 'female figures function
as crucially important forms of validation-by-opposition of the individual
poet's identity, in a (sometimes comically blatant) neo-Oedipal struggle'.
Cogent as she is, Coughlan in my view sometimes severely overstates the case.
The essay is reprinted in Michael Allen's *New Casebook* on Heaney, 185–205.

Thought-Fox' conjures 'foxness' – in the slither and melt of its own mimetic language and forms.[10] The mysterious inexorability of the eel's life-cycle also has its intimate symbolic connection with the major themes and motifs of the book. When the eel is 'a wick that is / its own taper and light / through the weltering dark', the actual eel of the Lough Neagh fishing industry becomes a representative of the volume's various kinds of darkness and of the will to confront them. Although the sequence is not uniformly successful, it is in places stealthily insinuating and subtle, its almost fearful astonishment acting as a prelude to the way similar emotions and means are deployed, with a new political charge, in the bog poems of *Wintering Out* and *North*:

> Against
> ebb, current, rock, rapids
> a muscled icicle
> that melts itself longer
> and fatter, he buries
> his arrival beyond
> light and tidal water,
> investing silt and sand
> with a sleek root. By day
> only the drainmaker's
> spade or the mud paddler
> can make him abort. Dark
> delivers him hungering
> down each undulation.

2 History

Gallarus Oratory on the Dingle peninsula in Co. Kerry is a tiny monastic chapel built in the early medieval period. When the poet enters it in 'In Gallarus Oratory', he senses a 'core of old

10 See the uncollected 'Deep as England', *Hibernia*, 1 December 1972, 13.

dark'; and in 'Whinlands', 'Shoreline', 'Bann Clay' and 'Bog-land', this 'old dark' of history and prehistory begins to be read out of the Irish landscape, in a way that points forward to some of the central poems in the two subsequent volumes, *Wintering Out* and *North*. 'Whinlands' and 'Shoreline' may owe some-thing to another element in Ted Hughes, the kind of effect he produces in 'Thistles' in *Wodwo* (1967). There, Hughes imagi-nes his thistles as a kind of vegetal persistence of the spirit of Viking invasion:

> Every one a revengeful burst
> Of resurrection, a grasped fistful
> Of splintered weapons and Icelandic frost thrust up
>
> From the underground stain of a decayed Viking.
> They are like pale hair and the gutturals of dialects.
> Every one manages a plume of blood.

Heaney's whins ('gorse', in England) are similarly, if rather less impressively, the emblematic inheritors of values attached to the history of a specific landscape:

> Gilt, jaggy, springy, frilled,
> This stunted, dry richness
> Persists on hills, near stone ditches,
> Over flintbed and battlefield.

The 'whinlands' characteristic of Northern Ireland become here – as Hughes's thistles do – the name for the persistence of a par-ticular kind of culture and character. In 'Shoreline', Heaney re-ceives the first of those visitations from the Vikings which are to constitute part of the mythology of *North*: 'Listen. Is it the Danes, / A black hawk bent on the sail?' Even if the Vikings are present not in the vegetation of Ireland, but in the tide 'rum-maging' at its coastline, Heaney's ear has probably been schooled to hear them there by 'Thistles', and also by another poem more directly about the Vikings in Hughes's *Wodwo*, 'The Warriors of the North', where, among several images for their invasions, Hughes includes their desire for 'the elaborate, patient gold of the Gaels'.

'Bogland', which concludes *Door into the Dark*, is very much a new beginning rather than an ending, appearing to contain within itself the excitement of the capacity for further extension and development, a different rhythm. In an interview, Heaney says that it 'was the first poem of mine that I felt had the status of symbol in some way; it wasn't trapped in its own anecdote, or its own closing-off: it seemed to have some kind of wind blowing through it that could carry on';[11] and the wind did, of course, carry on, through the sequence of 'bog poems' initiated by 'The Tollund Man' and 'Nerthus' in *Wintering Out*, and brought to fulfilment in *North*. 'Bogland' may be regarded as a kind of answering, Irish poem to Theodore Roethke's American 'In Praise of Prairie', in which 'Horizons have no strangeness to the eye' and 'distance is familiar as a friend. / The feud we kept with space comes to an end'. That American pioneering spirit, which looks outwards and upwards, to fulfilment through movement, advance, exploration, openness and, of course, conquest, is countered by Heaney's negative definition of Irish topographical experience: 'We have no prairies / To slice a big sun at evening'.[12] 'We' look 'inwards and downwards', into the bottomless centre of our own history, recovering there the traces and treasures of previous cultures and peoples, just as the bogland of Ireland literally preserves historical and prehistorical deposits which may be released by archaeology.

The sense of excited possibility in 'Bogland', however, derives

11 'A Raindrop on a Thorn', interview with Robert Druce, *Dutch Quarterly Review*, vol. 9 (1978), 24–37.
12 In 'The Parish and the Dream: Heaney and America, 1969–1987', *The Southern Review*, vol. 31 no. 3 (July 1995), 726–38, Michael Allen reads 'Bogland' in a subversive spirit as a first indication of the way Heaney's poetry includes America, alongside Ireland and England, as an 'intermittent presence'. This 'suggests,' he says, 'that the verse is searching out some empathy and support there'; the narrator of 'Bogland', 'despite the static Kavanagh aesthetic he claims to be promoting, has itchy feet'.

not only from Heaney's first use of the figure which is to act so powerfully in subsequent poems, but also from the fact that this poem itself describes its own lack of closure or containment, in the act of describing its overt subject:

> The ground itself is kind, black butter
>
> Melting and opening underfoot,
> Missing its last definition
> By millions of years.

Describing the ground here, the poem is also describing itself; its own falling rhythms and constantly enjambed lines 'melt and open' too, in a notification that the symbol of the bog itself will melt and open again. In embedding within itself a commentary on itself in this way, 'Bogland' initiates that process of almost constant self-commentary in Heaney's later work; and initiates, therefore, a more sophisticated and subtle kind of Heaney poem. 'The Forge', in Heaney's own terms, does remain 'trapped in its own anecdote'. The poem is too snug a fit for the metaphor: nothing remains promisingly inchoate or unreconciled; and the whole seems glazed with self-satisfaction. 'Bogland' is a much riskier kind of poem: tentative, exploratory, following its own instincts, testing its footsteps. In *Wintering Out*, Heaney's work clearly inherits this element of risk. Turning away from statement, assertion, the enforcing of a moral, his poems begin to turn inward on themselves, sometimes in an almost riddling self-delightedness; and they begin to take as theme their own material, language itself.

3 Similes and Windscreens

This movement is implied in *Door into the Dark* by two recurrent features of the book, the 'self-inwoven simile' (or the reflexive image), and the characterization of Heaney-as-driver. Christopher Ricks has noticed in Heaney, as in some other contemporary poets from Northern Ireland, a poetic figure shared with the seventeenth-century English poet Andrew Marvell which William Empson defined as the 'self-inwoven simile'; Ricks makes the point that both Marvell and the Northern Irish poets 'write out of an imagination of civil war', and that the reflexive image 'simultaneously acknowledges the opposing forces and yearns to reconcile them'.[13] There are instances of it in *Death of a Naturalist* (such as 'The burn drowns steadily in its own downpour' in 'Waterfall'), but it is more common in *Door into the Dark*, and persists variously in the later work. Ricks does not catalogue all the occurrences in *Door into the Dark*, but some of them are: 'a wick that is / its own taper and light', of an eel, in 'The Return'; 'under the black weight of their own breathing' in 'In Gallarus Oratory'; 'The leggy birds stilted on their own legs, / Islands riding themselves out into the fog' and 'things founded clean on their own shapes' in 'The Peninsula'; 'The breakers pour / Themselves into themselves' in 'Girls Bathing, Galway 1965'; the mosquitoes 'dying through / Their own live empyrean' in 'At Ardboe Point'.

In *Door into the Dark* these images or 'similes' connect with the structural circularity or reflexivity in 'A Lough Neagh Sequence'; with that disconcerting instance of metaphorical and syntactical reflexivity in 'Bogland', 'the eye ... / Is wooed into the cyclops' eye / Of a tarn'; and with those epigrammatically reflexive lines in the reticent and difficult poem 'The Plantation', 'Though you walked a straight line / It might be a circle you travelled', 'And having found them once / You were sure to find them again', and its concluding stanza:

You had to come back
To learn how to lose yourself,
To be pilot and stray – witch,
Hansel and Gretel in one.

13 See Christopher Ricks, 'Andrew Marvell: "Its own resemblance"', in *The Force of Poetry* (Clarendon Press, 1984), 34–59, 55, 59.

'The Plantation', indeed, even more thoroughly than 'Bogland', is a poem about itself, its Janus-face looking both at the wood (which is, presumably, that of a landed estate, since the poem's title is a political nod in the direction of the 'Plantation' of Ulster in the seventeenth century) and at the poem, all its statements held in an unresolved tension between the literal and the metaphorical. The stanza could be regarded almost as the 'philosophy' of this reflexivity in Heaney. Both pursuer and pursued, both in control and in surrender, the poet finds himself by losing himself in the language and in the form of his own poem. Poetic tradition or intertextuality is a desolation as well as a comfort, both envy and self-assertion: 'Someone had always been there / Though always you were alone'.

In the characterization of the poet-as-driver in *Door into the Dark*, the potential solipsism of the reflexive is given an accompanying poetic persona, as the perceiver is cut off from the object of perception by a car windscreen. In 'The Peninsula', the recommendation to 'drive / For a day all round the peninsula' is specifically dependent on your having 'nothing more to say', on being locked into your own silence; and the poem tellingly recreates the exhilaration of meditative solitary driving. 'Elegy for a Still-Born Child' discovers in a similar situation not exhilaration but the pain of loss, as the driver's consciousness is saturated by an awareness of the dead infant:

I drive by remote control on this bare road
Under a drizzling sky, a circling rook,

Past mountain fields, full to the brim with cloud,
White waves riding home on a wintry lough.

The poems 'Night Drive' and 'At Ardboe Point' complicate the characterization by being also love poems. In 'Night Drive', the solitude of the journey through France is tense with anticipation of the company which will end it, and the strong sexual feeling is, with reticent artfulness, diverted into evocations of the drive itself – the signposts which 'promised, promised'; the places 'granting ... fulfilment'; the thought of Italy laying 'its loin to France on the darkened sphere'. 'At Ardboe Point' modifies the figure: not now a solitary driver, but a pair of lovers together in the car, although curiously isolated nevertheless, at the centre of 'A smoke of flies' – 'they open and close on us / As the air opens and closes'. Even 'Shoreline', for all its recovery of a history of invasion from the Irish coastline, and for all that it eventually swells to embrace the whole island of Ireland, opens with a car 'Turning a corner, taking a hill / In County Down'.

The persistence of this figure in later Heaney is emphatic: it concludes *Wintering Out* (in 'Westering'), *Station Island* (in 'On the Road') and *The Spirit Level* (in 'Postscript'); and it is also central to some of his most-discussed other poems: the dedicatory poem of *Wintering Out* ('This morning from a dewy motorway'), 'The Toome Road', 'From the Frontier of Writing' and poem xxxi of 'Squarings' ('You drive into a meaning made of trees'). To compound its connection with the kinds of reflexivity I am discussing here, 'Postscript' may also be read as a revisiting of 'The Peninsula', and one whose possibly punning title suggests that something does, after all, come 'after script', survive textuality; in this case a heart-lifting response to the Irish coastline, specifically that of the much-mythologized Irish West. As the figure is initiated in *Door into the Dark*, it marks a move towards a more realistic reconciliation between the rural and the industrial or mechanical than the facile oppositions implied by 'The Forge'. The sense it conveys of a consciousness hermetically sealed off from its perceived environment and circumstances is also partly responsible for that poignant loneliness which is such a notable feature of some of Heaney's most interesting work. 'Something of his sad freedom / As he rode the tumbril / Should come to me, driving', he says in 'The Tollund Man'; and an element of this 'sad freedom' inheres in most of these driving poems, even in *Door into the Dark*.

4 Aggravations

In an interview, Heaney explains that the poem 'Docker', about a Northern Protestant, and a poem about Carrickfergus Castle (a former bastion of English power in Ireland) were among his first mature poetic efforts: 'my first attempts to speak, to make verse, faced the Northern sectarian problem. Then this went underground and I became very influenced by Hughes and one part of my temperament took over: the private County Derry childhood part of myself rather than the slightly aggravated young Catholic male part.'[14] It did not go completely underground, however, even in the first two books, since *Death of a Naturalist* does include 'Docker', with its prophetic second stanza ('That fist would drop a hammer on a Catholic – / Oh yes, that kind of thing could start again'); and, in *Door into the Dark*, 'A Lough Neagh Sequence' (with its dedication, 'for the fishermen') offers its tacit support to the clandestine 'poaching' activities of the group of fishermen who frequently came into violent conflict with the British company which officially owned the rights to eel-fishing on Lough Neagh. What lies behind the 'sectarian problem' is also articulated, in these books, in three poems devoted to specific moments of Irish history: the Famine of 1845–8 in 'For the Commander of the "Eliza"' and 'At a Potato Digging' in *Death of a Naturalist*; and the 1798 rebellion of the United Irishmen in 'Requiem for the Croppies' in *Door into the Dark*.

'For the Commander of the "Eliza"' and 'Requiem for the Croppies' are both dramatic monologues, the former spoken by the captain of a ship who sights a rowing boat of starving Irish off the coast of Co. Mayo, and the latter, posthumously, by one of the rebels killed by the English at Vinegar Hill, in Co. Wexford, in 1798. It is significant both that Heaney's early attempts at the dramatic monologue – a form he has used in

---

14 'Unhappy and at Home', with Seamus Deane, *The Crane Bag*, vol. 1 no. 1 (1977), 61–7, 63.

variously inventive ways since – should include these emphatic recreations of characters involved in crucial Irish historical events, and that Heaney's first use in his work of an Irish word should be, in the 'Eliza' poem, 'bia', repeated three times in desperation: the word for 'food'. Both poems also adapt to their own purposes pre-existent documentary sources – Cecil Woodham-Smith's study of the Famine, *The Great Hunger* (1962) in 'Eliza', and an impassioned and harrowing account of 1798 published by a survivor, P. O'Kelly, in Dublin in 1842, his *General History of the Rebellion of 1798*, in 'Requiem for the Croppies'. A use of documentary source material is later essential to the procedures of *North*, where Heaney constructs his own myth to articulate the 'sectarian problem'.

A comparison between poem and source for 'Eliza' reveals Heaney powerfully transforming the bleak original into a testimony to the humane but hopeless decency of the commander who speaks. In his report of the sighting –

> O my sweet Christ,
> We saw piled in the bottom of their craft
> Six grown men with gaping mouths and eyes
> Bursting the sockets like spring onions in drills

– the desperation of the apostrophe to Christ and the grotesque, quasi-expressionist simile are Heaney's own, as in the numerical particularity of that 'six' (the original has merely 'a boatload'). When, subsequently, the men are said to haunt the ship 'like six bad smells', the repeated precision conveys a kind of eerily discriminating accountancy not inappropriate to the English treatment of Ireland during the Famine.

'Requiem for the Croppies' was written in 1966, when Irish poets were commemorating the fiftieth anniversary of the Easter Rising of 1916. In what is to become a recognizably oblique way, Heaney celebrates not the Rising itself but what he considers its original seed in the rebellion of 1798. The boys of Wexford, or the 'croppy boys' (so named because they cropped their hair in the manner of the peasants of the French Revolution) were mercilessly killed at Vinegar Hill. Heaney's poem makes its nationalist sympathies clear when its final line ('And in August the barley grew up out of the grave') weaves into its image of seasonal renewal the sense of political resurgence. Irish Republicans were quick to read the implication here, and the poem became a popular one at Republican gatherings. Heaney has subsequently registered unease about how readily it could be appropriated. In this context, it is worth saying that it has stood up very well over the years as a text in which depth of empathetic feeling is imaginatively expressed with a kind of tragic economy. Its local details note the miseries of an actual history of hopelessness ('shaking scythes at cannon') without rhetorical heightening; and it risks, and justifies, an ironically Keatsian luxuriance in the line 'The hillside blushed, soaked in our broken wave', where the verb's vividly peculiar but appropriate personification dramatizes the sense of shame taken into the land itself by the atrocity committed on it.[15]

'At a Potato Digging' is artfully constructed, in its four sections, to uncover how, to the eye of the historical imagination, the Irish Famine, when the potato disastrously failed, remains as a 'running sore' infecting and blighting the contemporary activity of harvesting the potato crop. The present is made transparent to the past by the minatory and chilling puns which describe the diggers' fingers going 'dead in the cold', and their feeling 'Dead-beat' before lunch; and in the deft cinematic dissolve between the second and third sections, where the metaphorical description of potatoes in their pits as 'live skulls, blind-eyed' turns into the literal 'Live skulls, blind-eyed' of those starving to death in the nineteenth century. The continuity between past and present is enforced too by the figuring of the relationship between Irish agricultural labourer and the land as a religion propitiating 'the famine god'. Potato digging becomes a ritual of appeasement (with 'processional

15 In Keats's 'The Eve of St Agnes', 'A shielded scutcheon blushed with blood of kings and queens'.

stooping', 'humbled knees' and the labourers making 'a seasonal altar of the sod') to the earth as 'the black / Mother', the beneficial provider of food. When the crop fails during the Famine, the black mother becomes 'the bitch earth'; and, although this mother is subsequently partially demythologized as 'the faithless ground', the workers still spill their sacrificial 'Libations of cold tea'. The poem's quasi-Catholic rituals make it clear how deeply the sufferings of Irish historical experience are inscribed in the landscape itself and in the human psyche; and that 'black mother' will reappear in *Wintering Out* and *North*, in a newly mythologized form, as the goddess Nerthus.

Cold Beads of History and Home:
Wintering Out (1972)

It is a phrase associated with cattle, and with hired boys also.
In some ways, it links up with a very resonant line of English
verse that every schoolboy knows: 'Now is the winter of our
discontent'. It is meant to gesture towards the distresses that
we are all undergoing in this country at the minute. It is
meant to be, I suppose, comfortless enough, but with a
notion of survival in it.

    Seamus Heaney, explaining his title (*Listener*, 7 December 1972)

1 Obliquities

When it appeared in 1972, *Wintering Out* received a number of
rather indifferent reviews. Some lamented its apparent inability
to move far beyond the subject matter of the first two books,
while others regretted its lack of any obvious engagement with
the political situation in the North of Ireland. Heaney had been
writing, and publishing, poems which more straightforwardly
confronted the Northern violence after 1969, and some of them
eventually reappeared in *North*; but *Wintering Out*, like its title,
'gestures towards' the realities of the contemporary historical
moment rather than attempting to address them with any
specificity or intimacy. In the kinds of gesture it makes, however,
it does address, if not the conflict itself, then the context out of
which that conflict sprang. In doing so, it displays that peculiar
charge and vibrancy which is the essential signature of a poet of
distinction coming, for the first time, into possession of his
unique identity. In *Wintering Out*, Seamus Heaney, taking com-
mand of his proper material, seems hardly able to keep up with
himself; it is a volume in which the promise of future work is

almost as satisfying as the recognition of present achievement.

The reasons for Heaney's chosen obliquity are implicit in two poems which come closest to the contemporary violence: the dedicatory poem, 'This morning from a dewy motorway' (which reappears as section IV of 'Whatever You Say Say Nothing', in *North*) and 'A Northern Hoard'. The dedicatory poem situates Heaney once more behind a car windscreen, driving past the new internment camp, Long Kesh (subsequently known as the Maze prison), outside Belfast, built to house those detained after the introduction of internment without trial in August 1971. Heaney is now cut off from the landscape not only by the car window, but by the sense that what he is seeing for the first time has actually already been seen:

> There was that white mist you get on a low ground
> and it was déjà-vu, some film made
> of Stalag 17, a bad dream with no sound.

That 'déjà-vu' is the register of Heaney's anguished bafflement. The internment camp is as unlikely, in this familiar territory, as a Nazi concentration camp; it has defamiliarized the locale. Yet it is utterly familiar too, in all the received images of the Second World War that it summons to mind. The implicit question this asks the poet is how something so estrangingly familiar is to be described with any of the freshness necessary to poetry. The poet cannot simply describe again what has already been described once too often; and this poem, indeed, takes refuge in the public language of the stoically witty Belfast graffito, 'Is there a life before death?' In 'A Northern Hoard', Heaney actually asks himself the question about poetry more directly: 'What do I say if they wheel out their dead? / I'm cauterized, a black stump of home.' 'Cauterized': scarred or seared into insensibility, incapable of feeling or responding, having nothing to 'say'. *Wintering Out* attempts to find a voice for this abjection, and to find images of suffering, endurance and resistance which will not seem already seen.

It searches for this voice and these images within the 'home' itself. In 'A Northern Hoard', Heaney remembers trying to strike fire from flints when he was a child. Developing the memory into a symbolically resonant reaction to the present, he imagines these flints as 'Cold beads of history and home' which he 'fingered'. This memorial rosary may act as an image for the poems in *Wintering Out* too, which fondle memories, objects, names and words from Heaney's own original place, in order to evoke it now in its historical, political and linguistic complexity. In fingering such 'cold beads of history and home', Heaney writes, in *Wintering Out*, a poetry everywhere bruised by Northern politics, even though rarely confronting them directly. His obliquities are not evasive: they are, rather, subtly responsive and alert to present conflict, but concerned to be poetry, and not some other thing. As a result, the poems themselves hover intricately between the literal and the symbolic, realism and allegory, politics and philology. Restlessly missing their last definition, they avoid the snares of ideological declaration and received opinion. Instead, they feel tentatively along the lines that bind an individual to his people and a people to their history.

2 Geniuses of Place

The historical and political themes in *Wintering Out* are carried, in a number of poems in Part One, by particular imagined or recalled human figures: Edmund Spenser, the 'moustached dead' and the 'geniuses' of wood and glen in 'Bog Oak'; the 'Servant Boy' of the poem containing the phrase which gives the book its title; 'the last mummer'; Shakespeare's MacMorris and Joyce's Leopold Bloom in 'Traditions'; the 'girl from Derrygarve' in 'A New Song'; Henry Joy McCracken, executed after the 1798 rebellion, alluded to in 'Linen Town'; 'the Tollund man'; and the labourer of 'Navvy'. They are complemented, in mood and meaning, by various figures in Part Two, with its more miscellaneous poems: the 'mother of the groom'; the mad girl of 'A Winter's Tale'; the resentful wife of 'Shore Woman'; the mermaid (or suicide) of 'Maighdean Mara'; the mother who drowns her baby in 'Limbo'; the dumb victim of parental cruelty in 'Bye-Child'; and the lovers at angry, hurt odds in 'Summer Home'. In both parts of the book, many of the evoked figures suffer some kind of human diminishment: isolation, repression, disenchantment, exploitation or betrayal. They act as exemplars of suffering and endurance, and they are complemented by the volume's two references to Christ: at the end of 'Limbo', where he is a figure of the most intense exclusion and ineffectualness ('Even Christ's palms, unhealed, / Smart and cannot fish there'), and in the surreal image of the final line of 'Westering' – and therefore of the whole book – where, in a figure of lonely unconnectedness which perhaps draws on Salvador Dalí, the poem locates 'Christ weighing by his hands' in the moon's gravity.[1]

In 'Navvy', Heaney addresses the labourer who 'has not relented / under weather or insults' as 'my brother and keeper'; but Heaney himself could be said to act as the brother and keeper of his characters in 'Bog Oak', 'Servant Boy' and 'The Last Mummer', where he gives a place in poetry to those who have usually been excluded from it. In 'Bog Oak', he meditates on that familiar Irish building material, oakwood retrieved from bogland, and derives from it a colonial history in which the great poet of Elizabethan England, Edmund Spenser, is heavily implicated. As well as being the author of *The Faerie Queene*, that lengthy poetic celebration of Elizabethan monarchy, Spenser was one of the 'undertakers' in Ireland for the settlement of Munster; and in this capacity, in about 1598, he

1 'Limbo' is relatively neglected in critical studies of Heaney, but over the years it has assumed new significances in relation to modern Ireland. Its reading in a Northern Irish classroom is a crucial moment in the excellent television film *Hush-a-Bye Baby* made by Molly Harkin and the Derry Film and Video Workshop in 1989, with music by Sinéad O'Connor; this includes the song 'Three Babies' which is partly a response to 'Limbo'. Elizabeth Butler Cullingford's 'Seamus and Sinéad: From "Limbo" to *Saturday Night Live* by way of *Hush-a-Bye Baby*', in the *Colby Quarterly*, vol. xxx, no. 1 (March 1994), 43–61, is an illuminating reading of these cultural intersections.

wrote his prose account of the Irish 'problem', *A View of the Present State of Ireland*, from which 'Bog Oak' quotes a phrase on the starving Irish peasantry. Heaney's poem registers a sympathy for these historically dispossessed and maltreated, and for their successors, 'the moustached / dead, the creel-fillers'. As a poet writing in the English language, Heaney is inevitably part of the poetic tradition which contains *The Faerie Queene*; but 'Bog Oak' suggests how tangentially and suspiciously related to it he is when it reminds us that such literary perfections as that great Renaissance poem – written by Spenser 'dreaming sunlight' in Kilcolman Castle, his planter's estate in Co. Cork – were the flower of a culture whose roots lay in the brutal political realities described in the *State of Ireland*. Nevertheless, 'Bog Oak' is more saddened than resentful; it has, like those creel-fillers, its own 'hopeless wisdom'. 'Servant Boy', on the other hand, gives resentment its voice. The boy – servant, presumably, to one of the Big Houses of the Protestant Ascendancy – keeps a wily 'patience' and 'counsel', but ends 'resentful / and impenitent', a servant entirely without servility, carrying those eggs which may be 'warm' with the possibility of a different kind of future. In 'The Last Mummer', resentment breaks out into retaliation: the mummer, as the 'last' representative of the dying forms of rural life, 'trammelled / in the taboos of the country', casts his stone in anger at one of the homes in which the culture of television has rendered him obsolete and redundant.

It is the point of these poems, however, that they also imply Heaney's own kinship, as a poet, with the representative figures. Being watchful and alert is a wise recommendation for a poet as well as for a last mummer if both are 'picking a nice way through / the long toils of blood / / and feuding'; and, in the central stanza of 'Servant Boy', poet and character almost merge at the centre of their respective trails – the boy's wintering journey, the poet's written script:

Wintering Out

> ... how
> you draw me into
> your trail. Your trail
>
> broken from haggard to stable ...

Heaney has often quoted Robert Frost's dictum that, 'like a piece of ice on a hot stove, the poem must ride on its own melting';[2] and one of the characteristic effects of the new quatrain form he is inventing in these poems is of the melting, merging, dissolving of line into line and image into image, the poem perilously and precariously maintaining a grip on its own speedy unravelling. In the phrasal repetition which constitutes a single line of 'Servant Boy' ('your trail. Your trail'), this process perhaps reaches a vanishing point, even as it visibly pursues a trail; but it does suggest how useful the form could be to Heaney as an almost typographical enactment of sympathetic involvement with his subject, a testing, probing, tentative scrutiny of his material. In these poems of *Wintering Out*, this effect of the quatrain is reinforced by the beginnings of that use of the personal pronoun which is a vital element in the character of the poems of Part 1 of *North*: the poet's 'I' is detached from ordinary social circumstance, withdrawn to solipsistic meditation, ruminatively entranced, the hero of its own imaginative constructions and elaborations.

These uses of the personal pronoun and the slim quatrain form are crucially constitutive of 'The Tollund Man', which could be regarded as the culmination of these poems of representative figures in *Wintering Out*. That the Tollund man has a significance for Heaney comparable to that of the other figures of the book is made plain in an interview in which he says that when he first saw the man's photograph in P. V. Glob's book, *The Bog People*, he 'seemed like an ancestor almost, one

2 The axiom comes from Frost's 'The Figure a Poem Makes', his preface to his *Complete Poems*, reprinted in James Scully (ed.), *Modern Poets on Modern Poetry* (Fontana/Collins, 1966). See Chapter 9.

33

of my old uncles, one of those moustached archaic faces you used to meet all over the Irish countryside'.[3] He is one of the 'moustached dead' too, then; and we might remember that Heaney had already written a poem about one of these old uncles, 'Ancestral Photograph' in *Death of a Naturalist*. There is an element of special pleading in Heaney's account here of the Tollund man's photograph. He is not very obviously 'moustached', and he is younger and more elegant, in fact, than such moustached, archaic Irishmen seem to me. This only makes it more apparent, however, how greatly Heaney desires that 'The Tollund Man' should be also a poem about an ancestral photograph. He is beginning, here, to discover that suggestive analogy between Glob's bog-bodies and the victims of Irish political violence which culminates in the extended mythologizing of the 'bog poems' of *North*.

The analogy is not dependent only on physical appearance, of course; and Heaney emphasizes the deeper imaginative connection he is making when he publishes, alongside 'The Tollund Man', the very short poem 'Nerthus'. Nerthus is the fertility goddess to whom, Glob argues, some of the Iron Age people preserved in the peat bogs of Jutland were ritual sacrifices; their murder in winter, and the disposal of their bodies in bogs sacred to the goddess, would ensure the fertility of the crops the following spring. This is why the Tollund man is, in Heaney's account, a 'Bridegroom to the goddess', and why the processes of his burial and preservation are described in sexual terms. It is also why 'Nerthus' describes the grains of the ash fork 'gathering to the gouged split': in the photograph of the representation of the goddess Heaney has in mind here, this 'split' is a heavy incision, symbolic of the female sexual organ, cut at the fork of a wooden branch. The poem, however, implicitly translates the goddess out of Iron Age Jutland into modern Northern Ireland when the landscape she stands in is defined in Northern dialect terms: 'kesh', a causeway, and 'loaning', an uncultivated space

3 Interview with James Randall, *Ploughshares*, vol. 5 no. 3 (1979), 7–22.

between fields; the former, in particular, taking an edge from its use in the proper name 'Long Kesh', the internment camp Heaney drives past in the dedicatory poem of the book.

This compacting in Heaney's imagination of Jutland and Ireland was impelled, he tells us in 'Feeling into Words', by his sensing a kinship between these ancient sacrificial killings and 'the tradition of Irish political martyrdom for that cause whose icon is Kathleen ní Houlihan'; for, that is, the cause of Irish Republicanism. The implications of this recognition are fully pursued in *North*; but in 'The Tollund Man' it gives Heaney his first opportunity to bring into relation the Iron Age victim and the victims of recent Irish sectarian atrocity.[4] In this imagined continuity of sacrificial ritual, the Tollund man is worked to 'a saint's kept body' by the preservative powers of the peat. His corpse is therefore like the miraculously in-corrupt bodies of Catholic hagiology, a certain sign that he may be petitioned as a saint is. The hope in the poem's petition is that he may make these recent dead 'germinate' again, as his killers hoped he would make their next season's crops germinate. This concept has almost the startling force of a metaphysical conceit when it erupts into the second section of the poem; the poetic equivalent, perhaps, of the religious danger of 'blasphemy' which it also invokes. However, although the analogy it suggests clearly provides 'The Tollund Man' with its structure and its rationale, the connection which actually supplies its emotional sustenance is not that between Ireland and Jutland, but between the Tollund man and the

4 It is on this relation that negative criticism of the bog poems, mainly those of *North*, has centred. I quote Edna Longley's critique in my next chapter, and Ciaran Carson's in the appendix. Feminist criticism has also taken these poems as text, and Elizabeth Butler Cullingford's ' "Thinking of Her … as … Ireland": Yeats, Pearse and Heaney', in *Textual Practice*, vol. 4 no. 1 (1990), 1–21, is a notable contribution to the debate; she observes, for instance, that Heaney 'vacillates between the positions of detached anthropological observer and dismayed devotee of the Goddess', so that 'he seems unable to understand how the habit of thinking in immutable gender polarities helps to sustain the political problem he deplores'.

poet himself. Heaney's contemplative 'I' appears twice in the opening section in the repeated solemnity of a promise of pilgrimage; and the section tenderly and scrupulously disinters the man's body, carrying him, as it were, from the photograph into language.[5] The opening line of the second section – 'I could risk blasphemy' – is an admission of the man's power over him: he can compel a 'religious' reaction outside the norms of conventional piety. And the third section, which prophesies the poet's feelings when he gets to Jutland, establishes him and the Tollund man in exactly the kind of sympathetic relationship between subjective 'I' and object of attention to be found in 'Servant Boy'. Indeed, the 'trail' of that poem may be said to survive here as both the slight initial uncertainty about whether the adjectival phrases of the first section apply to man or poet, and as the poet's drive through the alien countryside, during which he shares the man's 'sad freedom' on the tumbril ride to his execution.

This empathetic involvement produces the strangely dream-like quality of the poem's paradoxical concluding lines, where the poet is both estranged and familiar, as he is in his condition of 'déjà-vu' in the dedicatory poem:

> Out there in Jutland
> In the old man-killing parishes
> I will feel lost,
> Unhappy and at home.

5 There is one sense in which the bog poems, for all their extraordinary originality, share in what is virtually a sub-genre of post-war poetry: the poem about the photograph, of which Philip Larkin's 'Lines on a Young Lady's Photograph Album' and Ted Hughes's 'Six Young Men' are classic cases. These in turn share in a long Western European tradition of 'ekphrastic' poetry, poetry about works of art. Heaney is discussed in this context in Jefferson Hunter, *Image and Word: The Interaction of Twentieth-Century Photographs and Texts* (Harvard University Press, 1987); and James A. W. Heffernan's *Museum of Words: The Poetics of Ekphrasis from Homer to Ashbery* (University of Chicago Press, 1993) is a valuable account of the whole context. See Chapter 7.

What the analogy has ultimately provided for Heaney in 'The Tollund Man' is this use of the word 'home', which goes beyond irony and sadness into tragedy, and is utterly comfortless and desolating.[6] The lines are the more blankly disconsolate for the blunt archaic abruptness of that 'man-killing', which strikes virtually with the peculiarity of neologism when one remembers that it is ousting the more conventional (and almost metrically identical) 'murderous'. In placing its emotional weight where it does, on the relationship between poet and evoked human figure, 'The Tollund Man' both inherits from less complex poems in *Wintering Out*, and also dissolves its more ambitious mythical elements into something sharply immediate: the pain of personal incomprehension, isolation and pity.

3 Tongues and Ears

Part of the dislocating effect of the final section of 'The Tollund Man' derives from Heaney's imagining himself uttering an alienating litany while driving through Jutland:

> Saying the names
>
> Tollund, Grauballe, Nebelgard,
> Watching the pointing hands
> Of country people,
> Not knowing their tongue.

'Tongue' is a word that reverberates through the volume, and the saying of other names – 'Anahorish', 'Toome', 'Broagh', for instance – is a common activity in the book. Not knowing the 'tongue' of the country you travel in is the deepest kind of estrangement; and Heaney's preoccupation with the tongue, in this book which subtly registers the contours of a divided

---

6 It may be said to find its analogue in Derek Mahon's rhyming of 'home' and 'bomb' in his poem 'Afterlives'.

culture, derives from the fact that the tongue, or language, he speaks, and uses as a poet – English – is not native or original to the land he comes from – Ireland – or straightforwardly iden-tifiable with the feelings or aspirations of the community from which he derives. English is, at least in the traditional national-ist reading of the case, the imposition of the colonial oppressor, dispossessing the native Irish of their own first 'tongue'.[7] The historical and political themes of *Wintering Out*, therefore, are necessarily implicit in the actual tongue spoken in Northern Ireland; and the book includes many poems about language itself.

'Traditions' acts, perhaps in a slightly self-conscious and programmatic way, as the major enunciation of this linguistic theme. A densely packed poem, it is centrally preoccupied with Shakespeare. Its first section imagines Elizabethan English as that 'alliterative tradition' ('alliterative', because the earliest metres of English poetry, in Anglo-Saxon and Middle English, were alliterative in form) which, following the Elizabethan Plantation of Ireland, has 'bulled' – raped, masculinely forced its will upon – the 'guttural muse' of the native Irish language, that virtually disappeared tongue commemorated in the poign-ant, glancing, allegorical elegy, 'The Backward Look'. In the lines in which the initial act of rape is followed by acceptance of 'custom, that "most / sovereign mistress"' who 'beds us down into / the British Isles', Heaney is drawing on *Othello* I.iii, where the Duke calls opinion 'a sovereign mistress of effects', and Othello begins his reply, 'The tyrant custom ... / Hath made the flinty and steel couch of war / My thrice driven bed of down'. The first section of 'Traditions' therefore adapts Shakespeare to

---

7 There are other views of the issue; and the whole matter of the relationship between the Irish and the English languages is one that itself becomes the focus of attention in a great deal of modern Irish literature. See, for instance, my own account of this in *After Yeats and Joyce: Reading Modern Irish Literature* (OUP, 1997) and Michael Cronin's historical survey, *Translating Ireland: Translation, Languages, Cultures* (Cork University Press, 1996), which makes reference to Heaney.

create a linguistic-sexual metaphor for Ireland's traumatic colonial history, a history whose crucial moment – the Elizabethan conquest and the Plantation of Ulster – occurred during Shakespeare's lifetime.

The second section then ironically notes some of the contemporary results of this 'bulling': the persistence, in the English spoken in Northern Ireland, of some 'correct Shakespearean' forms, and the currency of terms introduced by the Scots and English planters ('bawn', an English colonist's fortified farmhouse, and 'mossland', the Scots word for 'bogland').[8] The third part of the poem focuses its theme through two further emblematic figures; not now invented, or imaginatively elaborated from their sources, but quoted from literature: Shakespeare's MacMorris from *Henry V* and Joyce's Bloom from *Ulysses*. 'What ish my nation?' is MacMorris's brogue interruption, in the third act of *Henry V*, when he presumes that Fluellen, the Welshman, is about to criticize the Irish. In *The Irish Novelists 1800–1850*, Thomas Flanagan, to whom 'Traditions' is dedicated, calls MacMorris 'the first stage-Irishman'. The Irish as 'anatomies of death' is a further reference to Spenser's *State of Ireland*, to the same passage, in fact, quoted in 'Bog Oak'.

These Elizabethan English versions, or 'traditions', of Irishry – the comic buffoon; the deliberately starved victim – are finally countered in the poem by Leopold Bloom, the hero of Ireland's great modern epic (written, of course, in English), James Joyce's *Ulysses*. In the 'Cyclops' episode of that book, the Jewish Bloom

8 The forms are combined in the name of Heaney's first home, 'Mossbawn', as he tells us in 'Belfast' in *Preoccupations*, which is why they are chosen as representative here. Although Heaney's essay says that 'bawn' is the name the English colonists gave to their fortified farmhouses, the word in fact derives from the Irish *bábhún*. In Heaney's home town of Bellaghy there is a building called 'Bellaghy Bawn' which is now, in part, a museum devoted to his work. It is an excellent example of the kind of structure he has in mind here: a political lesson in stone in its skilful (and indeed beautiful) harmony of agricultural and military structures. I am grateful to John McVeagh for the round trip and good company from Portstewart to Bellaghy.

defends himself against an anti-Semitic Irish nationalist by insisting that Ireland is his nation because he was born there. The simple assertive dignity of his declaration – emphasized by Heaney's giving it two verbs of articulation, 'replied' and 'said' – is a criticism of the national stereotypes exhibited in the poem, and therefore, implicitly, of all such stereotyping. It is also an insistence on the achievement of the English language as it is spoken, and, written, in Ireland. Bloom, created out of the juncture between modern Irish urban experience and the English language, reveals James Joyce inheriting the language of Shake-speare, the 'alliterative tradition', but bending it to a 'guttural' Irish idiom, to produce – out of a sense of the futility of the received wisdoms and clichés of nationality – major literature.

'Traditions' reveals itself, then, peculiarly alert to the ways in which a spoken tongue might be the medium of a history and a politics; and the word 'ear' is consequently also prominent in *Wintering Out*, as the poet describes himself listening in to the language of his original place. He lies 'with my ear / in this loop of silence' in 'Land'; he remembers himself as 'small mouth and ear / in a woody cleft, / lobe and larynx / of the mossy places' in 'Oracle'; and, in 'Gifts of Rain', he takes 'soundings' into the flooded landscape, where the word punningly means both measurings of the depth of water and attunements to the sounds made on the land. The poem typifies the balance maintained between realism and allegory in *Wintering Out*. It begins as an evocation of the flooding of the Moyola, the local river, and discovers, in the wader's reaction to the flood, a compelling image of interdependence between man and land. A figure of circularity and reflexivity, the man is 'hooped to where he planted', the sky and ground 'running naturally among his arms / that grope the cropping land'. The knowledgeable intimacy of his mutuality is then refigured as the community's 'world-schooled ear' which can 'monitor' the language of the flood; and the poem pushes out of realistic evocation and allegory, as Heaney's meditative 'I' pushes out of the poem's previous third persons:

I cock my ear
at an absence –
in the shared calling of blood

arrives my need
for antediluvian lore.
Soft voices of the dead
are whispering by the shore

that I would question
(and for my children's sake)
about crops rotted, river mud
glazing the baked clay floor.

The 'absence' which the poet's ear picks up there is that of the older native 'lore' of pre-colonial Gaelic civilization ('antediluvian', presumably, because prior to the flood of colonization). It is the lore of native history and tradition which those 'soft voices of the dead' might speak; 'soft', no doubt, because they are speaking 'guttural' Irish, as well as because they are ghosts. The parenthesis represents the poem's ethical urgency: listening in to this lore is necessary to any more equitable future. When, therefore, the native Moyola river 'spells itself' in the flood of the final section, 'bedding the locale / in the utterance', its 'tawny guttural water' represents a new political possibility for Ireland: one which, in some harmonizing and reconciling way, will 'pleasure' the poem's 'I', making him a 'Dives', the paradigmatic biblical rich man, by establishing, on this divided soil, 'common ground'.

This is perhaps to spell out the poem's allegory in an over-insistent way, since its method, in which it 'spells itself', is a rich suggestiveness and implication; it manages a language stirring vibrantly with possible meaning rather than settling into declaration. When 'A New Song', in which the Moyola appears 'pleasuring' again, does attempt a greater declarativeness, the result is more problematic. A meditation on the name 'Derry-garve' issues in stanzas which are explicit but equivocal:

But now our river tongues must rise
From licking deep in native haunts
To flood, with vowelling embrace,
Demesnes staked out in consonants.

And Castledawson we'll enlist
And Upperlands, each planted bawn –
Like bleaching-greens resumed by grass –
A vocable, as rath and bullaun.

These are difficult lines, and they are glossed only partially by
the essay '1972' in *Preoccupations*, where, discussing his begin-
nings as a poet, Heaney writes, 'I think of the personal and Irish
pieties as vowels, and the literary awarenesses nourished by
English as consonants. My hope is that the poems will be voc-
ables adequate to my whole experience.' Unlike the flood over
'common ground' at the end of 'Gifts of Rain', however, the
flooding of a staked demesne seems much more an act of aggres-
sion; curiously remote, in fact, from a 'vowelling embrace'.[9]
The politically loaded words 'rise' (as in 'Easter Rising'?) and
'planted' (acquired by an act of dispossession during the Planta-
tion of Ulster), and the military 'enlist', hold the lines back from
any easily unitary vision. Similarly, as several commentators
have noted, the word 'must' is ambiguous, hovering between
its meanings of an inevitable process and an encouragement
to action. What is clear is the prophecy that the colonized terri-
tory of the Plantation will be 'resumed' – that is, taken back –
by entering into a new relationship with the native culture, as
the old bleaching-greens of the Protestant Ulster linen trade
have been 'resumed by grass', have gone 'native' again; and
the poem 'The Wool Trade' knows the historical cost of that in-
dustry when it ends with 'talk of tweed, / A stiff cloth with
flecks of blood'. The 'new song' of the poem's title is opposed

9 'Demesne', which appears frequently in Heaney, is the Anglo-French
word for a landed estate, obsolete in England, but still current in Ireland.

to the 'old song' which Robert Emmet, in 1803, called the story
of England's relations with Ireland. It will be sung in 'vocables'
which include not only the Irish words 'rath' (a hill-fort) and
'bullaun' (a hollowed stone mortar, found on archaeological
sites), but also the names of such places as Castledawson and
Upperlands, now captured and transformed by the poet's ima-
gination and put in the same class as these terms which emanate
affection and attachment.

Reticent, or uncertain, about how this new song might ever
come to be sung in the world of real politics as opposed to the
world of the poem, 'A New Song' has its origins in the
optimistic Civil Rights period in Northern Ireland. Despite its
ambiguities, its tone is light and it derives its politics from an
encounter which is initially playful or amatory, and as ani-
mated as a meeting in folksong ('I met a girl from Derrygarve'),
even if it also has behind it something aspiring to the resolved
balladic measure of the opening lines of the penultimate stanza,
with their echoes of political broadside. Its image of native
'river tongues' is at one with the way the poem makes the
Moyola itself a kind of mouth, its 'stepping stones like black
molars', just as 'Gifts of Rain' gives the same river a voice.
Heaney is here both playing with the usual applied usage, 'the
mouth of the river', and drawing out some implications of
Wordsworth's use of the word 'voice' in relation to water: 'the
voice / Of mountain torrents', for instance, in Book v of *The
Prelude*. In their conjuring of an articulate landscape, and in the
almost erotically satisfying 'pleasuring' which this offers, these
poems are clearly related to those shorter pieces of great
originality, the 'place-name poems' 'Anahorish', 'Toome' and
'Broagh'.

Heaney says of these poems in an interview:

I had a great sense of release as they were being written, a joy and
devil-may-careness, and that convinced me that one could be faithful
to the nature of the English language – for in some senses these poems
are erotic mouth-music by and out of the anglo-saxon tongue – and, at

the same time, be faithful to one's own non-English origin, for me that is County Derry.[10]

They are envisaged, then, as sudden, swooping retrievals of reconciliatory 'vocables' from within the etymology of the warmly cherished place-names of Heaney's home, and they may have been sanctioned by the Gaelic tradition of *dinnseanchas* which Heaney defines in 'The Sense of Place' in *Preoccupations* as 'poems and tales which relate the original meanings of place names and constitute a form of mythological etymology'.[11] The 'devil-may-careness' of their composition is reflected in the casual assurance and insouciance of their effect, and in what might be thought the audacity of their titles. The names of these small townlands of Co. Derry are made to register, in English poetry, with something of that defiant self-assertiveness shared by the otherwise scarcely known place-names which entitle Eliot's individual *Four Quartets* or Edward Thomas's 'Adlestrop'. They insist that the importance of a place depends not on the world's having heard of it, but on its significance for the poet who writes it. This presumptuousness is the origin of the inventive and fecund compression of these poems, as the place-name articulated by the tongue is made to yield, speedily, a local history; they are poems which rapidly seize a world from a word.

In 'Anahorish', the word is almost wooed by the poet lovingly celebrating its 'vocable': 'soft gradient / of consonant, vowel-meadow'. The shape of the landscape, which reconciles hill and meadow, is reconstituted in the word, which reconciles, with the 'consonant' of its English, the 'vowel' of its original Irish –

10 'Unhappy and at Home', with Seamus Deane, *The Crane Bag*, vol. 1 no. 1 (1977), 61–7.
11 They may also, however, owe something to Wordsworth's 'Poems on the Naming of Places', included in *Lyrical Ballads*; in his 'Advertisement' for them Wordsworth says, 'By Persons resident in the country and attached to rural objects, many places will be found unnamed or of unknown names, where little Incidents will have occurred, or feelings been experienced, which will have given to such places a private and peculiar interest.'

'anach fhior uisce', the 'place of clear water'. The world conjured from the word is one of an almost Arcadian freshness, the 'first hill in the world': 'first', because it is the hill of the poet's original place, and also because it is the site of a human continuity which allows him to imagine the farm workers of his childhood as primitive 'mound-dwellers', conveying a sense of what 'The Seed Cutters' in *North* will call 'our anonymities'. The poem offers the strong sense too, though, that this is now a 'first' place perceived from a different one, held in the mind and the memory as consolatory and comforting, an 'after-image'. Made 'my' place because, now, a place of the imagination, made out of words, the place-name has become the name of a poem, in a gesture which accommodates, even as it places, nostalgia.

'Toome', similarly but less pleasurably, recovers from the 'soft blastings' of its pronunciation 'a hundred centuries' of human habitation. Toome is situated in the Bann valley, the site of major archaeological finds, and one of the longest-inhabited areas in Ireland: hence the discovery of those 'torcs and fish-bones' in the souterrain (an ancient underground chamber) under the 'slab of the tongue'. It was also, however, one of the sites of the 1798 rebellion, and hence the military remains – 'flints, musket-balls' – of those eighteenth-century battles. Out of all this history and pre-history, the poet imagines himself 'prospecting what new';[12] attempting to search out, presumably, that alternative cultural and political possibility intimated in 'Gifts of Rain' and 'A New Song'. In fact, however, the prospector's search culminates not in the 'new', but in the very ancient indeed, as he finds himself

> ... sleeved in

> alluvial mud that shelves
> suddenly under

12 This is an odd usage – possibly dialectal? – which one might expect to read 'what's new'.

bogwater and tributaries,
and elvers tail my hair.

That compellingly quasi-surreal Medusa image probably owes something to the Medusa heads of Celtic Britain and Ireland, illustrations of which Heaney would have found in Anne Ross's *Pagan Celtic Britain* which he cites during his discussion of 'The Tollund Man' in 'Feeling into Words'. The poem therefore establishes a condition of primeval intimacy between poet and terrain, a sense that the existence of this 'I' is coterminous with its knowledge of this place, which goes beyond similar figurings in 'Gifts of Rain'. This knowledge, however, seems not enabling, or releasing, as it does in that poem, but dangerous. You lose your footing when the mud 'shelves / suddenly', particularly when the line-break enacts the shock of it; and those elvers retain the queasy power of that 'horrid cable' of eels in 'A Lough Neagh Sequence' in *Door into the Dark*, whose first section refers to Toomebridge, and whose final section prefigures this Medusa image, when the child is warned that the lice in his hair will 'gang up / Into a mealy rope / And drag him, small, dirty, doomed / Down to the water'. This sleeving and sudden shelving may thus be read as metaphorical versions of that complicitous 'understanding' of 'tribal revenge' articulated provocatively at the end of 'Punishment' in *North*. The Medusa, of course, turned anyone who looked at her to stone.

An intimacy with place is more simply conciliatory in 'Broagh', which draws from its place-name (the anglicization of the Irish 'bruach', a riverbank) the opportunity for the release, in an English poem, of the tongue of Co. Derry.[13] The first three

---

13 Tom Paulin thinks that the title is also ghosted by the word 'brogue', meaning both Irish dialect and a type of Irish shoe; the poem of course prominently contains both. He also notes that 'boortree' contains within itself the idea of the 'boor', which the Irish person has sometimes been considered by the English person. See 'Seamus Heaney's "Broagh"', a discussion between Paulin and Graham Martin, *The English Review*, vol. 2 no. 3 (1992), 28–9, the transcript of an Open University programme first broadcast in 1986.

lines of the poem all end with dialect words: 'rigs', for 'furrows', a word brought to Northern Ireland by the Scots planters of the seventeenth century; 'docken', a Scots and archaic English plural for 'dock-leaves'; and 'pad', an English and Scots dialect word for 'path'. Later in the poem 'boortrees', a variant of 'bourtrees', is the old Scots plural for the elderberry (Heaney makes a whole sonnet out of the contrast between the two words in the fifth of his 'Glanmore Sonnets' in *Field Work*). This very short poem, then, celebrates, along with the Irish-derived name of its title, the 'planted' words of the local dialect English; and, imagining the riverbank itself as an imitation, in nature, of the form of the word, the poem delights in the exclusivity of the pronunciation of 'Broagh'. Describing 'that last / gh the strangers found / difficult to manage' is a way of keeping the place private to his community, even while releasing it into the public articulation of a poem, since every reader not from Heaney's own place will also find that last 'gh' difficult to manage.

If 'Broagh' wilfully excludes some readers, however, it does so to create a paradigm of a certain kind of inclusiveness. Discussing the poem in the pamphlet *Among Schoolchildren*, Heaney says that the word 'Broagh' is 'a sound native to Ireland, common to Unionist and Nationalist, but unavailable to an English person'.[14] That he is almost certainly exaggerating here, and that therefore the poem is actually based on a convenient fiction, may be thought even to intensify one's sense that 'Broagh' has a significance in his work altogether disproportionate to its length. Exhilaratedly riding on its own melting, it acts as the linguistic paradigm for a reconciliation beyond sectarian division. Its point is that conflictual histories have resulted in a community whose individual members, whatever their political or religious affinity, now all speak the same language, whether derived from Irish or English or Scots roots. Hence the ability of everyone in this community, whether

14 Seamus Heaney, *Among Schoolchildren* (John Malone Memorial Committee, 1983), 9.

Catholic or Protestant, to pronounce the place name 'Broagh' is intended as a little optimistic or hortatory allegory of potential political, as well as linguistic, community. The poem is a celebration of exclusiveness, we might say, in the interests of local inclusiveness; although the note of exclusion undoubtedly carries its own political brunt too, since the final lines excluding the 'strangers' remind us that it is of course the English who have traditionally found the Irish 'difficult to manage' in the political sense.

Much of the poetic interest of this little political allegory, however, is not only that so much resonance and implication is compacted into such a tiny linguistic space – the poem is hardly more than a few breaths long – but that it is accompanied by a fiction which is both amatory and textual. 'Broagh' addresses a you, the companion, in a way that is attentive, hushed and almost secret. The reader, as it were, overhears what is said; and that poetic tone is entirely consistent with the allegory being described, which is one of shared privacies refusing to countenance disturbance. In addition, both place and place-name are being very self-consciously translated out of actual topography into what we might call the topography of the poem, or the place of the text, by the way it foregrounds that 'black O', the word '*Broagh*' itself, and the last '*gh*', by distinguishing them in italic font. The original place is, we might say, visibly displacing itself into the place of writing; the garden imprinted with the heel-mark becomes the paper imprinted with the text of the poem. In this sense, 'Broagh' is the strong forefather of many other Heaney poems in which such dualities are deeply inscribed, poems in which the eye and ear are scrupulously attentive to the objects of their sensuous evocation, while the writerly pen is turned towards its own tracks and traces too, in a play of self-reflexive figuration.

Despite the tone of 'Broagh', however, *Wintering Out* knows that it is easier to find emblems and paradigms than it is to create political realities; and 'The Other Side' hesitates before the fact of recalcitrance. The frail possibility of connection between

Catholic and Protestant neighbours, mined in any case by silences and embarrassments, is intruded upon by the mutual exclusiveness of their religious languages: the mournful litany of the Catholic rosary, and the Protestant's Old Testament arrogance. The Catholic's response to the Protestant's remark, 'It's poor as Lazarus, that ground', joins tongue and ear together, uniquely in the book, to almost surreal effect: 'my ear swallowing / his fabulous, biblical dismissal, / that tongue of chosen people'. An ear swallowing a tongue is an image of appalling engorgement, making it unsurprising that when Protestant turns away from Catholic, he leaves 'a wake of pollen / drifting to our bank, next season's tares'. Those 'tares' are also, ironically, biblical, deriving from the parable of the sower in Matthew XIII, where they are set deliberately among wheat by an 'enemy'. These are the tares and the enmities which Heaney's next book, *North*, exhausted or exacerbated almost beyond conciliatory gestures, attempts to render into words and images. Yet 'The Other Side' offers, in its third part, an image of *rapprochement* mutually desired, tentatively and tactfully entertained, as Protestant respectfully pauses before the ritual of the Catholic neighbour; and as Catholic poet, who has accorded him this primacy of approach, this willingness to cross to his 'other side', figures a possible communication, imagining himself into the consciousness of the 'other', and imagining it good-willed. A conversation about nothing much, but about a great deal too in an agricultural community, its potential is declared, and only partially undermined by the mode of declaration: an interrogative, not a statement; *rapprochement* balanced against rejection:

> Should I slip away, I wonder,
> or go up and touch his shoulder
> and talk about the weather
>
> or the price of grass-seed?

4 Mooning

If Part Two of *Wintering Out* seems disappointingly miscella-
neous compared to the singleminded purposefulness of Part
One, it nevertheless complements it in at least one significant
respect. I noted earlier that both parts share exemplary or
emblematic figures of suffering or endurance, those of Part
Two having a genuine role in establishing the chilly, disconso-
late mood of the book. These latter, who are predominantly
women, move out of prehistory, history and literature into the
contemporary world, although they acquire something of an
almost mythical or legendary quality too. This is created largely
by the imagery of moonlight and sea in which they are bathed,
and which they share with 'Roots', the opening section of 'A
Northern Hoard' in Part One. There, the woman's body is, like
one of Henry Moore's underground sleepers, 'moonstruck / To
drifted barrow, sunk glacial rock', and the poem's gruesome
symbolic mandrake is 'soaked by moonlight in tidal blood'. In
Part Two, the unhappy wife of 'Shore Woman' walks in the
moonlight to become almost disembodied in the final line, 'A
membrane between moonlight and my shadow'; the mermaid-
suicide of 'Maighdean Mara' lies in water, 'her cold breasts /
Dandled by undertow'; the victimized boy in 'Bye-Child' is a
'Little moon man', his dumbness a 'gaping wordless proof /
of Lunar distances / Travelled beyond love'. In the final poem of
the book, 'Westering', the poet is set under 'Rand McNally's /
"Official Map of the Moon"' in California, remembering
Donegal in the West of Ireland and the moon's 'bony shine'
throwing his shadow on whitewash, and imagining Christ
'weighing by his hands' in the moon's 'untroubled dust';
unlike the Earth's dust, we may take it, on which all of these
emblematic figures are personally 'troubled', and on which
Ireland is undergoing its political 'Troubles'.

These lunar associations suggest that Heaney is making the
figure of the poet emblematic in this poem in the way of the
volume's other such figures. His drive across Ireland to 'The

empty amphitheatre / Of the west' isolates and estranges him on his own home territory as, on Good Friday, he passes a succession of Irish congregations inside their 'still churches', he and his family only a 'dwindling interruption'. This supplies the book with its final image of being 'lost, / Unhappy and at home', an image created 'six thousand miles away' from home, while imagining the utter alienness of the moon. In its lostness and unhappiness, the poem is a fitting close to *Wintering Out*; but its image of the poet himself as estranged outsider is also appropriate to the personal, domestic distress evident in Part Two of the book, which complements the larger political and historical distress of Part One. It is in this primary sense that Part Two seems to me integral to the overall design of the volume. Lostness and unhappiness are located, in the end, 'at home': at, in fact, the poet's 'Summer Home'.

This poem painfully evokes an unhappy period in a marriage by conjuring images of unease, guilt, temporary assuagement, sexual desire and fulfilment, and sheer persistence. The presumably personal material is deflected away from the confessional towards the metaphoric and symbolic; and in this, as in some other elements of its technique, Sylvia Plath is an unexpected, but absorbed influence. The sourness of the marriage, for instance, is imagined as the air 'possessed' by the undiscoverable but insistent presence of a mat 'larval' with summer insects. The self-recriminating protagonist is glancingly mythologized as a kind of male Proserpine, desperately willing renewal: 'Bushing the door, my arms full / of wild cherry and rhododendron'. And there is a thrilled figuring of erotic intensity and focus: 'as you bend in the shower / water lives down the tilting stoups of your breasts', where the word 'stoups' (meaning vessels for carrying water) activates associations of healing at once dialectal, erotic and ecclesiastical (the 'stoup' in a church contains the holy water with which the members of the congregation bless themselves). Everything is directed towards composure, rather than confession. The final section of 'Summer Home' is a kind of reverse aubade, that traditional love poem in which the poet, delightedly in bed, laments the inevitable arrival of dawn which will separate the lovers. Here the couple are wakeful after argument, and the dawn becomes, rather, an alternative source of possible regeneration, however tentatively:

> My children weep out the hot foreign night.
> We walk the floor, my foul mouth takes it out
> On you and we lie stiff till dawn
> Attends the pillow, and the maize, and vine

> That holds its filling burden to the light.
> Yesterday rocks sang when we tapped
> Stalactites in the cave's old, dripping dark –
> Our love calls tiny as a tuning fork.

The difficulties are formally dramatized there by the heavy enjambements and caesurae which restrain the forward thrust of syntax: the future that the lines cry out to be released into is disrupted and postponed. The nervous irresolution of the half-rhymes completes the effect; and they reach their painful diminuendo in the sadly dissonant chime of 'fork' against 'dark', which complements the well-judged placing and full rhyming across stanzas of 'night' and 'light'. The poem's perfect pitch and control are fulfilled in its final simile. The little human noise resonating in the old dark of personal unhappiness and of overwhelming natural forces, as it has earlier resonated in the old dark of Irish historical and political experience, is the true tone of *Wintering Out*: comfortless enough, but with a notion of survival in it too.

3

The Appetites of Gravity:
North (1975)

> In Ireland at the moment I would see the necessity, since I'm
> involved in the tradition of the English lyric, to take the
> English lyric and make it eat stuff that it has never eaten
> before . . . like all the messy and, it would seem, incomprehens-
> ible obsessions in the North, and make it still an English lyric.
>
> Seamus Heaney in interview, 1973

1 Poetry and Politics

The decision to confront the crisis of Northern Ireland in a more
rigorous way must have come to seem almost inevitable to
Heaney after the publication of *Wintering Out*. Some of the
poems he had published, but not collected, did handle the
subject more directly; and his role as a public spokesman and
commentator was increasingly demanding both a scrutiny of his
own responses and position and a consideration of the kinds of
language appropriate to the occasion. His move from Belfast to
Dublin in 1972, particularly in the light of the media comment-
ary it received, no doubt gave these scruples a sharper edge and
urgency, while it also brought the perspective of at least
geographical distance. Above all, however, his anxieties about
confronting the subject had been mitigated to some extent by his
discovery of P. V. Glob's *The Bog People* and, in 'The Tollund
Man', of a way of using that material as analogy, of making it
render what he calls, in 'Feeling into Words', 'images and
symbols adequate to our predicament'. 'I felt it imperative', he
writes there, 'to discover a field of force in which, without
abandoning fidelity to the processes and experience of poetry, it
would be possible to encompass the perspectives of a humane

reason and at the same time to grant the religious intensity of the violence its authenticity and complexity.'

Heaney was also reading at the time, as his critical prose of the period makes clear, some modern and contemporary long poems, or poetic sequences: David Jones's *The Sleeping Lord* (published in book form in 1974, but available much earlier) and *The Anathemata* (1952), Geoffrey Hill's *Mercian Hymns* (1971) and – a sequence developed out of, and responding to, the Northern experience – John Montague's *The Rough Field* (1972). These are poems which, variously, set personal experience in a larger cultural and historical context and, as a result, display a studied and deliberate interest in archaeology and etymology. They are poems which retain, vestigially, some of the ambitions of 'epic' poetry and also attempt a kind of synthesizing historical myth, a form in which the confusions of the present may be articulated and understood with what will seem a more than merely individual authority. An extension and elaboration of the relationship between Ireland and Jutland proposed by 'The Tollund Man' provides Heaney with the basis for such a myth of Northern Ireland.

The sequence of 'bog poems' subsequently written out of this perception ('Come to the Bower', 'Bog Queen', 'The Grauballe Man', 'Punishment', 'Strange Fruit' and 'Kinship') lies at the centre of the meaning, effect and achievement of *North*; but the volume's myth is also developed from a variety of other sources. Separate poems meditate not only on bodies but also on objects retrieved from the northern ground (quernstones, a Viking longship, Viking trial-pieces – that is, pieces made as specimens for future designs – a white bone, a spade covered with moss, a turf cart), and on words retrieved from the language spoken on that ground ('moss', 'bawn', 'Dublin', 'bone-house' or 'banhus', 'bog'). These poems uncover a history of the conquest of Ireland first by the Vikings and later by the English. The myth is also advanced by poems in which territorial conquest is itself allegorized in terms of the Greek myths of Hercules and Antaeus and of Diana and Actaeon, and in sexual terms. Moreover, in

'The Digging Skeleton', the myth finds room for a translation from Baudelaire of a poem about anatomical drawings which imagines human misery persisting beyond the grave; in a pointed oxymoron, Heaney translates Baudelaire's word for the dead, 'forçats' (hard-labourers), as 'Death's lifers', which is chillingly appropriate to the bodies preserved for so long in the Danish bogs.

In the overall structure of *North*, however, the myth occupies only the first of its two parts, the second containing poems directly responsive to the Northern present, rather than to its past. In this sense, the book inherits the bipartite structure of *Wintering Out* and employs it to more radical effect. This duality has its correlative in Heaney's published responses as a citizen: in 'Belfast' in *Preoccupations*, for instance, he observes that 'At one minute you are drawn towards the old vortex of racial and religious instinct, at another time you seek the mean of humane love and reason.' However, its separation of the symbolic from the explicit is essentially the product of Heaney's sense of the varied, even contradictory ways in which matters of deep public perturbation might be articulated in poetry. In foregrounding possibility and difference in this way, *North* becomes a profoundly self-conscious book.

Such self-consciousness is apparent also in the way it places art itself, and Heaney's own art as a poet in particular, at its centre. The dedicatory poems under the title 'Mossbawn' evoke domestic and communal images of Heaney's first home, of human love and agricultural continuity, which recall Dutch and Flemish paintings. 'Sunlight', which remembers his aunt baking, has, with its composed stillness and its almost-archaism (dusting the board 'with a goose's wing'), something of the atmosphere of an interior by Vermeer. Robert Lowell, in 'Epilogue' in his volume *Day by Day* (1977), writes of 'the grace of accuracy / Vermeer gave to the sun's illumination', and Heaney's poem conjures a similarly accurate grace from its sunlight. 'The Seed Cutters', celebrating 'calendar customs', directly addresses a painter – 'Breughel, / You'll know them if

I can get them true.' These painterly images of beneficent tranquillity, of home-keeping and community, remain, as it were, outside the frame of *North*, implicitly commenting on the images of barbarism within the frame, particularly those derived from other, harsher artworks: the Viking longship incised by the child as a trial-piece in 'Viking Dublin'; the anatomical plates of 'The Digging Skeleton'; the Roman marble copy (after a lost Greek bronze) of a conquered Celtic warrior dying on his shield, known as *The Dying Gaul*, which is alluded to in 'The Grauballe Man'; Goya's 'Shootings of the Third of May' and his image of 'that holmgang / Where two berserks club each other to death / For honour's sake, greaved in a bog, and sinking' in 'Summer 1969'; and, indeed, the bog people themselves, iconically static in the frames of Glob's photographs.

These allusions to the plastic arts are accompanied in *North* by a very high density of reference to other writing; literary, historical and political. Occasionally very obviously signalled by quotation marks or italics, or by their use as epigraphs, but usually embedded more invisibly in Heaney's own texts, these allusions include, among many others: the Norse *Njal's Saga*; the Roman historian Tacitus's accounts of the Northern tribes in his *Germania* and *Agricola*; *Hamlet*; Joyce's *A Portrait of the Artist as a Young Man*; Synge's *The Playboy of the Western World*; Bede's *History of the English Church and People*; Yeats's poems and *Autobiographies*; Walter Ralegh's 'Ocean's Love to Cynthia' and John Aubrey's accounts of Ralegh; Lord Grey's account of the Battle of Smerwick, as dictated to Edmund Spenser; the Old English poem *The Battle of Maldon*; Conor Cruise O'Brien's *States of Ireland*; Horace's odes; R. H. Barrow's *The Romans*; Wordsworth's *The Prelude*; Patrick Kavanagh; Hopkins's *Journals*; Osip Mandelstam. Given the nature of its primary subject – Northern Ireland in crisis after 1969 – *North* is an astonishingly literary book which foregrounds the way it turns its material into text: literally so in 'Bog Queen', where 'My body was braille / for the creeping influences' and in 'Kinship' with its 'hieroglyphic' peat.

The allusions are integral and organic, not merely ornamental. They are made partly, no doubt, in the spirit of Walter Benjamin's striking, scandalous and probably now too-often-cited observation that 'There is no document of civilization which is not at the same time a document of barbarism';[1] but they are also made because *North* is a book almost as much about poetry itself as it is about Northern Ireland. The Greek myth of Hercules and Antaeus which encloses Part 1 in two separate poems seems primarily an allegory of colonization. In 'Hercules and Antaeus', Hercules is the stronger aggressor breaking the native Antaeus, son of Earth, by removing him from his source of strength in the soil and leaving him in the land in the shape of that persistent Celtic motif, the 'sleeping giant' who will one day wake to lead his people out of servitude. The myth which keeps an oppressed people hopeful but puerile, this figure is scathingly described as 'pap for the dispossessed'. In an interview Heaney acknowledges 'Hercules and Antaeus' as an allegory of Ireland, but describes its genesis in terms of poetry itself:

To me Hercules represents another voice, another possibility; and actually behind that poem lay a conversation with Iain Crichton Smith, a very fine poet but essentially different from the kind of poet I am. He's got a kind of Presbyterian *light* about him. The image that came into my mind after the conversation was of me being a dark soil and him being a kind of bright-pronged fork that was digging it up and going through it. . . . Hercules represents the possibility of the play of intelligence, that kind of satisfaction you get from Borges, the play and pattern, which is so different from the pleaures of Neruda, who's more of an Antaeus figure. That kind of thinking led into the poetry of the second half of *North*, which was an attempt at some kind of declarative voice.[2]

Heaney is clearly inviting here a reading of the poem as at least as much an allegory of poetry as of politics, as much an allegory

1 Walter Benjamin, 'Theses on the Philosophy of History', in *Illuminations* (1970; Fontana, 1973 edn.), 258.
2 John Haffenden, *Viewpoints: Poets in Conversation* (Faber and Faber, 1981), 69–70.

of the bipartite structure of *North* itself as of the relationship between England and Ireland, even if we are of course intended to take the weight of the denominational adjective 'Presbyterian' in this approbatory context. The two allegories are, we might say, coterminous.

Indeed, the poetic and the political are frequently coterminous in the book. The figure of the poet is present in Part I not only in the centrality of his 'I' (all those personal pronouns and possessive adjectives which open poems or sections of poems: 'I shouldered', 'I returned', 'Come fly with me', 'My hands come', 'I can feel', 'I found'), but also in the way the poetry discusses or exposes its own processes of composition. In the audacious conceit of the title poem 'North' itself, the Viking longship's 'swimming tongue' is one of the earliest, and strangest, of the exemplary voices which counsel Heaney in his own poetry, those voices sometimes coming out of nowhere in a radicalization and revision of the ancient poetic trope of prosopopoeia:

> It said, 'Lie down
> in the word-hoard, burrow
> the coil and gleam
> of your furrowed brain.
>
> Compose in darkness.
> Expect aurora borealis
> in the long foray
> but no cascade of light.
>
> Keep your eye clear
> as the bleb of the icicle,
> trust the feel of what nubbed treasure
> your hands have known.'

Heaney's fiction of being advised by a Viking voice establishes a frightening intimacy between the sources of his poetry and the brutal facts of Viking culture and power. The poem is not tender-minded or illusioned about the activity of making poems: when the poet lies down and burrows in the word-hoard to pursue the poem, he is engaged, like the Vikings, on a 'foray': a hostile or predatory incursion, a raid.

There is a marked degree of self-reflexivity in 'Viking Dublin' too, where the 'darkness' of composition is illuminated between section III and IV, when the Viking child's incised drawing of the longship – 'a buoyant/migrant line' – visibly insinuates itself into the poet's own script, as the longship 'enters my longhand, / turns cursive'. The longship entering longhand, the transference from one culture into another which is the historical conceit of these poems, is a further extension of the figure of the 'trail' in 'Servant Boy' in *Wintering Out*; but the greater self-referentiality here is almost the equivalent of that in an Escher drawing. The invitation it extends to the reader actually to enter the processes of the poem's composition is sustained in 'Bone Dreams', where the poet describes himself burrowing in an Anglo-Saxon word-hoard to retrieve a sense of the ancient culture from the word 'ban-hus'. In the bog poems, this poetic self-consciousness is as much thematic as structural, taking the form of an anxiety about making poems out of human suffering. The Grauballe man is an exemplary instance of the closeness between 'beauty and atrocity'; in 'Punishment', the poet is figured as an 'artful voyeur'; and in 'Strange Fruit', the beheaded girl resists all poetic attempts at 'beatification', that impulse which initiates the sequence in 'The Tollund Man', in which the corpse is read as a 'saint's kept body'.

In Part I, however, the volume's subtext of a poetry in dialogue with itself is most obvious in the sumptuously realized fourth section of 'Kinship', where the bog is evoked in terms which turn it into a kind of language. The opening line, 'This centre holds', offers a challenge to the doom-laden prophecy of Yeats's 'The Second Coming' that 'The centre cannot hold'; and, in the evocation of the bog's formation by autumnal decay, as it dies into its own life, there is also an echo of Eliot's description of autumn in *The Waste Land* ('the last fingers of leaf / Clutch and sink into the wet bank'). This bog is, therefore, already almost a poem too before Heaney makes an identification which suggests an analogy between the self-involved processes of the bog and the self-involved processes of poetic language, that compost of allusion and etymology which generates the composition of the new work. The poem's sonorous vowel music offers a rich metaphor for the bog:

> This is the vowel of earth
> dreaming its root
> in flowers and snow,
>
> mutation of weathers
> and seasons,
> a windfall composing
> the floor it rots into.
>
> I grew out of all this
> like a weeping willow
> inclined to
> the appetites of gravity.

'Grew out of' in the sense of 'was derived from', but also, perhaps, 'grew away from'; 'inclined to' as 'bent towards', but also 'predisposed to': the stanza's own ambiguities compose the floor it rots into. And the willow unites, in its apt simile, the opposed inclinations: it grows away from, but is also bent back towards, the ground which sustains it. Hercules and Antaeus intertwined, it is 'weeping' as a credible and proper reaction to 'all this' that the bog represents in *North*.

In Part II, this subtext rises to the status of text, as Heaney debates explicitly the relationship between poetry and public life (in the 'declarative' voice of 'Whatever You Say Say Nothing', in the fantasy of 'The Unacknowledged Legislator's Dream', and in the allegory of 'Freedman') and as, in 'Singing School', he describes, in realistic terms and under the aegis of autobiographical epigraphs from Wordsworth and Yeats, the immediate social circumstances and literary education which he, Seamus Heaney, 'grew out of'. The final poem of 'Singing School', 'Exposure', then acts as a kind of coda to subtext and text when it anxiously rehearses this poet's responsibilities and predicament in the light of 'all this'. Guilty, anxious and uncertain, 'Exposure' is an entirely appropriate conclusion to a volume in which the poet's own art of composition has itself been the focus of so much attention. The attention manifests a scrupulous unease about the ways in which poetry may properly engage the obdurate facts of political violence and death. This scepticism, suspicion and lack of presumption are the mark of the book's authority. Confessing its own artfulness, *North* discovers and sustains a humility and a gravity genuinely responsive to the urgency and intractability of its occasion.

2 Skull-handler

In the middle of 'Viking Dublin: Trial Pieces', immediately after the longship has entered his longhand, the poet makes a half-mocking, half-serious self-identification:

> I am Hamlet the Dane,
> skull-handler, parablist,
> smeller of rot
>
> in the state, infused
> with its poisons,
> pinioned by ghosts
> and affections,
>
> murders and pieties,
> coming to consciousness
> by jumping in graves,
> dithering, blathering.

The myth of Part I of *North* is made from such death-inflected identifications: Heaney constructs his 'parables' for the Irish present by contemplating objects, skulls and bodies retrieved from the ground and the grave. When 'Belderg' discovers in an excavated Norse settlement in Co. Mayo an exact replication of the 'stone-wall patternings' of the contemporary landscape, it describes this as 'persistence, / A congruence of lives'; and the whole of Part I is devoted to establishing a sense of these persistences and congruities. Yet it does so with the ironic knowledge that such an activity may be only 'blathering', that such word-spinning may be a helpless, Hamlet-like incapacity for action.

These poems are intensely, even claustrophobically obsessive and intimate. Sometimes organized into sequences, they revolve identical matters among themselves and, indeed, frequently share similar or identical images. The 'black glacier' of a funeral in 'Funeral Rites' reappears as the 'black glacier' of a sash in 'Bog Queen'; the 'neighbourly murder' of 'Funeral Rites' – that terrifying oxymoron – has its correspondence in the description of the Vikings as 'neighbourly, scoretaking / killers' in 'Viking Dublin'; the Bog Queen is wrapped in a 'swaddle of hides', and in 'Strange Fruit' the decapitated girl's hair is 'unswaddled' by her discoverer; the Bog Queen has 'dreams of Baltic amber' and, in 'Kinship', the word 'bog' itself is defined as 'pupil of amber'; and so on, through a number of other links and variations. The effect of this risky procedure is to make a certain monotony part of the poems' effect: they seem introverted, almost incestuously self-generated. They have, therefore, an exceptionally close family resemblance; and this seems appropriate to a sequence which includes a poem called 'Kinship' and which discovers an interconnectedness between contemporary sectarian atrocity in the North of Ireland, the behaviour of Viking invaders, and the ritual murders of Iron Age Jutland. It may also be thought appropriate to the subject of internecine, or civil, war.

The intimate relationship between these poems is most obvious, however, in their shared form: the thin quatrain, now grown almost skeletal. It is heavily stressed, characteristically with two stresses to a line (like the half-line of Anglo-Saxon alliterative metre); it often breaks its line to coincide with the grammatical phrase; and it makes great use of that punctuation mark of pause, definition and weighed apposition, the colon (every poem in the sequence has its colon or, in one or two cases, that quicker equivalent of the colon, the dash). As a result, the form is less airy and buoyant than it is in *Wintering Out*, and it has a certain archaic quality.[3] This is increased by the poems' characteristically arcane diction. They use and imitate Anglo-Saxon 'kennings' (periphrastic noun-phrases) in such forms as 'word-hoard', 'love-den', 'blood-holt', 'brain-firkin', 'oak-bone', 'mushroom-flesh', 'flint-find'; they employ Northern Irish dialect ('pash' for 'head', for instance, and 'bleb' for the icicle's bubble) and words from the Irish language ('crannog', 'pampooties', 'glib'); and they include the precisions of technical vocabularies ('zoomorphic', 'obelisk', 'felloes'). The poems are not aggressive towards the reader, exactly, but neither are they accommodating. Hard-edged, all elbows with their constantly jolting line-breaks and lexicographical diction, they disrupt the smoothness of English lyric in a way appropriate to the violence of their material, and with a certain political implication. In an interview Heaney explains that at the time he thought that 'the melodious grace of the English iambic line was some kind of affront, that it needed to be wrecked.'[4] This kind of disruption was probably sanctioned by Heaney's admiration for Robert Lowell's work of the late 1960s and early 1970s which practised violences upon the English sonnet; although the stylistic varia-tions of Yeats, as he wrote out his confusions in the post-1916 period of Irish history, would have supplied him with an available local model. *North* is heavily shadowed by Yeats, and explicitly so when it cites a politically charged passage from the *Autobiographies* as an epigraph to 'Singing School'. In addition, Heaney is interested in the typographical layout of

3 Heaney speaks of the influence of William Carlos Williams and 'the California spirit' on the forms of *Wintering Out*: see the Appendix. Even if this exaggerates the actual effect of most of the poems in that volume, nothing could be further from the 'spirit' of *North*, which is the spirit in chains. The alertness of Heaney's formal poetic intelligence is manifest in the way he can bend a similar structure to such different effect across succeeding volumes.
4 Interview with Frank Kinahan, *Critical Inquiry*, vol. 8 no. 3 (Spring 1982), 405–14, 412.

these quatrains and, in an interview, constructs an archaeological metaphor from them: 'those thin small quatrain poems,' he says, 'they're kind of drills or augers for turning in and they are narrow and long and deep'.[5] If this has its fanciful element, it is unsurprising that, in a book so interested in the plastic arts, Heaney should have been encouraged by the fact that his forms themselves can be thought to have the shape of archaeological implements, that they look like a means of returning to the light of human scrutiny what has lain so long underground. The slightly arcane word 'auger' may also suggest its homonym, 'augur': which is to say, a diviner, a 'smeller of rot / in the state'.

3 Vikings

In addition to establishing a link between the culture of the Vikings and Heaney's own writing in 'North' and 'Viking Dublin', the Viking poems which open Part 1 of *North* also draw together, in a pattern of analogy, the violence of the Vikings and the violence of contemporary Northern Ireland.[6]

5 Interview with James Randall, *Ploughshares*, vol. 5 no. 3 (1979), 7–22, 16.
6 This linkage has been the focus of derogatory critical commentary, notably from critics otherwise as polarized as Edna Longley and Seamus Deane. Longley, taking up an observation of Ciaran Carson's, writes that it amounts to a form of historical determinism: 'determinism, the plundering of the past for parallels, circular thinking (all incidentally features of Republican and Loyalist ideology) ... insist on "territorial piety", on a religious-anthropological, even slightly glamorous way of apprehending the conflict'; and Deane notes that 'the Viking myths do not correspond to Irish experience without some fairly forceful straining.' When he goes on to remark that, nevertheless, 'the potency of the analogy between the two was at first thrilling', Edna Longley might well think that he is aiding her case about the poems' spurious 'glamour'. See Edna Longley, ' "Inner Emigré" or "Artful Voyeur"? Seamus Heaney's *North*', in *Poetry in the Wars* (Bloodaxe, 1986) and Seamus Deane, 'Seamus Heaney: The Timorous and the Bold', in *Celtic Revivals* (Faber and Faber, 1985). Both essays are reprinted in Michael Allen's *New Casebook*. Heaney displays an alertness to such criticism when, in 'The First Flight' in the 'Sweeney Redivivus' sequence of *Station Island*, he has his persona say, 'I was mired in attachment / until they began to pronounce me / a feeder off battlefields.' There are indications in much of his self-revising work after *North* that he is, himself, subsequently

In 'Belderg', images of persistence from ancient to modern landscape are matched by possible elements of continuity in the name 'Mossbawn', when the companion in the poem suggests a Norse derivation for the word. The proposal leads the poet to a vertiginous vision in which, in his 'mind's eye', he sees 'A world-tree of balanced stones, / Querns piled like vertebrae, / The marrow crushed to grounds.' That 'world-tree' is the Yggdrasil of Norse mythology, the ash tree which sustained the Viking world. In this vision, its sustenance is a matter of terror and savagery; and the vision is a hideous reversal of the images of sunlight and community which go under the name 'Mossbawn' in the book's dedicatory poems. 'Funeral Rites' similarly yokes together the funerals of Heaney's own childhood, the present funerals of victims in the North, and the burial of Gunnar, one of the heroes of *Njal's Saga*. The hideous phrase 'neighbourly murder' establishes the connection between present and past: those who are 'neighbours' in Northern Ireland, Catholics and Protestants, kill one another, just as the Norsemen of the sagas, with their ferocious ethic of revenge, kill one another. The poem envisages a propitiatory and assuaging rite which may satisfy all those in the North who 'pine for ceremony, / customary rhythms', lines which ironically echo Yeats's 'A Prayer for my Daughter': 'How but in custom and in ceremony / Are innocence and beauty born?' Of its nature, this must be a rite which transcends the Christian rituals of the religions in whose name this 'neighbourly murder' is committed. If elsewhere in *North* Heaney registers deep solidarity with his Northern Catholic origins, here he is implicitly distancing himself into judgement when he has his relations' hands 'shackled in rosary beads'; the participle making the religion a kind of enslavement.

---

sceptical about some of its procedures. The entanglement of these poems in suspect or dangerous emotion may make them less exemplary as poetic acts but may leave them nevertheless revealingly symptomatic of a certain condition usefully available, in them, to the scrutiny of reader or critic or, in this case, the poet himself, apparently, in his later work.

The dreamlike procession imagined in the second section of 'Funeral Rites' goes beyond, or below, Christianity, as the poem wills a reconciliatory funeral rite into being:

> I would restore
>
> the great chambers of Boyne,
> prepare a sepulchre
> under the cupmarked stones ....
>
> Quiet as a serpent
> in its grassy boulevard,
>
> the procession drags its tail
> out of the Gap of the North
> as its head already enters
> the megalithic doorway.

David Trotter has written very interestingly about Heaney's use of the modal auxiliary 'would' in this passage, pointing out that it moves away from the simply commemorative sense of typical earlier instances in the work ('I would fill jampotfuls' in 'Death of a Naturalist', for instance) towards 'a fiercer optative mood'; and certainly the visionary grandeur of the lines is impelled by the solemn desire in Heaney's tone.[7] The Boyne, scene of the victory in 1690 still celebrated annually by Ulster Loyalists, is commemorated here not as the source of sectarian division, but as the site of the prehistoric burial chambers at Newgrange. The divisions of the present, therefore, are to be healed in a rite which insists on the common ground shared, in the North, by both Catholic and Protestant; it is a rite in which the 'whole country' can join, and its 'triumph' will be not a militaristic procession, as a 'triumph' was in imperial Rome, but in fact an overcoming of militarism.

The possibility of reconciliation is imaged, finally, in an

7 David Trotter, *The Making of the Reader: Language and Subjectivity in Modern American, English and Irish Poetry* (Macmillan, 1984), 191.

allusion to that pacific moment in *Njal's Saga* when, uniquely, there is a brief respite in the revenge cycle remorselessly catalogued in the rest of the tale. Gunnar, a victim (but previously an ardent perpetrator) of violence, is imagined 'joyful' in death, although 'unavenged'. The poem's hope is that those 'disposed like Gunnar' during the imagined funeral rites on the Boyne may remain similarly 'unavenged' by their mourners, who are suddenly figured as Norsemen when they drive back not past modern Strangford and Carlingford, but 'Strang and Carling fjords'; a reminder that the Vikings have left their names, as they might be thought to have left something of their ethical code, in the North of Ireland. 'Funeral Rites', however, is only 'optative'; it urgently desires an end to the terrible cycle, but it can imagine such a thing only in a mythologized visionary realm. The four lights burning in Gunnar's burial chamber are merely a flickering illumination in the darkness of the other Viking poems in the book, whose discovery of persistence and continuity obliterates much sense of optimism. When, in 'Viking Dublin: Trial Pieces', the poet prays to these forefathers, it is to insist on the repetitions of Irish history:

> Old fathers, be with us.
> Old cunning assessors
> of feuds and of sites
> for ambush or town.

The prayer recalls other Irish literary fathers: Daedalus at the end of *A Portrait of the Artist as a Young Man*, to whom Stephen prays, 'Old father, old artificer, stand me now and ever in good stead', and Yeats's 'old fathers ... / Merchant and scholar who have left me blood', of whom he asks 'pardon' in the prefatory poem to *Responsibilities*. Heaney's location of the Irish paternity theme in this Viking source is exhausted and despairing; it is at one, in 'Viking Dublin', with the devastating pun which – prompted by Jimmy Farrell in Synge's *The Playboy of the Western World* – figures the 'cobbled quays' of Dublin as 'the skull-capped ground'.

4 Bog Bodies

'Bone Dreams', which takes its images not from the Viking, but
from the English invasions of Ireland, effects a kind of
transition between the Viking poems and the bog poems of
Part I. Beginning in an act of aggression, when the poet – a little
David before a big Goliath – pitches a bone at England in 'the
sling of mind', the sequence moves to a close in metaphors of
lovemaking which imagine the English language and landscape
as a woman's body. These sections of the poem, IV and V, are
as strange as anything Heaney has written, fascinatedly creating
a sexual philology and topography; they may owe something to
Henry Moore's huge woman-landscape sculptures, and they are
not entirely unlike some moments in the work of David Jones
and of Heaney's contemporary, Michael Longley. They make
the reaction to 'England' conveyed by 'Bone Dreams' a complex
one: anger, but also rich philological delight in its language, and
an intimate imaginative infatuation with some of its landscapes
most redolent of succeeding phases of human habitation: the
prehistoric Giant of Cerne Abbas, priapic on the Dorset down-
land, evoked in IV; Hadrian's Wall; and Maiden Castle. The
poem as a whole, indeed, transforms its initial act of aggression
into a final tenderness, as the poet touches, for the first time, the
'small distant Pennines' of a mole's shoulders in Devon; the
mole which is native to England's 'strange fields', but unknown
in Ireland. 'Bone Dreams', then, announces the carnal theme
prominent in the bog poems which follow. The sexual is
implicit in the material itself, since the bog people, according
to Glob, were sacrificed in vegetation rites, and hence the
Tollund man in *Wintering Out* is described as a 'bridegroom
to the goddess'. A wholly new element is introduced, however,
when, as happens in several of these poems, we are made aware
of a male poet gazing on, and responding to, female victims.
Marked by the unease of their own reactions, these poems
nevertheless involve themselves in dangerous emotions. Famil-
iarity should not dull their edge of scandal: they are poems

whose artfulness operates within the vicinity not only of voyeurism, but of necrophilia.[8]

The confounding of the sexual and the political is managed quasi-allegorically in the first two poems, 'Come to the Bower' and 'Bog Queen', where the bog woman is not one of Glob's Jutland bodies, but the first properly documented body ever taken from a bog, that of the 'queen' discovered on the Moira estate, about twenty miles south of Belfast, in 1781. The fact that this was an Irish bog preservation, presumed to be the skeleton of a Danish Viking, is clearly important to Heaney, since it offers him a genuinely historical, not merely an imaginative, connection between Ireland and Jutland. In 'Come to the Bower', the 'bower' is the arbour sacred to Nerthus in which the body is sacrificed. It is the 'boudoir' which generates the poem's sexual metaphors, as the poem's 'I' - representing both poet and the original discoverer of the body – 'unpins' and 'unwraps' it, reaching towards the 'Venus bone'; and it is also the 'bower' of Ireland itself, that bower in the popular Republican song whose title Heaney has taken for his poem. In that song, the 'tradition of Irish political martyrdom' which he believes, he tells us in 'Feeling into Words', shares an 'archetypal pattern' with the religion of Nerthus, receives one of its most bloodily mystical expressions: the soil of its bower is 'sanctified by the blood' of the dead. 'Come to the Bower' appears to suggest in symbolic terms that such myths of blood sacrifice – which in modern Irish history are prominently associated with

8 Patricia Coughlan, in 'Bog Queens: The Representation of Women in the Poetry of John Montague and Seamus Heaney', in *Gender in Irish Writing*, ed. Toni O'Brien Johnson and David Cairns (Open University Press, 1991), offers a sustained critique of many of these tropes in Heaney and his near-contemporary, John Montague. She has very illuminating things to say about the unconscious compulsions of Irish Catholic male sexuality and gender attitudes as they may be read out of some of these poems, but when she presses her case so far as to accuse Heaney of coming close to 'pornographic fantasy', she is insensitive to nuance, tone and procedure which, in the bog poems, scrutinize and criticize any such tendency, rather than indulge it. The essay is reprinted, in part, in Michael Allen's *New Casebook*.

Padraig Pearse, poet and executed leader of the failed 1916 Easter Rising – continue to lie just below the surface of Irish political life, and continue also to exert an appeal in which the politics has an almost sexual allure and mystique.

'Bog Queen' itself, Heaney's most striking female monologue, pursues the allegory. The specific circumstances of the Moira bog woman, who was recovered from the bog after 'a peer's wife', Lady Moira, bribed the estate-worker who discovered her, ramify into associations in which she becomes a kind of Kathleen ní Houlihan, a Mother Ireland. She is placed 'between turf-face and demesne wall': between, that is, agricultural labour and leisured cultivation. Her native authority, symbolized by her diadem, is gradually undermined 'like the bearings of history'; her hair is 'robbed'. The poem is, on one level, a delicately accurate account of the processes of her decay, of the body being reclaimed by, and turning into, the land itself; but the implications raise the bog queen to the status of a symbol of disaffected native resentment, biding its time underground. The phrase 'I lay waiting' is uttered twice, ambivalently in promise or threat; and the monologue appears to celebrate the local turfcutter who, having initially discovered her, lays her delicately to rest again ('and packed coomb softly / between the stone jambs / at my head and my feet'), whereas the bribery of the peer's wife is the reprehensible act which releases her fury.[9] 'Bog Queen' may be, in fact, a differently gendered version – appropriate to the republican and nationalist feminization of Ireland – of the 'sleeping giant' theme criticized in 'Hercules and Antaeus'. It also draws some of its power from the fact that it appears structurally indebted to Sylvia Plath's scarifying poem 'Lady Lazarus', with its vengefully stampeding persona. Both are the monologues of unwilling female returnees from the dead; and

9 The word 'coomb' does not exist in the OED in the sense in which Heaney must mean it here. C. I. Macafee's *A Concise Ulster Dictionary* (Oxford University Press, 1996) gives 'coom', meaning 'leftover dust and fragments of peat'. Dr Macafee's excellent dictionary is to be recommended to students of Heaney and of the contemporary literature of Northern Ireland more generally.

the closing cadences of 'Bog Queen' ('and I rose from the dark, / hacked bone, skull-ware, / frayed stitches, tufts, / small gleams on the bank') parallel Plath's ('Out of the ashes I rise with my red hair / and I eat men like air').[10]

'The Grauballe Man' and 'Punishment' go beyond implicit allegorizing to make direct analogies between bog people and contemporary victims of sectarian atrocity: 'The Grauballe Man' concludes with an evocation of 'each hooded victim, / slashed and dumped', and 'Punishment' imagines the Windeby 'bog girl' of Glob's account, possibly punished for adultery, as the 'sister' of those Catholic women tarred in Northern Ireland during the early 1970s as a punishment for 'going with' British soldiers. Both poems explore Heaney's own perturbedly ambiguous responses. 'The Grauballe Man' admits the ways in which such suffering can be turned to artistic account, as the successive photographs in Glob's book, which show the man being gradually removed from the bog, suggest not death but childbirth, and make the victim almost an icon, his corpse a 'vivid cast', his body having its 'opaque repose'. Even the wound in his 'slashed throat' is 'cured', which puns on 'preserved' and 'healed'. The precision and meticulousness of Heaney's metaphors, which may be thought to appropriate the human victim to the poem's own form and order, to the calming stasis of further representation, are themselves criticized in the final stanza where the victim – the man himself, then, and each murdered corpse, now – sickeningly thuds out of artistic 'repose' into the realistic brutality of 'slashed' and 'dumped'. The Roman marble known as *The Dying Gaul* is a magnificent image of the pathos of heroic death, but it is an image made by the conquerors, and the Gaul's body is 'too strictly compassed / on his shield' by the demands of both art and ideology.[11] The Grauballe man's 'actual weight'

10 Note too that in 'Come to the Bower' the bog woman's hair is 'Reddish as a fox's brush'.
11 The sculpture known as *The Dying Gaul* is the subject of an essay by David Jones first published in *The Listener* in 1959 and subsequently reprinted in his collection *The Dying Gaul and Other Writings* (Faber and Faber, 1978), which

falls out of such compass and alignment as a rebuke to Heaney's own mythologizing tendency. Rarely has the word 'actual' carried so much weight, as it insists that murder, then as now, happens in 'act', not 'art', in deed, not word. Who will say 'corpse' to his vivid cast? This very poem itself.

In 'Punishment', the ambiguity of Heaney's response is a more specifically political one, as the almost-love poem ('My poor scapegoat, // I almost love you'), with its tender empathies, releases its concluding identification and self-definition:

> I who have stood dumb
> when your betraying sisters,
> cauled in tar,
> wept by the railings,
>
> who would connive
> in civilized outrage
> yet understand the exact
> and tribal, intimate revenge.

These lines have given rise to critical debate about precisely what position in relation to IRA violence the poem is assuming. If the 'civilized outrage' is 'connivance', with that word's implication of the underhand and the conspiratorial, and the revenge is 'exact' – appropriate, correspondent to the crime – then presumably the 'understanding' is also a condoning. In his review of *North*, Conor Cruise O'Brien thought so:

It is the word 'exact' that hurts most: Seamus Heaney has so greatly earned the right to use this word that to see him use it as he does here opens up a sort of chasm. But then, of course, that is what he

---

includes an excellent photographic reproduction of it. This photograph, taken from above, also accompanied the original *Listener* article; and it emphasises the way the figure is 'too strictly compassed' since, from this angle, he is notably supporting himself on a hand placed beyond his shield, and his foot extends outside its compass too. There is also a poem by Desmond O'Grady called 'The Dying Gaul' which appears in John Montague (ed.), *The Faber Book of Irish Verse* (Faber and Faber, 1974), 352.

is about. The word 'exact' fits the situation as it is felt to be: and it is because it fits, and because other situations, among the rival population, turn on similarly oiled pivots, that hope succumbs. I have read many pessimistic analyses of 'Northern Ireland', but none that has the bleak conclusiveness of these poems.[12]

Certainly the poem's business is to remind us, once again, of the persistence of atavistic emotions and responses in the North, and therefore also, to some degree, in any poet born into the community of Northern Catholicism who wishes to tell a truth about it. It is the point of the myth of *North* that it should do this, and that, in doing so, it should criticize the shallowness and inadequacy of many too casually assumptive rational understandings. Nevertheless, the poet's dumbness before the contemporary 'sisters' who have been vengefully tarred is itself implicitly criticized by the poem's biblical allusions, which bring a third religion, Christianity, into the reckoning, along with the Iron Age vegetation religion and the 'religion' of Irish Republicanism. When the poet says he 'would have cast... / the stones of silence', the 'Little adulteress' of 'Punishment' acquires another 'sister', the woman taken in adultery in the eighth chapter of St John's gospel, where Christ tells the crowd gathered to stone her, 'He that is without sin among you, let him first cast a stone at her.' Nobody does, of course; but this poet, like the others of his 'tribe', casts those equally blameworthy 'stones of silence'. 'Punishment' includes further, more subdued biblical references: the 'scapegoat' of Leviticus, which takes on the sins of the tribe and is driven into the wilderness, a usage applied to Christ in the Catholic liturgy; and the girl's 'numbered bones', which derive from one of the psalms also used of Christ in Catholic worship, 'They have pierced my hands and feet; they have numbered all my bones.' The desperate irony of these allusions is that they both judge this

12 Conor Cruise O'Brien, 'A Slow North-east Wind', *The Listener*, 25 September 1975, 204–5; reprinted in Michael Allen's *New Casebook*.

act of tribal revenge by the more merciful ethic enshrined in the biblical religion and also implicate that religion in precisely those sacrificial rituals which join Jutland and Irish Republicanism. The allusion to the woman taken in adultery, however, complicates the ethical questions raised by the poem: if the poet's dumbness is blameworthy, then neither 'connivance' nor 'understanding' can excuse it; and the poem's predominant emotion, an empathetic pity for the victim, confirms the self-judgement.

Self-recrimination is of course the essence of the phrase 'artful voyeur' which castigates, in its pun, the poet for his poetry: he is 'artful' in that he is the skiful maker of an art, but also in that he is underhandedly cunning in contriving an art from this kind of intrusiveness, with its inherent scopophilia. This figure makes poetry itself a connivance, and the poet the guiltily abashed manipulator of others' distresses. Only such a combination of obligation and self-rebuke can license and authorize such poems as these; although in 'Strange Fruit', the poem which follows 'Punishment', even self-rebuke is unsteadied by the actuality of the victim. Its title is that of a song, with words by Lewis Allen, made famous by Billie Holiday in a 1956 recording; a song about the lynching of black people in the American South, its 'strange fruit' is the hanged corpse on a Southern tree. Heaney's poem appears, in its opening line – 'Here is the girl's head like an exhumed gourd' – to be about to run a similar metaphorical progression on the theme of the head as fruit; but in fact it moves to an insistence on the irreducibility of this atrocity to any poetic metaphorizing:

> Murdered, forgotten, nameless, terrible
> Beheaded girl, outstaring axe
> And beatification, outstaring
> What had begun to feel like reverence.

The five adjectives there are simple and abjectly descriptive, aiming at nothing more than statement, standing up against any tendency to mythologization, whether religious or literary.

The poem's material here criticizes the poem; rejecting as, in the end, culpable, because too consolatory, its capacity for veneration. The repetition of the word 'outstaring' across succeeding short lines means that this head stares back too at the male gaze of the voyeuristic poet. Outstaring axe and reverence, she is also outstaring him; refusing, in that redeemed cliché of the poem's fourth line, to be 'made an exhibition' of.

The final bog poem, 'Kinship', is a summarizing hymn to the bog, in which the poet establishes his own intimacy with the terrain, reading out of its 'hieroglyphic' landscape his own 'kinship' to the victims of Jutland. The poem's six sections display different aspects of his relationship to the bog: his physical delight in it (I); his derivation of a history and a psychology from the word itself (one of the few importations from Irish into English), which figure the bog as both memory of the landscape and the 'outback of my mind' (II); his mythologizing of the bog by 'twinning' an old moss-covered turf-spade with the 'cloven oak-limb' representative of the goddess Nerthus (III); his imagining it as language or poem, which he and his work 'grew out of' (IV), as I discussed above; his memory of helping a turfcutter as a child, a section written in the heraldic, archaizing language of some of the *Stations* sequence of prose poems, which makes the turfcutter a Zeus-like 'god of the waggon' and the boy-poet his cup-bearing Ganymede (V); and, finally, an address to the Roman historian Tacitus, who wrote about Ireland in his *Agricola* and who, in the fortieth chapter of his *Germania*, describes the cult of the goddess Nerthus.

That chapter opens, in the phrase quoted by Heaney, 'In an island of the ocean is a holy grove ...', and it is the source of Glob's speculations about the religion of the bog people. Heaney's poem imagines the present in the North of Ireland in terms of Roman imperial conquest: 'a desolate peace' is a version of Tacitus's observation about the nature of empire that 'They make a desolation and call it peace', and the Roman 'legions' who 'stare / from the ramparts' presumably figure the 'occupying' forces of the British Army. In a conclusion which,

like that of 'Punishment', has proved controversial, Tacitus is
invited to

> Come back to this
> 'island of the ocean'
> where nothing will suffice.
> Read the inhumed faces
>
> of casualty and victim;
> report us fairly,
> how we slaughter
> for the common good
>
> and shave the heads
> of the notorious,
> how the goddess swallows
> our love and terror.

Edna Longley has written of the 'astonishingly introverted
Catholic and Nationalist terms' of this section of 'Kinship',
and Blake Morrison, failing to find any 'civilized irony' in the
phrase 'slaughter / for the common good', has said that Hea-
ney's poetry here 'grants sectarian killing in Northern Ireland
a historical respectability which it is not usually granted in
day-to-day journalism'.[13] However, although this poem cer-
tainly marks the most intimate conjunction in these bog
poems between the Nordic religion and modern Ireland (that
'goddess' is both Nerthus and Kathleen ní Houlihan), there
surely is irony in the phrase. The country in which this slaugh-
ter is carried on is an island in which 'nothing will suffice'
(Yeats had asked, in 'Easter 1916', 'O when may it suffice?',
after warning that 'Too long a sacrifice / Can make a stone
of the heart'); and this 'nothing' must include such slaughter.
It will not 'suffice', will not be adequate to the end in view; par-
ticularly if the end in view is the 'common good'. To bring into

---

13 Edna Longley, *Poetry in the Wars*, 154, and Blake Morrison, *Seamus
Heaney* (Methuen, 1982), 68.

causal connection the barbarity of 'slaughter' and the civility of that English translation of the Roman ideal of civility, the *res publica*, is indeed an irony, and one not necessarily directed only against the native practice. Those legions who stare from the ramparts are also quite capable of slaughtering for the common good; they are, after all, the ones who, in Tacitus's account, make a desolation and call it peace.

5 Politico-sexual Allegories

Some such civilized, or barbarous, irony informs those allegorical poems which draw Part 1 of *North* to a conclusion, 'Ocean's Love to Ireland' and 'Act of Union'. Both allegorize crucial moments in the making of that desolation – and therefore in the history of Ireland's relationship with England – in sexual terms. 'Ocean's Love to Ireland' (its title an echo of Walter Ralegh's long poem to Elizabeth, 'Ocean's Love to Cynthia') ingeniously draws on a passage from John Aubrey's life of Ralegh to transform that 'love' into a rape. The relevant passage from *Brief Lives* reads:

He loved a wench well; and one time getting up one of the Mayds of Honour up against a tree in a wood ('twas his first Lady) who seemed at first boarding to be something fearful of her Honour, and modest, she cryed, sweet Sir Walter, what doe you me ask? Will you undoe me? Nay, sweet Sir Walter! Sweet Sir Walter! At last, as the danger and the pleasure at the same time grew higher, she cryed in the extasey, Swisser Swatter Swisser Swatter. She proved with child, and I doubt not but this Hero tooke care of them both, as also that the Product was more than an ordinary mortal.

Heaney's poem, imagining the maid backed by Ralegh to a tree 'As Ireland is backed to England', folds the Aubrey story around an evocation of the massacre at Smerwick in Co. Kerry in 1580, in which Ralegh was instrumental. A small Spanish-Catholic defence force sent by the Pope to the aid of the Irish was murdered there after surrendering. The quotation in the poem's second section is taken from an account of the massacre dictated by the English commander, Lord Grey, to his secretary, the poet Edmund Spenser. In 'Ocean's Love to Ireland', then, Ireland is the maid 'ruined' by Ralegh's imperial, plundering rape, and forced to surrender her language to the 'Iambic drums' of these English poet-courtiers. This is a poem in which, it might be said, Ralegh and Spenser are caught in the act of slaughtering for the common good; or at least for the common good of 'Cynthia' (Queen Elizabeth) and those English colonists who dispossessed the rebel landholders after Smerwick.

'Act of Union' is almost as strangely inhabited a monologue as 'Bog Queen'. If in that poem it is, in a sense, Ireland who speaks, here it is England. The Act of Union of the title is the parliamentary act of 1800 – England's response to the 1798 rebellion – which created, from 1 January 1801, the 'United Kingdom of Great Britain and Ireland'. The poem, carrying further the sexual-political topography of 'Bone Dreams', allegorizes the act as one of sexual congress between England and Ireland: England 'imperially / Male'; Ireland the woman made pregnant with the child whose 'first movement' is now being recognized by its father. Whether this child is Northern Ireland itself, or the Republican and/or Loyalist presence in Northern Ireland, the poem clearly regards the Act of Union as initiating a process which 'Culminates inexorably' in the present Troubles; in this child whose 'parasitical / And ignorant little fists' are raised against both Ireland and England. Its conclusion is hopeless and exhausted, the rhyme of 'pain' and 'again' insisting on the apparent endlessness of political suffering in Irish history:

> No treaty
> I foresee will salve completely your tracked
> And stretchmarked body, the big pain
> That leaves you raw, like opened ground, again.

6 An Inner Emigré

Part I of *North* includes exceptionally original and striking poems: a fact confirmed by the way in which they have, over the years, attracted a great deal of critical attention which, even when it is negative, is also testimony to their power. It is inevitable that the more ordinarily discursive poems of Part II have tended to suffer less attention as a result. However, they do complement Part I in a necessary way, raising again, in a more discursive or declarative manner, some of the same besetting pre-occupations. 'The Unacknowledged Legislator's Dream', 'Freedman' and 'Whatever You Say Say Nothing' address the relationships possible between poetry and the public life; 'Singing School' explores some of the conditioning cultural circumstances of the poet's own biography, culminating in 'Exposure', a classic modern poem on a poet's anxiety about the place and function of his own art in relation to an ideal of civic responsibility.

The experiment with fantasy in 'The Unacknowledged Legislator's Dream' is interestingly uncharacteristic, in a mode Heaney has not worked again. The poem – which is, despite its lineation, in fact a prose-poem – could be said to undermine Shelley's Romantic conception of poets as 'the unacknowledged legislators of the world' in the *Defence of Poetry* with something more akin to Auden's disillusioned modernist insistence that ' "The unacknowledged legislators of the world" describes the secret police, not the poets'.[14] The poem, indeed, is a kind of parable of how, in Auden's view, 'poetry makes nothing happen': in Heaney's fantasy, the poet-as-liberator is simply imprisoned by the secret policeman, and his heroically or ludicrously Tarzan-like act is rendered even more futile by the policeman's mild-mannered solicitude ('You'll be safer here, anyhow'). In 'Freedman', however, poetry, if it is not morally heroic, does provide the means of release from the most defining

14 W. H. Auden, 'Writing', *The Dyer's Hand and other essays* (Faber and Faber, 1963; 1975 edn.), 27.

marks of tribe and caste (imaged as the ashes on one's forehead – 'a light stipple of dust' – which make a Catholic automatically identifiable in Northern Ireland on Ash Wednesdays); but the release is paid for with reproach – 'Now they will say I bite the hand that fed me.' And in Heaney's most 'public' poem, 'Whatever You Say Say Nothing', poetry, in the form of allusion and of the poet's desire 'To lure the tribal shoals to epigram / And order', must contend with journalistic cliché (one way of saying nothing) and with 'The famous // Northern reticence, the tight gag of place', those sly obliquities of inspection and scrutiny operated by both communities. Heaney himself ends up saying not nothing, but what he has said before: the dedicatory poem of *Wintering Out*, repeated now as the final poem of this sequence.

'Exposure', which closes 'Singing School' and *North* itself, was written after Heaney's move away from Belfast to Wicklow in 1972. It hovers between different meanings of its title: the greater openness to the elements that comes with living again in a rural environment; confessional self-revelation; and the media publicity which the move occasioned. Literally self-questioning, the poem sets its poet in his first Wicklow winter, anxiously meditating on his own motivation and moving towards a moment of declaration in which unease is balanced with self-justification. The literal December, with its 'damp leaves, / Husks, the spent flukes of autumn', is a correlative for the poet's state of mind and therefore produces those symbolically instructive and prosopopoeic voices of the rain which both 'Mutter about let-downs and erosions' and also recall 'The diamond absolutes'. This is a dual-mindedness, a wavering between disappointment and assurance, that is also present in the poem's raising the possibility of a symbolic winter comet, only to have the poet 'miss' it in the final lines.

The movement between literal and symbolic in 'Exposure', which effects a kind of linkage inside this one poem of the predominant modes of Parts I and II of the book, is accompanied by an allusiveness which exposes the Heaney of 'Exposure' to the example of the great modern Russian poet, Osip Mandelstam. This may be thought an exercise in the exemplary entirely appropriate to the culminating poem of a sequence which takes its title from Yeats's 'Sailing to Byzantium': 'Nor is there singing school but studying / Monuments of its own magnificence'. When Heaney has himself 'Imagining a hero / On some muddy compound, / His gift like a slingstone / Whirled for the desperate', he is crossing an image of an Irish political prisoner (on the 'compound' of an internment camp) with an image of Mandelstam in one of Stalin's camps, after he had written his one explicitly anti-Stalin poem: 'David had faced Goliath with eight stony couplets in his sling,' Heaney says of this poem in 'Osip and Nadezhda Mandelstam' in *The Government of the Tongue*. The case of Mandelstam, and the kinds of decision he had to make about the writing of political poetry, is present to 'Exposure' also in the way the poet weighs his 'responsible *tristia*'. *Tristia* is the title of one of Mandelstam's books, which itself echoes the title of the Roman poet Ovid's *Tristia*, written during his exile from Rome. Heaney's self-description as an 'inner émigré' also has a Mandelstamian association: as Nadezhda Mandelstam, Osip's widow, tells us in her memoir, *Hope Against Hope*, both Mandelstam and Anna Akhmatova were branded 'internal émigrés' while still living in Moscow: émigrés, that is, from the assumptions of the Soviet regime.[15] Heaney is an 'inner émigré', presumably, both in his status as an emigrant from the North to the Republic of Ireland, and in his internal psychological status as an emigrant from certainty and self-assurance to a transitional zone of anxiety and insecurity.

The adduction of the Mandelstamian example would, however, seem intolerably presumptuous and self-aggrandizing if it did not provoke the poet of 'Exposure' into a saddened, but unapologetic self-defence:

15 Nadezhda Mandelstam, *Hope Against Hope: A Memoir*, trans. Max Hayward (1970; Penguin Books, 1975), 205.

I am neither internee nor informer;
An inner émigré, grown long-haired
And thoughtful; a wood-kerne

Escaped from the massacre,
Taking protective colouring
From bole and bark, feeling
Every wind that blows;

Who, blowing up these sparks
For their meagre heat, have missed
The once-in-a-lifetime portent,
The comet's pulsing rose.

The peculiarly negative affirmation of that is emphasized by the way it 'incubates a cadence' from Eliot (as Heaney has said, in 'The Fire i' the Flint' in *Preoccupations*, Eliot's 'Marina' incubates a cadence from Seneca): the wan anti-heroics of Prufrock's 'No! I am not Prince Hamlet, nor was meant to be; / Am an attendant lord'. Yet if the offered opportunity for action, or for the action of a particular kind of poem, has been 'missed', it is nevertheless an honourable position which has been won through to. The poet may not be an 'internee', the hero on a compound, but he is not an 'informer' either, or betrayer. He is 'a wood-kerne', one of those rebels who, during the earlier course of Irish history, took to the woods, when defeated, to prepare for further resistance. The word implies that Heaney's 'emigration', and the poetry he will compose during it, will not lack their political dimension; but the politics will take their 'protective colouring' from the obligations to the art of poetry itself. In this sense, 'Exposure' defines the poems Heaney has actually written in *North* which, with their hard-earned 'diamond absolutes' – of poetic excellence and of public accountability – do indeed themselves constitute the 'weighing' of 'responsible *tristia*'.

4

Opened Ground:
Field Work (1979)

> I suppose that the shift from *North* to *Field Work* is a shift in
> trust: a learning to trust melody, to trust art as reality, to
> trust artfulness as an affirmation and not to go into the
> self-punishment so much. I distrust that attitude too, of
> course. Those two volumes are negotiating with each other.
>
> Seamus Heaney in interview, 1982

1 Fortification

'I'm certain that up to *North*,' Heaney said in 1979, 'that was
one book; in a way it grows together and goes together.'[1]
Turned inward in scrutiny of the self, and of the culture
which had produced the self, the work from *Death of a
Naturalist* to *North* had established a relatively narrow range
of images and procedures as the characteristic Heaney territory,
and its predominant virtues were those of intensity, scrupulous-
ness and precision. The second part of *North*, however, gave
notice of a desire to turn a voice prone to self-entrancement
outwards in a more sociable form of address; and in several
interviews Heaney has spoken of his attempt in *Field Work* to
bring a sense of his ordinary social self into his poetry. The
abandonment of the very short, clipped, curt line of *North* in
favour of a return to the longer line, and the iambics, of his
earliest work is regarded as the entering into a 'rhythmic
contract' with an audience, a formal guarantee that the poetry
is intended as communication as well as self-communication.

Field Work is certainly more relaxed in its structure than

1 John Haffenden, *Viewpoints: Poets in Conversation* (Faber and Faber, 1981),
64.

North, less concentratedly intent on its own coherence. It brings together poems in a variety of kinds: political poems, 'pastoral' poems, elegies, love or 'marriage' poems, and a translation. In place of the previous book's chastened, ascetic restraint, there is a relished sensuousness of natural imagery; and the self-communing, withdrawn 'I' of *North* is replaced by a more relaxedly personal pronoun, the signal of a more conversational self. The desire to write about the ordinary world and the ordinary social self is balanced in the volume, however, by a strong sense of the ways in which the personal and domestic life can seem merely tedious or narcissistically presumptuous in contemporary poetry. His aim in *Field Work*, he observed in 1982, had been 'to fortify the quotidian into a work';[2] and it was in the poetry of Robert Lowell that he discovered the most compelling exemplification of how such a 'fortification' might occur. Lowell's impact on Heaney is pervasive in *Field Work*. Occasionally this can be disconcerting, when he appears merely to have taken over a Lowellian mannerism: the adjectival run, for instance ('Acrid, brassy, genital, ejected', of bullets, in 'The Strand at Lough Beg'), or the oracular rhetorical question ('How perilous is it to choose / not to love the life we're shown?' in 'The Badgers'), or the plaintively intimate colloquial question ('Remember our American wake?'in 'September Song', which seems to remember queries in Lowell such as 'Remember our lists of birds?', 'Remember summer?' 'Remember standing with me in the dark, / escaping?'). However, there is also a much deeper assimilation of some Lowellian procedures. In particular, Heaney has caught from the American poet that very artful combination of intent concentration and almost-inconsequentiality which, in a range of poems from *Life Studies* (1959) to *The Dolphin* (1973), deflects confessional narcissism into a taut drama of self-perception.

The major poetic presence in *Field Work*, and in much of Heaney's subsequent work, however, is Dante. *The Divine*

2 Interview with Frank Kinahan, *Critical Inquiry*, vol. 8 no. 3 (Spring 1982), 405–14, 412.

Comedy is present in the epigraph (from the *Purgatorio*) to 'The Strand at Lough Beg', and in that poem's haunting conclusion, where the poet wipes his murdered cousin's face with dew and moss, as Virgil wipes Dante's at the opening of the *Purgatorio* itself. It supplies the witty conceit of 'An Afterwards', which sets the poet in the ninth circle of the *Inferno* for the domestic treachery of too great a devotion to his art. In 'Leavings', Thomas Cromwell, despoiler of the English monasteries, is similarly imagined in one of hell's circles, 'scalding on cobbles, / each one a broken statue's head'; and the opening line of 'September Song', 'In the middle of the way', is a version of the opening line of the *Commedia*, 'Nel mezzo del cammin di nostra vita . . .'. Above all, Dante figures in the translation from Cantos 32 and 33 of the *Inferno*, which Heaney calls 'Ugolino' and uses to bring *Field Work* to a conclusion. Dante is of crucial value to Heaney as the greatest of all poetic communers with the dead. *The Divine Comedy* is a series of encounters in which they offer explanations of their fate and advice, encouragement and instruction to the poet and his companion, Virgil. *Field Work* is full of encounters with its poet's own dead. There are the violently dead of Northern Ireland: Colum McCartney, Heaney's second cousin, the victim of a random sectarian killing in 1975; Sean Armstrong, a Belfast social worker whom Heaney had known at university, in 'A Postcard from North Antrim'; the victim in 'Casualty' (unnamed in the poem, but in fact a friend of Heaney's called Louis O'Neill); the 'murdered dead' and the 'violent shattered boy' of 'The Badgers'. Dead artists are also commemorated in the book's elegies: Sean O'Riada, the Irish composer who died at the age of forty in 1971; Robert Lowell himself, who died in 1977; and Francis Ledwidge, the Irish poet killed fighting for England during the First World War. Such encounters, shadowed by the Dantean example in *Field Work*, achieve a further pitch of intensity in the title sequence of Heaney's next book, *Station Island*, in which the idea of example becomes structural.

In an interview in 1979, however, Heaney also remarked on a

less obvious focus of his interest in Dante when he said that 'the first person singular and the historical life, the circumstances of the time and the man's personal angers, are all part of the forcefulness of the utterance'.[3] Dante therefore, like Lowell, proposes a different way of saying 'I' in a lyric, a new mode for the expression of subjectivity; and in fact the more personal voice of the poems which open *Field Work* is actually fortified by an awareness of the intimate relationship between the personal and the political or historical. In the volume's opening poem, 'Oysters', the apparently innocent eating of a meal with friends, that paradigm of good-natured sociability, becomes the basis for a meditation on the difficulty of ever avoiding the larger contingencies. These oysters, 'Alive and violated', 'ripped and shucked and scattered', have their innocence violated too by the knowledge of their place in the history of human taste. As the delicacy of the Romans, the oysters come tainted with the savagery of European imperialist history and with the pride of caste or class: they are the 'frond-lipped, brine-stung / Glut of privilege' which refuses the poet any easy luxuriating in 'the cool of thatch and crockery'. His final anger grows from resentment that such self-punitive knowledge keeps him from untrammelled enjoyment of the meal, that such conscience prevents him from reposing his trust 'In the clear light, like poetry or freedom / Leaning in from sea'.

Such 'clear light' would presumably be the opposite of the 'dark' of Irish history and self-scrutiny given expression in the work from *Death of a Naturalist* to *North*. It is a light 'like poetry', leaning in temptingly, invitingly, a poetry of the sea, not the land, transcending the diminishments of human history; poetry as alternative, as delight and consolation, as the free play of imagination. When this poet eats the day 'Deliberately, that its tang / Might quicken me all into verb, pure verb', it is an impatient response to such a cajoling invitation. Being quick-

3 'In the mid-course of his life', interview with Dennis O'Driscoll, *Hibernia*, 11 October 1979, 13.

ened into verb will remove him, once and for all, from the enclosing, static nouns of earth and myth and place-name; and the movement is conveyed in lines as rich in etymological implication as anything in Heaney, in which the Old English and Old Norse derivations 'ate', 'day', 'tang' and 'quicken' propel their penitential abruptness into the greater relaxedness of the Latinate 'Deliberately' and 'verb, pure verb'. Yet the repose of such unfettered imagination, however deeply it is desired (and 'Oysters' makes it seem sweetly desirable), cannot be attained by mere effort of will. After such knowledge, light can never be so easily 'clear' again, nor verb so pure.

Indeed, as if to emphasize the equivocal nature of this meal with which *Field Work* opens, the book closes with the eating of a kind of meal too. In 'Ugolino', Count Ugolino gnaws at Archbishop Roger's head in a grotesque parody of a meal. He and his sons and grandsons had been starved to death by Roger, and this is the eternal punishment fitting the crime. In translating Dante here, Heaney introduces a metaphor and a simile not in the original, which point up the comparison between this hideous act and the eating of a meal: the 'sweet fruit of the brain', and the head 'As if it were some spattered carnal melon'. The picture of enemies eternally locked in a literal enactment of 'devouring hatred' has, of course, its relevance to Northern Ireland, just as dying of hunger has its reverberations in Irish history and politics.[4] The 'clear light' of the poetry desired in 'Oysters' is in fact darkened frequently in *Field Work* by such shadows from the old conflict; and the poems which follow 'Oysters' – 'Triptych' and 'The Toome Road' – are, once again, consumed by it.

Both make use of an oracular, vatic, quasi-Yeatsian rhetoric.[5]

4 In 'The Flight Path' in *The Spirit Level* Heaney revisits this translation and makes the contemporary connection explicit. See Chapter 8.
5 The best account I know of this element in Heaney, although not written with specific reference to these poems, is Alan Peacock, 'Mediations: Poet as Translator, Poet as Seer', in Elmer Andrews (ed.), *Seamus Heaney: A Collection of Critical Essays* (Macmillan, 1992), 233–55. Peacock asks, 'Can the oracular

It is a manner which can be used only very sparingly by a contemporary poet if it is not to seem presumptuously over-weening; but in 'Triptych' it gives a persuasively magisterial and authoritative air to the poem's pained view of the present state of Ireland: now, for the first time in Heaney's work, the South with its mercenary acquisitiveness, as well as the North with its sectarian violence. The panels of this triptych propose, very tentatively, images of some kind of comprehension, or consolation, or simple endurance. In 'After a Killing', which was written after the murder of the British ambassador to Ireland, Christopher Ewart-Biggs, in July 1976, the 'small-eyed survivor flowers', the 'Broad window light' and the young girl's gift of vegetables are literal, if symbolically resonant, natural compensations for the obdurate persistence of the images of violence and desolation with which the poem opens. Those images include, however, the comparison of, presumably, members of the Provisional IRA to 'the unquiet founders' – that is, the revolutionary, violent establishers of the Irish Free State in the 1920s – who are also described as 'Profane and bracing as their instruments' (that is, their rifles). Those adjectives work against each other in a self-cancelling way: the unholy and therefore damnable is corrected by the defiant (and 'bracing' is elsewhere a term of strong approbation in Heaney); and the word 'instruments', used of firearms, both renders the rifles as neutral as musical 'instruments' would be, and also suggests their function as agents of purpose or end. Despite what appear, then, the poem's pacific gestures at its close, there is a glamour and 'quickening' inherent in these images at its opening which attach it – almost, as it were, despite itself – to some of the persistent tropes and tones of republican rhetoric. 'Who's sorry for our trouble?' is a

---

voice be assumed without compromising private loyalties, ordinary reticences? It is a question central to any interpretation of Heaney's *oeuvre*.' This is surely right; and the question abides its answer(s).

rhetorical question which appears to elide those other questions of guilt and responsibility in a pathos of intractable hopelessness: 'I'm sorry for your trouble' is the tenderly Irish way of acknowledging bereavement, and it figures in Heaney's own 'Mid-Term Break' in *Death of a Naturalist*; but in 'Triptych', of course, it also echoes with the euphemism which describes the current situation as the 'Troubles'.

In 'Sibyl', the girl – who had been, glancingly, a kind of Ceres-figure in 'After a Killing' – is more deliberately mythologized, as she utters her prophecy, with its faint hope of 'forgiveness'. The extraordinary image of new life returning to the 'helmeted and bleeding tree' may derive from the trees which bleed in the underworld of Virgil's *Aeneid VI*, and from the frontispiece drawing by David Jones for his poem about the First World War, *In Parenthesis*, which entangles a naked but prominently helmeted soldier in a landscape of blasted trees in an image which joins together savagery and vulnerability. In this image, Heaney has risen to his occasion, drawing together the grandiose and the tenderly human (those 'buds like infants' fists') to create a powerful sense of alternative possibility. Nevertheless, the hope is, realistically, wearily conditional, abrupted before the clause in which it is uttered can become a sentence, and the oracular tone is licensed only by its being articulated in character and quotation:

> 'Unless forgiveness finds its nerve and voice,
> Unless the helmeted and bleeding tree
> Can green and open buds like infants' fists
> And the fouled magma incubate
>
> Bright nymphs ...'

That Lowellian ellipsis is the voice failing to find its nerve; and this makes the tentative optimism a sudden brief eruption into a poem which otherwise throws its attention back on to the prophecy of what will happen without such 'forgiveness' – the change of human form into a bestial or insectile alternative – and forward to the evocation of the actual Irish present, in which the profit motive is unidealistically pursued ('My people think money / And talk weather'). Heaney's 'bleeding tree', as an emblem for such an Ireland, reduced by both political violence and capitalist mercenariness, may also be an undermining revision of Yeats's magnificent unitary, harmonizing symbol in 'Among School Children', the 'chestnut tree, great-rooted blossomer'; and the impulse to a revision of the image may also suggest that, in Heaney, the Yeatsian rhetoric itself will not be given its head. In 'Sibyl' the language of vision-ary possibility engages the stubborn compunctions of the actual; which makes it appropriate that the sibyl's final line is an ironic and despairing allusion to, and modification of Shakespeare. 'Our island is full of comfortless noises' remem-bers, and reverses, Caliban in *The Tempest* – 'Be not afeard: the isle is full of noises, / Sounds and sweet airs, that give delight, and hurt not' – by remembering that, when Gloucester's eyes are put out in *King Lear*, he is left 'all dark and comfortless'.

This comfortlessness is the concluding mood of 'Triptych' when its final poem, 'At the Water's Edge', sets the poet amid the ancient Christian and pagan remains on the wooded islets of Lough Erne, one of the oldest inhabited sites in Ireland, longing for the humbling postures of Christian penitence:

> Everything in me
> Wanted to bow down, to offer up,
> To go barefoot, foetal and penitential,
>
> And pray at the water's edge.

The religious desire, however, is held in abeyance by the memory of actual politics; and the Christianity whose site this is, a religion which recommends 'forgiveness', offers only 'silence', its 'stoup' now 'for rain water', not for the holy water of Christian blessing. In its concluding lines 'Triptych' disconsolately collapses back out of any visionary or religious possibility, into the 'irrevocable' political fact: the British

Army helicopter 'shadowing' the march at Newry which followed as a protest against Bloody Sunday (30 January 1972).

That march is 'our march', and they are 'my roads' which the poet drives down when he meets the armoured convoy in 'The Toome Road'. The possessives are the signal of the outraged native challenge to the colonizing aggressor. Indeed, the British soldiers become, briefly, continuous with the forces of the Roman *imperium* evoked in 'Oysters', when they are anachronistically addressed as 'charioteers'. Against their presumption, Heaney insists on the sustaining, 'vibrant' presence of 'The invisible, untoppled omphalos'. This reference to the navel-stone at Delphi, the location of the Delphic Oracle, suggests that the Toome road (which has strong associations with the 1798 rebellion of the United Irishmen) is, to this poet, a place with oracular significance. The navel-stone of nationalist Irish feeling, it maintains a persistent, defiant opposition to the colonial power; and Heaney deliberately assumes, in the poem, a representative role as the articulator of such feeling: 'I had rights-of-way, fields, cattle in my keeping'.[6] 'The Toome Road', 'Triptych', the implied allegory of 'Ugolino', and the

6 Peter McDonald, in his subtle, painstaking book *Mistaken Identities: Poetry and Northern Ireland* (Oxford University Press, 1997), 52–8, has a lengthy reading of this poem which asks what he calls the 'hard questions' about it. He quotes my identification of the 'omphalos' and observes that it 'seems to hint at possibilities of irony ... which the rhetorical drive of the last three lines simply rules out'. I have to confess that McDonald sophisticates me here: I did not intend to hint at irony, sympathizing, as I did, with what is undoubtedly Heaney's nationalist position in the poem. Although my own position has become more complicated over the years, it still seems to me that 'The Toome Road' articulates an emotion appropriate to its time and place; it is certainly one that anyone who drove around Northern Ireland with Northern Irish Catholics in the mid-1970s, and particularly in the year or two following Bloody Sunday, will recognize and remember. McDonald admits to the ways in which his own critique may be ideologically underpinned; and when he says that 'the coherence which the "omphalos" supplies must obscure the kinds of actual violence which have given rise to the military presence', he may be thought to beg the question of where that violence actually had its origin; and that of course is the hard question that divides unionist from nationalist.

Northern Ireland elegies ensure that, for all its poems of the personal life, *Field Work* retains a large political resonance; and that, for all its trust in the healing and consolatory affirmations of the artistic act, and the married life, it remains uncomplacently open to the urgencies of its historical moment, and responsively alert to the world beyond poem and home.

2 Elegies

The elegies for artists in *Field Work* are manifestly, in the way of elegy, deeply self-involved too, proposing images of the artistic life relevant to, or exemplary for, Heaney himself. Sean O'Riada's melding of a sophisticated international musical culture with native Irish folk melody is figured as his conducting the Ulster Orchestra 'like a drover with an ashplant / herding them south', where the word 'south' has clear political implications picked up in the subsequent identification of O'Riada as 'our jacobite, / ... our young pretender'. Robert Lowell's promulgation of 'art's / deliberate, peremptory / love and arrogance' takes up terms of ambivalent approval which Heaney uses in his critical writing too, for instance in 'Yeats as an Example?' in *Preoccupations*, and which elements of his own work suggest he desires for himself, even while he acknowledges his own more pliable artistic temperament. Francis Ledwidge's fate ('"To be called a British soldier while my country / Has no place among nations ..."') makes him into 'our dead enigma' in whom 'all the strains / Criss-cross in useless equilibrium': the poem's implied aspiration is, presumably, that in this later poet in whom similar strains are crossed the strain might prove more useful. The political complication and the empathetic poignancy give 'In Memoriam Francis Ledwidge' real strength,[7] but the other artistic elegies in *Field*

---

7 Particularly when, in *New Selected Poems 1966–1987*, Heaney cuts a redundant stanza, aware, presumably, of the poem's tendency to corpulence. Heaney is a notable post-publication reviser of his own work, not always with the gain he makes here.

Work seem over-deliberate. The Lowell elegy in particular is too knowing when it sets Heaney and Lowell together 'under the full bay tree' in Glanmore, sharing a moment of intimacy which reads very like a poetic laying-on of hands. 'My sweet, who wears the bays ... ?', the poet will ask in 'An Afterwards', where such arrogance earns its infernal rebuke. Where there is leisure for ambition there is, perhaps, too little grief.

The elegies for dead friends are another matter. The immediacy of Heaney's sympathy forces him, for the first time in his work, to confront directly – as he did not in the mythologized obliquities of *North* – the actual circumstances of sectarian murder. Colum McCartney is blessed, at the end of 'The Strand at Lough Beg', with a Dantean asperging, but he is also imagined 'with blood and roadside muck in [his] hair and eyes'; and before the poet can plait those 'green scapulars' for his cousin's shroud – which have connotations at once patriotic, Christian-resurrectionary and pastoral-elegiac – he must lift the actual weight of the Irish countryman 'under the arms'.[8] Sean Armstrong is urged, in the banter of desperation, to 'Get up from your blood on the floor' in 'A Postcard from North Antrim'. And Louis O'Neill, the fisherman in 'Casualty', is particularized in the moment of being blown to pieces, 'Remorse fused with terror / In his still knowable face'; where 'still knowable' insists not only on what will become of his face a split-second later, but also on how he survives, now, in the poet's memory and in this commemorative poem.[9]

In the context of these specific deaths, Heaney is also compelled to confront his own evolving responses to the

8 A scapular is a short cloak covering the shoulders worn by the members of some religious orders.
9 The lines following this – 'His cornered outfaced stare / Blinding in the flash' – vividly and terribly pick up the image of the 'face'. O'Neill is 'outfaced' by the bomb both because it literally takes his still knowable face away, making it no longer knowable; but also because he has attempted to 'outface' the bomb by defiantly braving the curfew, and the bomb (and those who detonate it) are more than capable of defying him.

North. In 'The Strand at Lough Beg', this takes the form of a rueful acknowledgement of his family's incapacity for facing some of the violent realities of sectarianism: 'For you and yours and yours and mine fought shy, / Spoke an old language of conspirators / And could not crack the whip or seize the day'; the implication of which is, presumably, that this family are constitutional, not revolutionary nationalists. The attitude is probed no further, but the poem makes it clear that McCartney has been killed by those who have cracked their whip and seized their day; and the assassination itself takes on an aspect of even greater horror in that it intrudes into a landscape with associations sacred to Northern Catholics. The poem's close, therefore, attempts to restore to the violated place an element of quasi-sacred ritual deriving from its allusion to the moment in *The Divine Comedy* when his guide Virgil washes the grime of Hell from Dante's face with the dew of Purgatory. As the grieving poet raises his cousin from the ground, the poem's solemnly mournful iambics and direct visionary address to the dead man place these lines as the most moving Heaney has written:

> I turn because the sweeping of your feet
> Has stopped behind me, to find you on your knees
> With blood and roadside muck in your hair and eyes,
> Then kneel in front of you in brimming grass
> And gather up cold handfuls of the dew
> To wash you, cousin. I dab you clean with moss
> Fine as the drizzle out of a low cloud.
> I lift you under the arms and lay you flat.
> With rushes that shoot green again, I plait
> Green scapulars to wear over your shroud.

When McCartney's shade subsequently appears in 'Station Island', it is to complain bitterly that this exquisite Dantean close to 'The Strand at Lough Beg' is a continuance in literature of family incapacity. Heaney now punctiliously identifies McCartney as 'my second cousin', where the earlier poem had indulged in the pathos of an address simply to a 'cousin'. So identified, he in turn addresses the poet in recrimination:

> 'You confused evasion and artistic tact.
> The Protestant who shot me through the head
> I accuse directly, but indirectly, you
> who now atone perhaps upon this bed
> for the way you whitewashed ugliness and drew
> the lovely blinds of the *Purgatorio*
> and saccharined my death with mourning dew.'

This is the supreme instance in Heaney's self-corrective work of the poet blaming himself for the act of writing: an attitude which is, indeed, so pervasive as to constitute an always restless, mobile aesthetic. In these self-cancelling passages great rhetorical and visionary capacity exposes and undermines itself, marking anxiety as a fundamental principle of creativity.

In 'Casualty' Louis O'Neill, who has broken an IRA curfew after Bloody Sunday, has been blown up in the reprisal bombing of a Protestant pub. As well as being a perfectly judged elegy for O'Neill, deftly evoking the quality of the man's life, and genuinely grieved, 'Casualty' is also a meditation on the ethics of betraying 'our tribe's complicity', the complex loyalties of a Northern Catholic. The poem is formally ironic: written in the rhyming, triple-stress metre of Yeats's 'The Fisherman', which conjures from the Celtic Twilight an idealized West of Ireland peasant as the perfect, if unlikely, dedicatee of his work, Heaney's poem contains its fisherman too, but a rather less idealized one, 'dole-kept'. Knowing the poet only in the pub and on the boat, he finds that 'other life' of poetry 'Incomprehensible', although he is curious. 'Casualty' joins the two lives and two worlds together when it brings O'Neill, uncondescendingly, into this poem. The poet initially notices the fisherman's 'turned observant back', and subsequently offers the ambivalent lines, 'But my tentative art / His turned back watches too.' The inversion in these lines makes it impossible to say whether the poet subjectively watches the turned back or whether the turned back subjectively watches his tentative art, in a variation of the cliché 'to have eyes in the back of your head'. This undecidable grammatical reciprocity is entirely consonant with the poem's ending, which implicitly joins the poet's lines to the fisherman's lines through the use, once more, of that word prominent also in Heaney's earliest negotiations between his primary and his secondary worlds in 'Digging' and 'Churning Day' in *Death of a Naturalist*, the word 'rhythm': 'As you find a rhythm / Working you, slow mile by mile / Into your proper haunt'; and the poem, having effected this close conjunction of the poet and his fisherman subject, concludes in an invitation which makes the poet himself the object of scrutiny and inquiry:

> Dawn-sniffing revenant,
> Plodder through midnight rain,
> Question me again.

The 'question' is one which Heaney's meditation on O'Neill's fate has earlier made him ask himself: 'How culpable was he / That last night when he broke / Our tribe's complicity?' When O'Neill's fishing and Heaney's poetry are joined in these concluding lines, their mutual lonely 'beyondness' takes them 'well out' from that image of community, the 'common funeral' of the thirteen dead of Bloody Sunday, which occupies the central section of 'Casualty'. The terms of that description are ambivalently poised between solidarity and constraint:

> The common funeral
> Unrolled its swaddling band,
> Lapping, tightening
> Till we were braced and bound
> Like brothers in a ring.

The funeral swaddles the mourners in a metaphor of maternal protectiveness which also infantilizes them; and 'braced' links them together in a participle which also straitens them (and perhaps throws retrospective light on the word 'bracing' in 'Triptych'). The concluding evocation of fisherman and poet sharing the boat, on the other hand, is light with release: 'I tasted freedom with him' ('like poetry or freedom / Leaning in from sea', we remember, in 'Oysters'). The poem locates them together in the boat with 'The screw purling, turning / Indolent fathoms white'; and the word 'turning' picks up the already prominent – because repeated – attitude of the fisherman's 'turned back'. These prominences are complemented by the poet's imagining of the moment of the man's death: 'I see him as he turned / In that bombed offending place.' Turning, and turning away, are the ethical gestures found deeply compelling in 'Casualty', but not firmly assented to; and in this sense also Yeats's 'The Fisherman' is a ghostly intertext for Heaney's poem. There, the fisherman is imagined into being 'In scorn of this audience': of, that is, the audience which Yeats, perhaps arrogantly, always found disappointing. The fisherman of 'Casualty' similarly offers a figure for the 'proper haunt' of a poet who would not be curbed or constrained by even the most compelling expectations of an audience or a 'tribe'. The apparently confident analogies between poetry and rural crafts in the earlier work, which 'bound' the poet to the community, have been replaced, in the analogy of 'Casualty', by something much edgier, more uncertain, more 'tentative' and 'turned'. To the republican or nationalist mind, 'Casualty' is therefore a scandalous poem, one that proposes an image of divorce even in the act of memorializing the worst of the atrocities perpetrated by the British Army in Ulster: the one poem of Heaney's which explicitly includes Bloody Sunday is an elegy not for its thirteen dead, but for one 'Casualty' – that neutrally exculpating, statistical term of the military strategist – killed in reprisal. The poet's invitation of O'Neill to 'Question me again' may be regarded, therefore, as Heaney's own questioning of the fixed positions, loyalties and 'complicities' which sanction those automatic reprisals and acts of vengeance which, despite themselves, in fact make no sectarian discriminations. As such, it initiates the elaborate self-questioning of 'Station Island', whose first revenant is another one who turns his back, the 'old fork-tongued turn-coat', William Carleton.

3 Marriage Poems

Although the love poem is a staple of the lyric tradition, the 'marriage poem' – that is, the poem celebrating a continued, fruitful, collaborative relationship – is not. Some instances of the kind are notoriously embarrassing: Eliot's 'A Dedication to my Wife', for instance, which F. R. Leavis was rumoured to have sellotaped down in his edition of the poems. The strongest poems of marriage are either addressed to a dead wife (from Henry King's 'Exequy', to Eugenio Montale's *Xenia*) or they are poems of a deeply troubled marriage (Lowell's *For Lizzie and Harriet* and *The Dolphin*), or they are both (Thomas Hardy's poems of 1912–13). But, even if there is little direct competition, Heaney's achievement in the marriage poems of *Field Work* is a large one. He has written a poetry of ordinary domestic happiness, of the dailiness and continuity of married love, entirely lacking in either sentimentality or self-satisfaction.

The poems manage this partly by not disguising the difficulties. In 'High Summer', there is the teething child who cries 'inconsolably' at night; in 'Polder', there are 'the sudden outburst and the squalls' of a domestic row; and in 'The Otter', marriage as an evolving process is gracefully figured in the correlative of the changing weathers of Tuscany:

> The mellowed clarities, the grape-deep air
> Thinned and disappointed.
> Thank God for the slow loadening,
> When I hold you now
> We are close and deep
> As the atmosphere on water.

In 'An Afterwards', the constant accommodations to be made between domestic obligation and poetic responsibility – the conflict notably defined by Yeats as the requirement that one choose 'perfection of the life or of the work' – are treated in an unsolemn register. The tensions are figured in the conceit which renders Ugolino's punishment of Roger comically bathetic, depicting the hell of poets who are concerned only with the 'bays' of critical renown as 'a rabid egotistical daisy-chain'. For all the poem's affectionately wry comedy, however, the wife's question, with its heart-sinking enjambement, sadly rebukes the poet's self-absorption:

> 'Why could you not have, oftener, in our years
>
> Unclenched, and come down laughing from your room
> And walked the twilight with me and your children –
> Like that one evening of elder bloom
> And hay, when the wild roses were fading?'

She lets him off the hook, nevertheless, for his 'kind, / Indifferent, faults-on-both-sides tact'; but he is not so lightly dismissed in 'A Dream of Jealousy'. Even if the opportunity for jealousy is being given only in 'a dream' in that poem, there is nevertheless no remedy for the hurt it causes. Neither in the order of aesthetics ('these verses', with their beguiling allurements, including a setting that seems taken from Manet's *Le Déjeuner sur l'Herbe*), nor in the ethical order ('my prudence'), is there balm for the woman's 'wounded stare', which survives the sonnet's apology, as the bog woman's stare survives 'Strange Fruit'.

By admitting the difficulties, then, these poems refuse to idealize human love; and they also refuse to idealize the human body. In a series of zoomorphizing analogies which are perhaps partly indebted to Robert Lowell, whose work is full of animal and piscine life, the woman is an otter, a skunk, and a sandmartin's nest. The poet is himself self-deprecating too: he is 'tense as a voyeur' in 'The Skunk'; he is the sandmartin desperate for the 'occlusion' of the nest in 'Homecomings'; and he is 'like an old willow' in the lovely 'Polder'. The analogies and the anti-romantic attitudes insist on the embodied nature of love, and on the body's inevitable imperfections. As in the strange religio-erotic ritual which closes the 'Field Work' sequence itself, however, – that sequence which gazes on the imperfection of vaccination marks stretched on arm and thigh – these are imperfections which, through the intent devotion of sexual love, may be 'stained, stained / to perfection'. Being 'stained to perfection' is, we might say, a renovation of the Christian concept of the Fall as a *felix culpa*, a happy fault: it is the paradoxical conjunction of nature and art, of the human body and the human will which may bring about the 'anointing' (the word of 'Field Work') of a happy marriage.

Yet this is to overstate what these poems delicately understate, nowhere more than in 'The Skunk'. Its title, and the glimpse of the poet as voyeur, recall Robert Lowell's 'Skunk Hour' in *Life Studies*; but the mood of that disconsolate, desolating poem is contrastively remote from Heaney's. Lowell's 'skunk hour' is a time of intense, infernal isolation ('I myself am hell, / nobody's here'), whereas Heaney's skunk acts as an emblem for the way the poet's aloneness is a mere physical accident, suffused with his wife's presence when, away from her in California, he writes her a love letter. The skunk – 'intent and glamorous', 'ordinary, mysterious', 'mythologized, demythologized' – takes on the 'oxymoronic' qualities of the woman much known and much missed: so that the risky comparison, made while he is with her again in their bedroom, is charged with affection and intimacy, turning a faintly ridiculous human posture into an unconscious erotic invitation:

> It all came back to me last night, stirred
> By the sootfall of your things at bedtime,
> Your head-down, tail-up hunt in a bottom drawer
> For the black plunge-line nightdress.

The unromanticizing exactitude of the poem, its trustful certainty that it cannot put a foot wrong, or strike a false note, is clinched by the word 'sootfall'. A delightful neologism, like Eliot's 'smokefall' in 'Burnt Norton', it is accurate in the way it listens to the clothes falling to the bedroom floor, but it also remembers that the clothes are, like all clothes falling from a human body at bedtime, dirty. To be 'stirred' by such a 'sootfall' is to give witness to the ordinary mysteriousness of a marriage; and 'The Skunk' is a loving comedy of the consolations of the habitual. Like others of these marriage poems, it is tender without being cosy, personal without being embarrassingly self-revealing. They are poems of a disinterested maturity, managing an intensely difficult tone: honest, and quite without self-regard.

4 Glanmore

The sequence of ten 'Glanmore Sonnets' which lies physically at the centre of *Field Work* is a concentration of preoccupations apparent in its other poems too. The presence of a sonnet sequence, after the disruption of the lyric in *North*, is the most open acknowledgement in *Field Work* of an allegiance to the English lyric tradition; and the tenth sonnet alludes to Thomas Wyatt, the first English sonneteer. This allegiance is fused, however, with a further acknowledgement of Patrick Kavanagh, whose sonnet sequence 'Temptation in Harvest' delicately registers the rural world of his native Co. Monaghan; in *Preoccupations* Heaney observes that some poems in the sequence 'beautifully and wistfully annotate ... his move to Dublin in 1939'. The 'Glanmore Sonnets' also annotate a move, from Belfast to Co. Wicklow, out of an urban environment back into a rural one. On one level then, the sonnets are what Kavanagh's sequence is: a sensuously exact evocation of living eye-level close to the processes and seasons of the natural world, its animal life and its vegetation. Unlike Kavanagh, however, Heaney discovers in the site a new point of confirmation and resolution, a firmer ground.

'Ground' is the word which ends the first line of the first sonnet, in the phrase 'opened ground', which glances back at 'Act of Union' in *North*, where the 'opened ground' is the raw wound left on Ireland by England's siring on her of the North. In the 'Glanmore Sonnets', the phrase is deliberately translated out of that historical agony into the realm of aesthetics: the 'ground' is now that of poetry itself. The phrase 'vowels ploughed into other' of that opening line is not easily interpreted, but it may mean, self-reflexively, 'vowels ploughed into other vowels', and hence suggest the almost self-entranced process of poetic composition, as the line forms itself when one vowel-sound suggests and prompts another; but it may also contain the idea of the vowels of Irish speech being worked into the otherness of the English iambic line, or even the words of the poem as they take into themselves the otherness of reality, hence opening a further linguistic and rhythmic path for the poet. That process of interpenetration is figured vividly in the line 'Each verse returning like the plough turned round', a simile suggested by the derivation of 'verse' from the Latin *versus*, which meant both a line of verse and the turn made by the ploughshare from one furrow into the next. This original linguistic juncture between agriculture and culture is at one with the identifications made elsewhere in the sequence between nature and poetry: an evening 'all crepuscular and iambic', and a wind which 'Is cadences'. This delighted, sensuous merging of facts of nature and facts of culture may derive its originating impulse from a poem of Osip Mandelstam's, no. 62, in the W. S. Merwin and Clarence Brown translation of 1973. It is a poem which the 'Glanmore Sonnets' could be said secretly to nurture and address:

> Orioles in the woods: length of vowels alone
> makes the metre of the classic lines. No more
> than once a year, though, nature pours out
> the full-drawn length, the verse of Homer.

> This day yawns like a caesura: a lull
> beginning in the morning, difficult, going on and on:
> the grazing oxen, the golden languor powerless
> to call out of the reed the riches of one whole note.

If Mandelstam is a hidden presence in the sequence, other writers are there too, in varying degrees of visibility, in allusions

which make the literary as much a mode of the perceiving con-
sciousness in these poems as it is in *North*. Boris Pasternak's
'Hamlet' ends with a Russian proverb which Lowell translates,
in *Imitations*, 'To live a life is not to cross a field'; and Heaney's
opening sonnet remembers this when it says of the relaxed ease
of the Glanmore life, 'Now the good life could be to cross a
field.' Wyatt, as I have noted, is alluded to in the tenth
sonnet, where the eroticism of the poet's 'first night' with his
wife is allied to one of the most tenderly erotic moments in Eng-
lish poetry, Wyatt's 'They flee from me':

> When her lose gowne from her shoulders did fall,
> And she me caught in her armes long and small;
> Therewithall sweetly did me kysse,
> And softly saide, dere hert, howe like you this?

More glancingly, Joyce is alluded to in the 'inwit' of IX (Stephen
meditates in *Ulysses* on the medieval English phrase 'agenbite
of inwit', remorse of conscience); Philip Sidney's *Apology for
Poetry* in X ('What is my apology for poetry?'); Shakespeare,
also in X, with the eloping lovers Lorenzo and Jessica from
The Merchant of Venice; and Diarmuid and Grainne in the
same sonnet, lovers pursued in the Ulster mythological cycle.

Above all, though, it is Wordsworth who shadows the
sequence, as obviously present here as he is in *Death of a
Naturalist*. In II, 'sensings, mountings from the hiding places'
is Wordsworthian in its gerunds and in its reference to 'the
hiding places of my power' in *The Prelude*. In III, the poet is
about to make a direct comparison of his wife and himself, in
their 'strange loneliness', to Dorothy and William in Dove
Cottage, but the hyperbole is deflated by his wife's interrupting
demurral. Sonnets IV, V and VI are also Wordsworthian in the
way they seek out moments analogous to the 'spots of time' in
The Prelude, moments from the poet's childhood through
which, in memory, an imaginative extension occurs. In IV, the
child misses the reputed 'iron tune' of the train when he puts his
ear to the line, but the adult retrieves a poem from the memory,

lying now with an ear to the poetic line. In v, the meditation on a tree associated with early sexual experience, and already named in 'Broagh' – in dialect the 'boortree', in standard English the 'elderberry' – is offered as one instance of what has made this poet an 'etymologist of roots and graftings' in the 'tree' of language. And in vi, the legendary story of 'the man who dared the ice' is an implied analogy from the poet's childhood for the daring, attack, inspiration and impetuousness of a particular kind of poem, whose risk is also 'a cold where things might crystallize or founder'. It is to the point also that it is in an essay in *Preoccupations* which makes reference to Wordsworth's ambulatory compositional methods that Heaney traces the derivation of 'verse' from *versus*.

Poem vi refers to 'the unsayable lights'; but these are all poems which manage to 'say' complex experiences, even while reminding us of the difficulty with which any experience struggles out of its 'hiding place' into the articulation of a poem. Formed partly from other poems, and gratefully allusive to them, the 'Glanmore Sonnets' are nevertheless directed out towards the world as well as inwards towards writing itself, seeking their ideal in a harmoniously reciprocal relationship between culture and nature. The sequence discovers its finest metaphor for these correspondences not in literary creation, but in sculpture, when, in ii, Oisin Kelly is imagined 'hankering after stone / That connived with the chisel, as if the grain / Remembered what the mallet tapped to know'. An understanding of these relationships, however, is not simply given, but must be slowly acquired; and this is why Glanmore is a 'hedge-school' in which the poet tries to learn a voice that might 'continue, hold, dispel, appease'. The 'hedge-schools' were the only means the native Irish had of gaining an education during the period of the Penal Laws, and we can take it that what this voice must dispel and appease is, at least in part, the inheritance of a history of violence and repression. For all that the sonnets find their comforts in pastoral calm, in literature, and in the achieved mutuality of marriage, these consolations are set against insistent reminders of the world's pain. In VIII, the innocent sight of a magpie inspecting a sleeping horse summons to mind the 'armour and carrion' of a historical battlefield; in IX, a rat 'Sways on the briar like infected fruit', terrifying the poet's wife, and other rats killed in threshing leave their 'Blood on a pitch-fork, blood on chaff and hay'; and the final sonnet evokes a dream in which husband and wife lie down together and apart, in the attitude of death, as well as the embrace of sexual love.

In 'Yeats as an Example?' in *Preoccupations*, Heaney claims that in Yeats's poems 'the finally exemplary moments are those when [the] powerful artistic control is vulnerable to the pain or pathos of life itself.' The strength of the 'Glanmore Sonnets' is that, for all the control of their artistry, and the self-delight of their literariness, they never forget this vulnerability. Characteristic moments, then, are the conclusions of sonnets VIII and X. Sonnet VIII:

> Do you remember that pension in *Les Landes*
> Where the old one rocked and rocked and rocked
> A mongol in her lap, to little songs?
> Come to me quick, I am upstairs shaking.
> My all of you birchwood in lightning.

The poignant memory of human suffering there is countered with the urgent imperative of sexual desire, as if the one could occlude the other. It is the vulnerable desperation which registers most powerfully, however, in the phrase 'My all of you', which effects a grammatical conjunction (of his possessive adjective and her personal pronoun) responsively imitative of the sexual conjunction itself, which is urgently and vividly imagined now, in anticipation – which is 'all' he has of her until she comes to him – as birchwood seen in, or consumed by a flash of lightning. It is the humbled expression of overwhelming need, as well as of irresistible desire. And X, with its echo of Wyatt:

And in that dream I dreamt – how like you this? –
Our first night years ago in that hotel
When you came with your deliberate kiss
To raise us towards the lovely and painful
Covenants of flesh; our separateness;
The respite in our dewy dreaming faces.

'Deliberate' is a beautifully tactful word, drawing love, responsibility and inexperience into its net; and 'raise' similarly entraps both sexual tumescence and spiritual uplifting. 'Lovely and painful' is a telling paradox, just as these are 'covenants' which leave husband and wife, nevertheless, in their 'separateness'. The kind of art Heaney longs for in 'Oysters' is one in which his trust might 'repose'; but the saving grace of his own in the 'Glanmore Sonnets' is that it culminates not in the permanence of 'repose', but only in the temporary relief of 'respite'; implying that the covenants made by flesh – in poetry and in marriage alike – are always, in the end, vulnerable.

5 The End of Art

Field Work is a more miscellaneous collection than some of Heaney's, as its title proposes, with its suggestion of a collection of samples gathered together. There are other poems I have not yet discussed which powerfully contribute to its character; and two of them, 'The Singer's House' and 'The Harvest Bow', dramatize the sense of the relationship between art and politics which Heaney has acquired in his hedge-school. Both oppose instances of particular kinds of artistic perfection – the folk-singer's song and the harvest bow – to the depredations of human life and history, and both include an implicit benediction for the future. 'The Singer's House' contains one of Heaney's saddest generalized reflections:

What do we say any more
to conjure the salt of our earth?

So much comes and is gone
that should be crystal and kept

and amicable weathers
that bring up the grain of things,
their tang of season and store,
are all the packing we'll get.

The song celebrated in the poem is one of the things that might be 'said' in response to the query of the opening lines there. With 'a hint of the clip of the pick', it brings the predominantly Northern Protestant salt-mining culture of the seaport Carrickfergus to the singer's 'house' in Gweebarra, the bay in Co. Donegal; and it therefore implies a new harmony between North and South. When the seals are imagined as 'drowned souls' drawn towards the singer's voice, they become emblems of muted hope and possibility. That they might 'change shape' is an optimistic version of that metamorphosis so terrifyingly prophesied in 'Sibyl' (where the changed form would be a 'saurian relapse', a reversion to a reptilian condition). The poem's final peremptory address to the singer – 'Raise it again, man. We still believe what we hear.' – is an affirmation of an art which, in the face of human loss and diminishment, still presumes to offer a model of pacific reconciliation.

Its presumption is, however, in the word of 'Casualty', 'tentative' in the face of the apparent ineradicability of violence. The motto of the harvest bow is also uninsistently subjunctive: the bow is a 'frail device', easily destroyed, whose motto 'could be' 'The end of art is peace'. The way the motto reads itself out of the bow, on behalf of its tongue-tied maker, may remind us of the prosopopoeic 'foster-child of silence', the urn, in Keats's 'Ode on a Grecian Urn'; but the comparison reveals too how very provisional this device is.[10] The motto is offered not as

10 The slightly unexpected word 'device' accrues strength from knowledge of its etymology: it can mean, or once meant, both 'an emblematic design usually accompanied by a motto' and 'a conversation'. Both senses are clearly relevant;

discovery and revelation ('Beauty is truth, truth beauty'), but as
fragile aspiration. It is, nevertheless, a hope offered by the most
benign aspects of a particular rural inheritance: the 'spirit of the
corn' is an apotheosis of the patient, devoted effort of agricul-
ture. In this sense, the poem may be considered a revision of
'Digging'. There, the poet's pen became an agricultural imple-
ment like the father's spade; in 'The Harvest Bow', the
(assumed) father plaits, in the bow, a paradigm of art. The
hands which plait the bow have also, however, 'lapped the spurs
on a lifetime of game cocks', and the urgency of the poem's
desire for 'peace' does not slip into any sentimentalizing of the
threats always offered to it. The concluding simile makes this
plain when the motto is said to be 'Like a drawn snare'; the
beneficent removal of the cause of pain reminding us of the
animal who may be relieved but is still, of course, wounded. The
motto itself may even warily acknowledge that, if the 'end' (the
aim and fruit) of art is peace, then peace may also be the 'end'
(the termination) of art, since so much art, and certainly the art
of this poet, has been nourished by what is not 'peace'.[11]

   Such realism concludes *Field Work* not with the conciliatory
and absolving gestures of 'The Harvest Bow' and 'The Singer's
House', but with the violence of 'Ugolino'. The end of that poem
makes out of Dante's invective against Pisa a venomous sibilance
which hides a snake in its grass: 'Pisa! Pisa, your sounds are like
a hiss / Sizzling in our country's grassy language.' The denuncia-
tion is, presumably, not directed only against medieval Pisa; and
when it dilapidates to its conclusion in the pathos of naming the

---

and this is one of the notable cases in Heaney where poems appear almost to
pause as they concentrate a ramifying etymological appropriateness into
themselves.

11 Bernard O'Donoghue, in *Seamus Heaney and the Language of Poetry*
(Harvester Wheatsheaf, 1994), 86, observes that 'It also brings to mind another
familiar declaration in Dante's *Paradiso* which sits uneasily in the context of
these elegies for the victims of violence: Piccarda's *e'n la sua voluntade è nostra
pace* (in God's will is our peace).'

dead – 'Your atrocity was Theban. They were young / And innocent: Hugh and Brigata / And the other two whose names are in my song' – we remember too the names of those other dead in the 'song' of *Field Work* itself. The art of the volume is that it has held tensely in the same balance the song of possible reconciliation and the memorial lament. If *Field Work* offers comfort, it is a comfort earned well on the other side of distress.

5

Writing a Bare Wire:
Station Island (1984)

There are some lines in poetry which are like wool in texture and some that are like bare wires. I was devoted to a Keatsian woolly line, textured stuff, but now I would like to be able to write a bare wire.

Seamus Heaney in interview, 1984

1 Modes of Scrutiny

Station Island is in three separate parts: an opening section of individual lyrics which take their occasions from the occurrences and memories of the ordinary life; the central section, the title sequence itself, which narrates, or dramatizes, a number of visionary encounters with the dead; and a concluding sequence, 'Sweeney Redivivus', which, as Heaney puts it in one of his own notes to the volume, is 'voiced for Sweeney', the seventh-century king transformed into a bird in the medieval Irish poem *Buile Suibhne* which Heaney has translated as *Sweeney Astray*. Despite its separate parts, however, the book has a formal unity, signalled by the presence, in all three parts, of the Sweeney figure. He is there in the poem which ends Part One, 'The King of the Ditchbacks' (which is, partly, about the act of translation itself); then in the opening section of 'Station Island', in his manifestation as the unregenerate Simon Sweeney, one of a family of tinkers remembered from Heaney's childhood; and finally, of course, in the 'Sweeney Redivivus' sequence itself. What 'The King of the Ditchbacks' calls Sweeney's 'dark morse' is therefore tapped throughout the volume; and it spells out a rigorous scrutiny by this poet of his own commitments, attachments and responsibilities. This self-scrutiny proceeds through the three parts of *Station Island* in different modes. In Part One, it occurs in separate lyrics originating in autobiographical experience; in 'Station Island', this contemporary self undergoes a penitential and confessional exercise on a mythologized pilgrimage; and in 'Sweeney Redivivus', the newly steadied self is released into the freedom of a kind of anti-self or parallel-self, as Heaney's voice or script is twinned with that of the character whose name rhymes with his own, 'Sweeney'.

The different modes of the volume – the lyric; the narrative and dramatic; the disguised or ventriloquial – are no doubt designed partly to offset the dangers of self-importance in this very self-involved book. In this respect, the shortest poem in *Station Island*, and one of its most perfect, 'Widgeon', may be read as an allegory of the book's deflective procedures:

> It had been badly shot.
> While he was plucking it
> he found, he says, the voice box
>
> like a flute stop
> in the broken windpipe –
>
> and blew upon it
> unexpectedly
> his own small widgeon cries.

This tiny anecdote about the shot wild duck is a story already told ('he says') – like the Station Island pilgrimage which is already well written into Irish literature, like *Buile Suibhne* – which the poet now tells again, in his own words. The bird is 'badly shot', as some of the shades in 'Station Island' have been badly (wickedly, cruelly) shot, in Northern sectarian murders. 'He' in 'Widgeon' blows his own cries on the dead bird's voice box, just as Heaney briefly and poignantly returns a voice to the dead in the 'Station Island' sequence, a voice which remains, nevertheless, entirely his own voice too; and as, in 'Sweeney Redivivus', his own voice sounds through the 'voice box' of Sweeney, the bird-man.

In this dartingly implicit allegory of the way the individual poetic voice speaks through the real and the legendary dead – through biographical experience and literary tradition – it is the word 'unexpectedly', given a line to itself, which carries the greatest charge of implication. The poet who would properly articulate his own small widgeon cries through encounters with the dead must seem uncalculatingly preoccupied with his subject or with the form of his own poem, having something of the intent self-forgetfulness of one who would, testingly and probingly, attempt to blow upon a dead bird's voice box. The preoccupation may then release, 'unexpectedly', and almost distractedly, a genuine self-illumination or self-definition, just as 'Widgeon' releases allegorical implications most 'unexpectedly' too. It is precisely this unexpectedness which characterizes *Station Island*. Ambitious and perhaps not equally successful in all its parts, it nevertheless gives notice that Heaney's poetry, in its dissatisfied revision of earlier attitudes and assumptions, and in its exploratory inventiveness as it feels out new directions, is now in the process of successfully negotiating what is, for any poet, the most difficult phase of a career: the transition from the modes and manners which have created the reputation, to the genuinely new and unexpected thing. In *Station Island* this makes for a poetry bristling with the risks of self-transformation and, at its high points, triumphantly self-vindicating too.

2 Sermons in Stones

I want to spend most of the space available to me in this chapter discussing the sequences in *Station Island*, since they present particular difficulties which may be aided by sustained consideration. The individual lyrics of Part One, however, complement them in various ways. Introducing a new acerbity and astringency to the Heaney lyric, many of them offer rueful self-scrutiny as objects and occasions from the ordinary world (rather than, as in 'Station Island', the visitations of ghosts) insist their ethical claims. In 'An Aisling in the Burren', there are, literally, sermons in stones: 'That day the clatter of stones / as we climbed was a sermon / on conscience and healing'; and in poem after poem Heaney listens to similar, if less explicit, sermons, as the natural world offers instances of the exemplary. Sloe gin, in the poem it gets to itself, is 'bitter / and dependable'; a lobster is 'the hampered one, out of water, / fortified and bewildered'; a granite chip from Joyce's Martello tower is 'a Calvin edge in my complaisant pith'; old pewter says that 'Glimmerings are what the soul's composed of'; the Pacific in Malibu is an instruction in how this poet is indissolubly wedded to the ascetic Atlantic; visiting Hardy's birthplace is an education in displacement; flying a kite is to know 'the strumming, rooted, long-tailed pull of grief'; and listening in to 'the limbo of lost words' on a loaning (that is, a lane or a track) is to hear how:

> At the click of a cell lock somewhere now
> the interrogator steels his introibo,
> the light-motes blaze, a blood-red cigarette
> startles the shades, screeching and beseeching.

These instructive moralities make Part One of *Station Island* severe and self-admonitory, and the tone is predominantly chastened, restrained and even wearied. 'What guarantees things keeping / if a railway can be lifted / like a long briar out of ditch growth?', 'Iron Spike' asks; and self-chastening is accompanied now by a sense of diminishment, transience and the perilous fragmentariness of memory. If the newly tart lyric manner is a departure of the kind recommended in 'Making Strange' by the voice of poetry itself – 'Go beyond what's reliable / in all that keeps pleading and pleading' – the departure is nevertheless fully conscious of how much must be left behind: 'The Loaning' confesses that:

> When you are tired or terrified
> your voice slips back into its old first place
> and makes the sound your shades make there.

Despite the new departures of these lyrics, however, what nevertheless keeps pleading at some level in a number of them is the political reality of the North. In 'Sandstone Keepsake', another stone acts as the spur to a meditation in which Heaney paints a wry self-portrait of the artist as political outsider which is characteristic in its shrug of uneasy self-deprecation. The poem remembers how the stone was 'lifted' from the beach at Inishowen. At the northern tip of Co. Donegal, Inishowen is at the opposite side of Lough Foyle from the Magilligan internment camp. Heaney is therefore prompted into mythologizing the stone in the terms of a Dantean analogy, imagining it as 'A stone from Phlegethon, / bloodied on the bed of hell's hot river'; yet he rejects the grandiose comparison in deflating embarrassment ('but not really'), before concluding in the self-deflating contemplation of how the poet might appear to the Magilligan guards:

> Anyhow, there I was with the wet red stone
> in my hand, staring across at the watch-towers
> from my free state of image and allusion,
> swooped on, then dropped by trained binoculars:
>
> a silhouette not worth bothering about,
> out for the evening in scarf and waders
> and not about to set times wrong or right,
> stooping along, one of the venerators.

The incapacity for the political role is rebuked in those lines by the pun which makes over the 'Irish Free State', which was bitterly fought for in a revolutionary and a civil war, into a phrase for the disengagement of poetry, and by the allusion itself which refuses the obligation Hamlet finds so overwhelming, to 'set right' the times that are 'out of joint'. 'Sandstone Keepsake' inherits, it may be, the guilt and anxiety of 'Exposure', but seems more ironically assured of the poet's peripheral status: the most the poem can aspire to is the 'veneration' of the political victim. This self-presentation, with its let-downs and erosions, casts its shadow far into *Station Island*.

3 Going on Pilgrimage

Station Island, or St Patrick's Purgatory, is a small, rocky isle in the middle of Lough Derg in Co. Donegal which, since early medieval times, has been a place of pilgrimage for Irish Catholics. The three-day pilgrimage involves a self-punitive routine of prayer, fasting and barefoot-walking around stone circles or 'beds', thought to be the remains of ancient monastic cells. From the very earliest times, Lough Derg has inspired popular legend and writing, in particular medieval accounts of miracles and visions, and historical narratives about the suppression of the pilgrimage in the eighteenth century, under the anti-Catholic Penal Laws. As a result, 'Station Island', is the name for a nexus of Irish Catholic religious, historical and cultural affiliations. Since the nineteenth century, it has also been the subject of more specifically literary treatments: William Carleton's mocking but fascinated prose account, 'The Lough Derg Pilgrim' (1828); Patrick Kavanagh's lengthy *Lough Derg: A Poem* (written in 1942, but published only posthumously in 1978); Denis Devlin's poem, *Lough Derg* (1946); and Sean O'Faolain's classic short story, 'The Lovers of the Lake' (1958), a story about the uneasy coexistence of sexuality and the Irish Catholic conscience.

In an uncollected essay, Heaney says that it was partly the anxiety occasioned by these numerous earlier literary versions of the pilgrimage which turned him to Dante's meetings with ghosts in the *Purgatorio* as a model for his own poem: Dante showed him how to 'make an advantage of what could otherwise be regarded as a disadvantage'.[1] Hence in 'Station Island' the imaginary pilgrimage to the island becomes a series of meetings with ghosts of the type Dante meets in the *Purgatorio*: friendly, sad, self-defining, exemplary, admonitory,

---

1 Seamus Heaney, 'Envies and Identifications: Dante and the Modern Poet', *Irish University Review*, vol. 15 no. 1 (Spring 1985), 5–19, 18.

rebuking. A central passage from this essay illuminates Dante's usefulness for Heaney:

What I first loved in the *Commedia* was the local intensity, the vehemence and fondness attaching to individual shades, the way personalities and values were emotionally soldered together, the strong strain of what has been called personal realism in the celebration of bonds of friendship and bonds of enmity. The way in which Dante could place himself in an historical world yet submit that world to scrutiny from a perspective beyond history, the way he could accommodate the political and the transcendent, this too encouraged my attempt at a sequence of poems which would explore the typical strains which the consciousness labours under in this country. The main tension is between two often contradictory commands: to be faithful to the collective historical experience and to be true to the recognitions of the emerging self. I hoped that I could dramatize these strains by meeting shades from my own dream-life who had also been inhabitants of the actual Irish world. They could perhaps voice the claims of orthodoxy and the necessity to recognize those claims. They could probe the validity of one's commitment.[2]

The shades Heaney meets in the poem, then, have all been 'inhabitants of the actual Irish world', whether personally known friends and acquaintances, or writers known from their work; and their conversations turn on the living of a proper life or on the production of significant art. The revenants are advisers, from beyond the grave, on the poet's responsibilities in the realms of ethics and aesthetics.

In I, a prelude to the pilgrimage itself, the encounter, on a Sunday, is with the unregenerate 'sabbath-breaker', Simon Sweeney, a figure of fascination as well as fear, with his advice to 'Stay clear of all processions.' The advice is set against the orthodox pieties of a crowd of women on their way to mass, in a scene which contains (in 'the field was full / of half-remembered faces') a sudden echo of the opening of the medieval poem of vision and pilgrimage, *Piers Plowman*, and its 'field full of folk'; a reminder that poetry in English, as well as in Italian, has its

2 Ibid., 18–19.

tradition of the dream-vision, and that 'Station Island' self-consciously draws on it. In II, the ghost is William Carleton, encountered appropriately on the road, not on the island itself, since, after visiting Station Island in his youth, he subsequently renounced Catholicism and wrote 'The Lough Derg Pilgrim' as a denunciation of its barbarities and superstitions (hence his being named 'the old fork-tongued turncoat'). The 'ghost' of III is the inanimate 'seaside trinket' which, to the poet as a child, had been redolent of the death of the girl who owned it (her original was Agnes, the sister of Heaney's father, who died of TB in the 1920s). In Section IV the poet meets a priest who had died on the foreign missions shortly after his ordination (his original was Terry Keenan, still a clerical student when Heaney knew him). The section meditates on the ratifying role of the priesthood in Irish society, and its effect on the priest himself, 'doomed to the decent thing'. V includes three separate encounters with teachers or mentors of the poet's, including his first teacher at Anahorish School, Barney Murphy, and Patrick Kavanagh. VI evokes, with affectionate tenderness, an early sexual experience and, after 'long virgin / Fasts and thirsts' under the dominion of Catholic sexual morality, a later satisfying and fulfilling one. The ghost of VII is a man Heaney had played football with in his youth, the victim of a sectarian murder in Northern Ireland (Heaney is remembering William Strathearn, killed by two off-duty policemen in a notorious incident in Co. Antrim). The victim's description of the circumstances of his death impels the poet into a confession of what he regards as his own evasive, uncommitted politics. VIII confronts the poet with two further ghosts whose challenges provoke self-rebuke: an archaeologist friend (whose original was Tom Delaney, who died at thirty-two), towards whom he feels 'I had somehow broken / covenants, and failed an obligation', and Colum McCartney, the subject of 'The Strand at Lough Beg' in *Field Work*, who utters the most unrelenting accusation in the sequence, reproving the poet for, precisely, his poetry itself, as we have seen in Chapter 4.

Section IX gives a voice to one of the ten IRA hunger-strikers who died in Long Kesh prison between March and September 1981 (Heaney is thinking of the second of them to die, Francis Hughes, who came from his own district, Bellaghy, and whose family he knows). The certitude which could lead to that kind of political suicide is juxtaposed with a dream of release and revival in which the symbol of a 'strange polyp' ('My softly awash and blanching self-disgust') appears, to be supported and illuminated by a candle, and is followed by a further symbol of possibility, an 'old brass trumpet' remembered from childhood. X has another inanimate ghost, a drinking mug removed from the poet's childhood home by actors for use in a play, and returned just as Ronan's psalter is miraculously returned from the lake by an otter at the opening of *Sweeney Astray*; a further symbol, therefore, for the unexpected translations which the known, ordinary and domestic may undergo. In XI the ghost is a monk to whom the poet once made his confession, who requires him, as a penance, to translate a poem by St John of the Cross, the sixteenth-century Spanish mystic; the poet responds now, belatedly, with a version of 'Cantar del alma que se huelga de conoscer Dios por fe', the 'Song of the soul that is glad to know God by faith': a hymn to the 'fountain' of the Trinity and the sacrament of the Eucharist, that sign of the believing Church in harmonious community. Finally, in the concluding section of the poem, the poet, returned to the mainland, meets the ghost of James Joyce, who recommends a course antithetical to that of orthodox Catholic pilgrimage, a striking-out on one's own in an isolation which, he claims, is the only way the poet's proper work can be done.

These encounters find their structural shape in the nature of the pilgrimage itself, as the pilgrims leave the ordinary social world, cross the waters of Lough Derg, perform their penitential exercises, and return. The irony of 'Station Island', however, is that this pilgrimage leads to no confirmation in the religion and values of the Catholic community, but to something very like a renunciation of them. The sequence may be read as a kind of retraction or palinode directed at some of the innate assumptions and attitudes of Heaney's own earlier work. When the poet does 'repent' in IX, his contrition is for the guilt of these old attachments with their self-restricting immaturities: ' "I repent / My unweaned life that kept me competent / To sleepwalk with connivance and mistrust." ' The poem itself remains aware of all the ways in which a consciousness must stay permanently 'unweaned' from such powerful formative influences and experiences; it retains, throughout, the poignancy of anxiety and misgiving. Nevertheless, 'Station Island' uses the structural metaphor of its Irish Catholic pilgrimage to define some of the constrictions which that religion and culture have imposed and to suggest how, under alternative mentors, and through the agency of poetry itself, a newly enabling freedom might be won.

A subtext of accusations against Irish Catholicism may be read out of the earlier parts of the poem: in I, where the poet is set behind pious women on a 'drugged path', that it acts as a mere opiate, numbing the obedient conscience with its assertions of authority; in II, where the radical Ribbonmen of Carleton's day have become, by the time of the poet's childhood, a drunken band who 'played hymns to Mary', that it keeps you patient and enduring, incapable of the anger of action; in III, where the child's death, held in pious memory, is juxtaposed with the brute reality of a dog's death, that, in attempting to account for death, it in fact sentimentalizes it; and in IV, with its 'doomed' priest, that its clericalism thwarts the lives of those who represent it, and bolsters platitudinous pieties. In the poem's latter sections, Catholicism is heavily implicated in the poet's adolescence of sexual dissatisfaction and guilt, and in his unease and regret about his lack of any firmer political commitment: the 'timid circumspect involvement' for which he begs forgiveness of Strathearn, and that confusion of 'evasion and artistic tact' of which McCartney accuses him. These charges generate the outburst of rejection in IX:

'I hate how quick I was to know my place.
I hate where I was born, hate everything
That made me biddable and unforthcoming.'

Here, knowing his place is not so much establishing an identity
with a particular territory – which is celebrated as a virtue often
enough in Heaney's earlier work – as meekly accepting a servi-
tude to the mores of a community; where to 'know your place'
is to stay put.[3] Even though it is quickly undercut with rueful
qualifications, the venom of that climactic attack makes it un-
surprising that, despite appearances, no true pilgrimage is actu-
ally undertaken in the poem. In IV, the poet is 'ready to say the
dream words I renounce ...', the renunciation of worldliness
which is the essential prelude to repentance, when he is inter-
rupted by the priest reflecting that he may be there only to
take 'the last look' since 'the god has, as they say, withdrawn.'
No praying is done on the pilgrimage: when he kneels in III, it is
only 'Habit's afterlife'; and the poem-prayer in XI could be
thought to undermine its song of faith with its constant refrain,
'although it is the night'. In John of the Cross this is the 'dark
night of the soul', in which the mystic feels himself temporarily
abandoned by God; but, to a secular consciousness, it could re-
present the sheer inability to believe.

The poet is also sometimes in physical positions which
dissociate him from the other pilgrims: in V, he is 'faced
wrong way / into more pilgrims absorbed in this exercise',
and in VI, the others 'Trailed up the steps as I went down
them / Towards the bottle-green, still / Shade of an oak'. That
same section goes so far as to appropriate, from the beginning of
the *Divine Comedy*, the moment when Dante is impelled on his
journey by learning from Virgil of Beatrice's intercession, in

---

3 There are numerous ways in which Heaney's one-time pupil Paul Muldoon,
the dedicatee of 'Widgeon', engages with Heaney's work in his own poetry.
This may be one of the places where Heaney glancingly alludes to Muldoon,
whose first pamphlet publication was entitled *Knowing My Place* (Ulsterman
Publications, 1971).

order to describe the poet's own sexual awakening after the enforced virginity of his Irish Catholic adolescence. His truancy from the pilgrimage there turns the tradition of the vision-poem on its head, making sexual not divine love the object of the exercise; but it reminds us too that Dante's great poem of Christian quest discovers its images of heavenly bliss in transfigured womanly form. At the centre of this pilgrimage, however, there is not presence but absence, figured frequently as a 'space'. It is 'a space utterly empty, / utterly a source, like the idea of sound' in III; 'A stillness far away, a space' in VI; 'the granite airy space / I was staring into' in VIII; and, in XII, after the pilgrimage, 'It was as if I had stepped free into a space / alone with nothing that I had not known / already'. This final linking of the blank space with freedom comes after the Joyce figure counsels the poet; he is, implicitly, the repository of a new kind of personal and cultural health when the poet takes his hand 'like a convalescent' and feels an 'alien comfort' in his company. In this sense, the pilgrimage to the island in the poem is a large parenthesis, the brackets of which are closed by William Carleton at one end, and by James Joyce at the other: highly politicized artists offering, on the mainland, their alternatives to the orthodoxies of the island, which ironically echo the first advice given in the poem, the unregenerate Simon Sweeney's 'Stay clear of all processions.'

Carleton's significance is clarified by another of Heaney's uncollected essays in which 'The Lough Derg Pilgrim', with its portrait of a culturally and materially deprived Ireland, is opposed to Synge's much better-known account, in his plays and prose, of the Aran Islands which is, in Heaney's view, a glamorizing of the reality in accordance with the literary-political programme of the Irish Literary Revival.[4] The 'two islands' of the essay, 'Station' and 'Aran', represent two different

4 Seamus Heaney, 'A tale of two islands: reflections on the Irish Literary Revival', in P. J. Drudy (ed.), *Irish Studies* 1 (Cambridge University Press, 1980), 1–20.

Irelands, realities put to virtually opposed literary and ideo-
logical uses. Carleton, in fact, is regarded very much as a
nineteenth-century equivalent of Patrick Kavanagh: a teller of
the true tale, from the inside, but also from a position of
estrangement, about Irish rural life, which is 'not ennobling
but disabling'. In his appearance in 'Station Island', he counsels
the poet in a righteous anger and also in the redemptive
necessity, for the Irish writer, of a memory and sensibility
schooled by politics as well as by the natural world: ' "We are
earthworms of the earth, and all that / has gone through us is
what will be our trace." ' The word associated with Carleton in
'Station Island' is 'hard'. Defining his 'turncoat' politics, Heaney
has him say, ' "If times were hard, I could be hard too" '; and
when he departs in the final line, he 'headed up the road at the
same hard pace'. His hardness is matched by Joyce's 'straight-
ness'. In XII, 'he walked straight as a rush / upon his ash plant,
his eyes fixed straight ahead'; and when he departs, 'the down-
pour loosed its screens round his straight walk.' This is the
straightness of his decisiveness and authority, as he counsels the
more pliable poet in a course opposed to communal and local
fidelities.

What this sequence wryly calls the 'Feast of the Holy Tundish'
is a very secular feast, constructed from Stephen Dedalus's diary
entry for 13 April, at the end of *A Portrait of the Artist as a
Young Man*.[5] The entry is 'a revelation // set among my stars'
because 13 April is Seamus Heaney's birthday. In the passage
referred to, Stephen reflects on an earlier conversation with his
English Jesuit dean of studies about the word 'tundish'. The
priest has never heard the word before, but it is a common usage
for 'funnel' in Stephen's Dublin:

5 In the version of the poem published in Heaney's *New Selected Poems 1966–
1987* this reference is omitted. It could be that, in retrospect, it appeared self-
regarding. This seems to me a revealing instance of authorial indecision in
relation to a precursor. I discuss some implications of the Joyce figure of
'Station Island' in 'Heaney's Joyce, Eliot's Yeats', *Agenda*, vol. 27 no. 1 (Spring
1989), 37–47.

That tundish has been on my mind for a long time. I looked it up and find it English and good old blunt English too. Damn the dean of studies and his funnel! What did he come here for to teach us his own language or to learn it from us? Damn him one way or the other![6]

The damnation of the Englishman is a register of Joyce's supreme confidence in his own language, and this is an enabling moment, a 'password', for this later writer too, who inherits in his own art the Joycean example of an Irish writer who bends the once alien English language suitably to his own purposes. Hence Heaney's apparent delight in the biographical coincidence, and hence also the poem's addressing Joyce as 'old father', which is how Stephen addresses the mythical Daedalus at the end of the *Portrait*. The confidence is combined, in Joyce, with that arrogant pride and disdain which enabled him to subvert various deleterious conceptions of Irishness in his work and which also impelled his brave self-exile from Ireland. Hence the concluding advice from the Joyce figure of 'Station Island' to the poet engaged on a not entirely dissimilar project, to 'keep at a tangent', to:

> 'swim
>
> out on your own and fill the element
> with signatures on your own frequency,
> echo soundings, searches, probes, allurements,
>
> elver-gleams in the dark of the whole sea.'

There are excellent passages in 'Station Island': Section III, for instance, with its extraordinarily inward and intimate evocation of the way the young poet is almost erotically possessed by the child's death; and its most Dantean moments – McCartney's rebuke, and the fading of some of the shades, notably Strathearn's in VII ('And then a stun of pain seemed to go through him // and he trembled like a heatwave and faded')

6 James Joyce, *A Portrait of the Artist as a Young Man*, ed. Seamus Deane (Penguin, 1992), 274.

– which are unforgettably poignant and intense. Nevertheless, it seems to me that the narrative and dramatic structure of the sequence inhibits Heaney's truest poetic strengths, which are lyric strengths. In particular, the dialogue can be heavy-handed: 'Open up and see what you have got' and 'Not that it is any consolation, / but they were caught' seem stilted, especially in their context of deep emotional perturbation and distress.[7] Some of the symbols are over-insistent, particularly compared to the grace and delicacy with which the literal slides into the symbolic in the earlier work. There are moments of bathos: when, in IX, after seeing the vision of the trumpet, the poet tells us he 'pitched backwards in a headlong fall', and we are suddenly closer to slapstick than to symbolic reverie; and, more subtly perhaps, when the Joycean voice of XII seems so much more accommodating, concerned and hortatory than anything Joyce ever wrote himself – for the good reason, perhaps, that the passage's marine imagery is much more Heaney-like than Joycean, much closer to 'Casualty' and 'Oysters' than to the *Portrait*. Finally, there are occasional uncertainties in the handling of verse form, particularly in Heaney's sometimes ragged variations on the Dantean *terza rima*. The form is notoriously difficult in English, but Heaney's variations on it are bound to summon much too closely for comfort Eliot's tremen-

---

7 Bernard O'Donoghue, in *Seamus Heaney and the Language of Poetry* (Harvester Wheatsheaf, 1994), 93–4, rebukes me for this remark and makes a case for Heaney's language in the poem as genuinely Dantean. The 'language of the exchange,' he says, 'is not rhetorically recast ... but occurs unprocessed', just as in the *Divine Comedy* the characters 'act with passion, but they speak without it'. This is a reasoned and sophisticated defence from someone whose knowledge of Dante is much greater than mine, and in a book which is subtle and illuminating on Heaney's language; but in fact I dispute that 'unprocessed'. Surely, at the very least, the verbs in these exchanges would be elided in unprocessed form: not 'you have' but 'you've'; and not 'it is' but 'it's'? A small point, maybe, but, as Heaney himself writes in another context, 'minute incisions' matter in poems. Peter McDonald, in *Mistaken Identities: Poetry and Northern Ireland* (Oxford University Press, 1997), 12, describes 'Station Island' as 'only intermittently successful'.

dous imitative approximation of it in the second section of 'Little Gidding', and Yeats's use of it in a poem Heaney admires in *Preoccupations*, 'Cuchulain Comforted'.[8] 'Station Island' is, nevertheless, clearly a necessary poem for Heaney to have written, one that defines a painful realignment between himself and his own original culture, and brings him to that point of newly steadied illumination where it might be said of his work, as it is said of one of its symbols, that 'the whole bright-masted thing retrieved / A course and the currents it had gone with / Were what it rode and showed.'

4 The Mask of Sweeney

Heaney's engagement with the figure of Sweeney lasted over ten years: from his earliest attempts at a translation in 1972 until its eventual publication, as *Sweeney Astray*, in 1983. In that poem Sweeney is an Ulster king who offends the cleric St Ronan, and is punished by being cursed after the Battle of Moira in 637. Driven mad and changed into a bird, he flies, exiled from family and tribe, over Ireland and as far as Scotland. The poem's narrative is frequently interrupted by Sweeney's poignant lyric expressions of his own misery, and by his equally sharp and tender celebrations of the Irish landscape, particularly its trees. Sweeney is therefore also a lyric poet; and in Robert Graves's account of *Buile Suibhne* in his 'grammar of poetic myth', *The White Goddess*, he describes it as 'the most ruthless and bitter description in all European literature of an obsessed poet's predicament'.[9] Heaney recognizes in the poem a crucial point

---

8 Again, O'Donoghue, ibid., 99, counters this with his own belief that Heaney's *terza rima* is 'his most impressive achievement in poetic form', although he is also thinking of what he regards as variations on it in the 'Squarings' sequence of *Seeing Things*. I agree that the verse is managed wonderfully in 'Squarings', but it does not echo *terza rima* so closely as 'Station Island', even though it does, indeed, have other strongly Dantean elements, as I suggest in Chapter 7.
9 Robert Graves, *The White Goddess* (Faber and Faber, 1961), 455.

in the move from a pagan to a Christian culture in Ireland, and he is interested in it for political and topographical reasons too; but in the introduction to his version he additionally spells out some of the implications of a recognition similar to Graves's:

... insofar as Sweeney is also a figure of the artist, displaced, guilty, assuaging himself by his utterance, it is possible to read the work as an aspect of the quarrel between free creative imagination and the constraints of religious, political and domestic obligation.

A further aspect, in fact, of that 'quarrel' already evident in 'Station Island'; and it is difficult to read far into *Sweeney Astray* without noticing some of the ways in which Sweeney's voice is harmonized with, or subdued to, Heaney's own. Sweeney draws on a lexicon familiar from the poems: 'visitant', 'casualties', 'recitation', 'trust', 'philander', for instance, as well as using the thin quatrain as his most frequent lyric form. At one point, indeed, the original is 'translated' in lines which are openly self-referential, when Sweeney says:

> I have deserved all this:
> night-vigils, terror,
> flittings across water,
> women's cried-out eyes.

This is another version of a sentence which concludes 'The wanderer', one of the prose-poems in *Stations*, which mythologizes Heaney's departure from his first school: 'That day I was a rich young man, who could tell you now of flittings, night-vigils, let-downs, women's cried-out eyes', lines which are of course evocative of the situation of Northern Ireland.[10]

That 'rich young man' reappears in the final poem of the 'Sweeney Redivivus' sequence, 'On the Road'. In Matthew's gospel the man asks Christ what he must do to be saved, and the answer is the uncompromisingly absolute one repeated in the poem, 'Sell all you have and give to the poor and follow me.' The

10 Seamus Heaney, *Stations* (Ulsterman Publications, 1975), 19.

demand, whether it is made in the realm of religion or of art, and whether a response to it is a real possibility or a chimera, is one that haunts the sequence and in a sense encloses it, since 'The King of the Ditchbacks' in Part One ends in lines which bind together poet, Sweeney and the rich young man. That poem has evoked the mesmerized and obsessive process of poetic translation before its final section effects this further 'translation' which carries the poet over, in an imagined magical rite, into Sweeney:

> And I saw myself
> rising to move in that dissimulation,
>
> top-knotted, masked in sheaves, noting
> the fall of birds: a rich young man
>
> leaving everything he had
> for a migrant solitude.

The poet translates himself into Sweeney, then, in the context of a biblical allusion which summons to the metamorphosis concepts of urgent demand, of striking out on one's own, of exile, of attempting to go beyond what is recognized and known. This is all implicit in Heaney's explanation in an interview of how he felt he had found in the figure of Sweeney 'a presence, a fable which could lead to the discovery of feelings in myself which I could not otherwise find words for, and which would cast a dream or possibility or myth across the swirl of private feelings: an objective correlative.'[11]

This 'migrant solitude' is manifestly akin to the 'tangent' recommended by the figure of Joyce at the end of 'Station Island', and the actual form of the poems of 'Sweeney Redivivus' seems to bear some relation to Heaney's description of Joyce's voice there, 'definite / as a steel nib's downstroke', which remembers how, in *Ulysses*, Stephen refers to 'the cold steelpen'

11 'Unhappy and at Home', with Seamus Deane, *The Crane Bag*, vol. 1 no. 1 (1977), 61–7, 65. The interview is reprinted in M. P. Hederman and Richard Kearney (eds.), *The Crane Bag Book of Irish Studies (1977–1981)* (Blackwater Press, 1983), 66–72.

of his art. There is a definiteness, a hard edge, a sense of the thing suddenly and speedily, but finally, articulated in the free forms of these poems. In this, their forms may also derive from Heaney's view of medieval Irish lyric, as he expresses it in 'The God in the Tree' in *Preoccupations*, where he compliments Flann O'Brien (who had made his own use of Sweeney in the novel *At Swim-Two-Birds*), for his characterization of the 'steel-pen exactness' of Irish lyric. Heaney describes such lyric himself in terms appropriate to his own sequence: its 'little jabs of delight in the elemental', its combination of 'suddenness and richness', and its revelation of the writer as 'hermit' as much as 'scribe' ('Sweeney Redivivus' includes poems called 'The Hermit' and 'The Scribes'). It is worth adducing this larger context for 'Sweeney Redivivus' since the Sweeney of *Buile Suibhne* is really only one element in the construction of this 'objective correlative'; and, despite Heaney's description, in a note, of the poems as 'glosses' on the original story, there are in fact remarkably few obvious points of correspondence. 'Sweeney' in 'Sweeney Redivivus' is the name for a personality, a different self, a congruence of impulses, a mask antithetical to much that the name 'Seamus Heaney' has meant in his previous books; and in the essay already cited in relation to Dante and 'Station Island', the Yeatsian mask is defined in terms which seem relevant to 'Sweeney':

Energy is discharged, reality is revealed and enforced when the artist strains to attain the mask of his opposite; in the act of summoning and achieving that image, he does his proper work and leaves us with the art itself, which is a kind of trace element of the inner struggle of opposites, a graph of the effort of transcendence.[12]

Yeats himself seems prominent in the construction of the figure of 'The Master' in the poem of that title in the sequence, which could be written almost as an allegory of what the critic Harold Bloom has called the 'anxiety of influence': the 'master' as the precursor, the poet against whom Heaney's own art must

12 'Envies and Identifications', loc. cit., 5.

struggle in order properly to define and articulate itself. The poem figures the master as a 'rook' in a 'tower'; Yeats refers in a major poem to 'the cold and rook-delighting heaven', and of course he lived for a while in a tower, Thoor Ballylee in Sligo, and entitled a book *The Tower*. The gradual coming to terms with him is the discovery that 'his book of withholding / ... was nothing / arcane, just the old rules / we all had inscribed on our slates', the discovery, it may be, that Yeats's notoriously private mythology and the otherness of his Protestant Ascendancy culture conceal an apprehensible human and political meaning and relevance. Heaney's measuring of himself against this magisterial authority, which has sounded the Sweeney note of enterprising, wily self-assertion, is also, however, combined with an envious humility:

> How flimsy I felt climbing down
> the unrailed stairs on the wall,
> hearing the purpose and venture
> in a wingflap above me.

As a result, the poem is the trace not so much of a struggle, as of a bold but wary inspection; it is a demonstration of the way in which fearfulness, by being confronted, may become a move towards authority.

That this poem is an allegory is typical of the sequence, in which allegory and parable, the puzzling and the hermetic, are constant modes. In fact, one of Heaney's major derivations from the original source is – as the master-as-rook suggests – a series of ornithological correspondences which contribute to the poems' parabolic design. 'The First Flight', for instance, views the poet's move from Belfast to Glanmore as a bird's migration; 'Drifting Off', a version of a medieval 'Boast' poem, ascribes different human (or poetic) qualities to birds; 'A Waking Dream' imagines poetic composition as the attempt to catch a bird by throwing salt on its tail (as the popular recommendation has it), but in fact being transported into flight oneself; and 'On the Road' actually locates the moment when the poet, previously behind the wheel of a car, is lofted into flight ('I was up and away'). Apart from this system of analogy, what the original story offers 'Sweeney Redivivus' is little more than a medieval anchorite colouring in some poems, and a tolerant hospitality to others which could just as easily have appeared without its support-system: 'In the Beech', for instance, which imagines the young poet in a tree, and the brilliant 'Holly'. Indeed, three poems which appear towards the end of the sequence – 'An Artist' (on Cézanne), 'The Old Icons' (on republican politics) and 'In Illo Tempore' (on the loss of religious faith) seem written more straightforwardly in Heaney's own voice, though by now clearly schooled into a 'Sweeney' scepticism and mistrust.

Although the mask, then, is not worn consistently in the sequence, 'The Master' suggests its usefulness to Heaney. There, it allows him the opportunity to articulate in a parable what would otherwise be virtually impossible without pretension or overweening vanity, the measuring of himself against Yeats. Elsewhere, it allows him a similar pride in his own achievement, and a tangential, dubious, sideways-on inspection of some matters already handled more straightforwardly in his earlier work. This is why 'The First Gloss' steps from its 'justified line / into the margin' only after recalling, in the metaphor, 'the shaft of the pen', the first poem in Heaney's first collection, 'Digging'. And it is why, in 'Sweeney Redivivus' and 'Unwinding', Heaney pursues the metaphor of the head as 'a ball of wet twine / dense with soakage, but beginning / to unwind'. The 'twine' – the string made by joining together, 'twinning', two separate strands – is both Heaney and Sweeney. Its 'unwinding' is Heaney's studied attempt to dry out the 'soakage' of his heritage and, perhaps, of the more sociable self on display in *Field Work*. The whole sequence defines different stages in this process of unwinding as Heaney reviews his life and reputation in a newly suspicious perspective.

'In the Beech' and 'The First Kingdom' suggest how selective his earliest accounts of the world of his childhood were. The former sets the young poet in a 'boundary tree' between the old rural ways and modern military industrialism, with specific reference, presumably, to the airforce bases in Northern Ireland during the Second World War which made no appearance in *Death of a Naturalist*. 'The First Kingdom' takes a more jaundiced view of the inhabitants of that world than one would have believed possible from the author of Heaney's first book: 'And seed, breed and generation still / they are holding on, every bit / as pious and exacting and demeaned'; where 'exacting' perhaps looks back rebukingly to the 'exact' revenge of 'Punishment'. Similarly, 'The First Flight', 'Drifting Off' and 'The Scribes' imply a more unapologetic confidence in his own work than is apparent in anything Heaney has previously written. 'The First Flight' celebrates, with a Joycean disdain, the outwitting of adverse criticism ('they began to pronounce me / a feeder off battlefields' leaps out of the parable into contemporary literary battlefields for anyone taking stock of some Northern accounts of *North*); 'Drifting Off' ends with Heaney not as the Joycean 'hawklike man', but as the hawk himself, 'unwieldly / and brimming, / my spurs at the ready'; and 'The Scribes' is an almost contemptuous jousting with, again, his critics or his peers which culminates when Heaney/ Sweeney throws this poem itself in their faces: 'Let them remember this not inconsiderable / contribution to their jealous art'. That 'not inconsiderable' is finely judged, keeping its temper along with its hauteur, utterly certain that it is 'considerable'; and the poem has something of the insolence Heaney in *The Government of the Tongue* admires in Nadezhda Mandelstam's treatment of the Soviets: 'the unthinking authority of somebody brushing a fly from her food'. This is the reverse of accommodating, it is dangerous; and one would not like to get on the wrong side of it: but its tone allies Heaney with an Irish tradition to which he has not previously given great allegiance, one that includes eighteenth-century Gaelic poetry and Austin Clarke, for instance, as well as Joyce. Heaney has chosen – temporarily, perhaps – to call this tradition 'Sweeney'; but, under whatever name, it is a salutary protection against certain kinds of sweetness and lushness which have whispered at the edge of earshot in some of his poetic kinds.

These asperities of tone are softened by a certain regretfulness in those poems which once again review Heaney's attitude to religion and to politics. 'The Cleric', on Catholicism, seems to acknowledge ruefully at its close that, having once placed faith in all of that, any future sense of freedom from it will be defined by it; which is the familiar enough double-bind of the devout lapsed Catholic, but phrased here, in the tones of the still-pagan Sweeney reflecting on St Ronan, in a way that gives genuinely new life to the old song:

> Give him his due, in the end
>
> he opened my path to a kingdom
> of such scope and neuter allegiance
> my emptiness reigns at its whim.

'In Illo Tempore' – its title taken from the words which introduced the reading of the gospel in the Latin mass – is perhaps Heaney's most straightforward and personal rehearsal of the theme; released, it may be, by the Sweeney mask, but not much indebted to it. Imagining Catholicism as a language one has lost the ability to speak, consigning it to 'illo tempore', 'that time', the poem is sadly resigned rather than gratefully released; and in this it is at one with the reverence still felt for the outgrown republican images in 'The Old Icons' – 'Why, when it was all over, did I hold on to them?' In these poems resolve and regret merge to create a tone at the same time both chastened and determined.

The poem which closes 'Sweeney Redivivus', and the whole of *Station Island*, 'On the Road', may be read as a kind of summary of Heaney's career to date, and the statement of an intention for the future, as it inherits and brings to fulfilment the volume's imagery of journeying, pilgrimage, quest and migration. It opens with that figure common in the earlier work, the poet-as-driver; but now the driver is placed behind the steering wheel's 'empty round'. This is an emptiness, a space suddenly filled with the rich young man's question about salvation. Christ's invitation, accompanied by the sudden 'visitation' of the last bird in *Station Island*, provokes a response in which the poet is translated out of that early figure and its present emptiness, into the figure of Sweeney. The flight which follows, with its swooping and dipping rhythms, seems similarly to translate Christ's injunction out of the realm of religion – Heaney/Sweeney migrating from 'chapel gable' and 'churchyard wall' – into the realm of art, as it ends inside a 'high cave mouth' beside the prehistoric cave drawing of a 'drinking deer'. This is presumably related to that 'deer of poetry ... / in pools of lucent sound' which appears in 'A Migration' in Part One; but in 'On the Road', its nostril is 'flared // at a dried-up source'. It is a source, nevertheless, which provides the poet with at least the possibility of some arid renewal:

> For my book of changes
> I would meditate
> that stone-faced vigil
>
> until the long dumbfounded
> spirit broke cover
> to raise a dust
> in the font of exhaustion.

The 'font' in a church usually contains holy water, used to make the sign of the cross; but this dry 'font of exhaustion' may well be Heaney's equivalent of Yeats's 'foul rag-and-bone shop of the heart' at the end of 'The Circus Animals' Desertion', that point of desolation from which, alone, the new inspiration may rise.[13]

13 Stan Smith in 'The Distance Between: Seamus Heaney' in Neil Corcoran (ed.), *The Chosen Ground: Essays on the Contemporary Poetry of Northern Ireland* (Seren, 1992), 35–61, says 'Neil Corcoran sees this as a holy water font, and so it is. But it is also the font of print itself, which is where all new texts find their origins.' I concur; and such a reading projects itself forward to the very

In that poem, Yeats reviews the stages of his career in some detail, and in 'On the Road', Heaney may be said to review his own, more glancingly, in little verbal echoes of his earlier work. The road 'reeling in' remembers the roads that 'unreeled, unreeled' in that other poem of flight, 'Westering', at the end of *Wintering Out*; 'soft-nubbed' and 'incised outline' recall the archaeological diction of *North*, as the poem's chain of optatives ('I would roost', 'I would migrate', 'I would meditate') make again one of the characteristic grammatical figures of *North*; the 'undulant, tenor / black-letter latin' recalls the 'sweet tenor latin' of 'Leavings' in *Field Work* and the phrase 'broke cover' recollects the badger that 'broke cover in me' in 'The Badgers', also in that volume. The self-allusiveness makes it plain how much in Heaney's earlier 'source' is now 'dried-up', and also implies how high a degree of directed energy and effort must go into the construction of a new 'book of changes'. In this way, the mask of Sweeney has become the name for a restless dissatisfaction with the work already done, a fear of repetition, an anxiety about too casual an assimilation and acclaim, a deep suspicion of this poet's own reputation and excellence. Sweeney is therefore the name, too, for what Helen Vendler has called 'the breaking of style';[14] and, as such, he continues to tap his restless morse through Heaney's subsequent books which, as soon as they seem to resolve a style into composure, disturb and abrupt it once again.

---

writerly book, *The Haw Lantern*. Smith's essay is reprinted in Michael Allen's *New Casebook*.

14 Helen Vendler, *The Breaking of Style: Hopkins, Heaney, Graham* (Harvard University Press, 1995).

6

Strange Letters:
The Haw Lantern (1987)

1 Hermes

The god Hermes figures centrally in 'The Stone Verdict' in *The Haw Lantern*, and in several ways he may be considered the presiding genius of the volume. In Greek mythology Hermes is responsible for leading the dead to the underworld, and he therefore appropriately appears in this poem, an elegy for Heaney's father; and his elegiac function may also be said to shadow other poems in the book, notably the sonnet sequence 'Clearances', written in memory of the poet's mother. 'The Stone Verdict' imagines a last judgement fit for a taciturn man: its prayer is that he be given a version of 'the judgement of Hermes'. When Hermes was tried for killing the dog Argos, he was acquitted not by a spoken verdict but by the gods silently casting their voting-pebbles at his feet until he was left at the centre of a pile of stones. This is why the poem calls Hermes 'God of the stone heap'. This association with trial or testing therefore means that he stands over the volume's several poems of ethical scrutiny or inspection; and the connection with stone means that he inheres in the book's many uses of it as image, symbol and emblem. The resisting, dangerous obduracy of stone is almost as necessary to *The Haw Lantern* as the yielding, preservative qualities of bog peat are to *North*.

Hermes is also the god of writing itself, whose name may be read out of the words 'hermetic' and 'hermeneutic'; and *The*

Haw Lantern, inheriting the mode of 'Sweeney Redivivus', prominently figures both secret meanings and the act of interpretation. The book's parable poems encode, in cryptic or allegorical ways, a set of ethical and political attitudes and responses; in these, the lyric 'I' disguises itself more than it declares itself. Their forms, which sometimes sound so unrecognizably different from earlier Heaney styles as to appear almost like translations from another language, are a further way in which this poet makes himself strange to himself.[1] They too act as a kind of mask, persona or alternative self, an alibi or alias. As a consequence, the lyric becomes what it has never been in Heaney's work before: abstract, diagnostic, analytic, dispassionate, admonitory, forensic, post-mortem. Similarly, poems take ideas of interpretation as theme: beginning with a poem called 'Alphabets' and concluding with one called 'The Riddle', *The Haw Lantern* foregrounds both the materiality of script and the hermeneutic issues involved in telling what 'The Riddle' calls a 'story'.

The word 'writing', or one of its cognates, in fact figures ten times during the book's thirty-one poems, and the prefatory poem to 'Clearances' prays that his mother might teach him 'To strike it rich behind the linear black': behind, that is, the lines of type, of printed writing, that form these poems. This preoccupation is continuous with the volume's epigraph poem:

> The riverbed, dried-up, half-full of leaves.

> Us, listening to a river in the trees.

Connecting with, and advancing from, the 'dried-up source' at the end of *Station Island*, these lines suggest that the concentration on the act of writing and its ethics – its function as self-advancement, as political or historical interpretation, and as

1 It is revealing in this context that, apparently, *The Haw Lantern* is the most widely translated of Heaney's individual volumes; see the introduction to Hans-Christian Oeser, *Transverse* II: *Seamus Heaney in Translation* (Irish Translators' Association, 1994). I am grateful to Dennis O'Driscoll for bringing this publication to my attention.

problematic entry to personal experience and memory – is the consequence, in the first instance, of the fact that this poet has reached a point at which the difficulty of access to sources of potential has become an urgent creative issue. When the dried-up riverbed is replaced by an imaginary river heard in the trees, it is a figure for enlivening imaginative endurance and for the requirement that early instinct and spontaneity be replaced by subsequent calculation and resource.

If the new writerly self-consciousness of *The Haw Lantern* is impelled by personal necessity, however, it also sets the book very much in tune with its literary and cultural moment, since an extreme self-consciousness about the act of writing, and about the ways in which language itself constructs subjectivity and identity, has characterized the academic study of literature since the late 1960s. The congruence between the poetry of *The Haw Lantern* and this mood of literary criticism and theory may be measured in at least two ways. Firstly, there is Heaney's willingness to appear a *doctus poeta*, a learned poet in the classical sense. That he is, from the first, learned is apparent to anyone who recognizes the allusions, intertexts and analogies in the work; but previously the learning has usually operated from well below the surface of the poems, informing and generating rather than explicitly declaring. *The Haw Lantern* is less sceptically reticent. Many poems in the book bristle with citation. These include 'The Stone Verdict' which is, as we have seen, dependent on some relatively esoteric information about Hermes; 'Alphabets', which contains references to the Renaissance Neo-Platonist Marsilio Ficino and to the Roman Emperor Constantine; 'The Haw Lantern', which depends on a story about the Greek Cynic philosopher Diogenes; 'A Daylight Art', which takes off from Plato's account in the *Phaedo* of the philosopher Socrates's dream that he may have practised the wrong art all his life, and of his therefore choosing to versify Aesop's fables in his death-cell; and 'Grotus and Coventina', which draws on a Roman iconic stone inscription. These references, usually having a strong narrative element, act as the initiation of poems in a way quite different from the modes of image and metaphor in the earlier work.

In addition, *The Haw Lantern* evinces a congruity between poet and critic in Heaney which has previously been relatively muted. The representation of the poet as professor in an auditorium in the opening poem 'Alphabets' may be thought a signal of this alignment; and *The Government of the Tongue*, Heaney's second volume of critical essays, published the year after *The Haw Lantern*, may be read as virtually a companion to the poems, the essays sometimes fleshing out in discursive terms what the poems encode more obliquely. The phrase 'I governed my tongue' figures prominently in the fourth of the 'Clearances' sonnets; and its use there is partly glossed by the title essay of the collection. The closing sonnet makes use of the image of a chestnut tree planted to commemorate the poet's birth and subsequently cut down; and the same autobiographical reminis- cence opens the essay 'The Placeless Heaven', on Patrick Kavanagh. 'Hailstones' strikingly uses the word 'dilation', as does the essay 'The Main of Light', on Philip Larkin, where Heaney says of the poem 'Deceptions' that 'It is this light-filled dilation at the heart of the poem which transposes it from lament to comprehension', an observation which may feed usefully back into an interpretation of the Heaney poem itself. 'From the Canton of Expectation' offers a view of contemporary Irish history as a grammar of varying verbal moods, culminating in a desire for the 'right action' of the indicative; and in the essay 'The Impact of Translation' Heaney celebrates the 'indicative mood' of modern Russian writers, with its implicit challenge to the indeterminate conditional mood of much contemporary Western European and American poetry. 'A Daylight Art' is the poem which uses the story of Socrates versifying Aesop; and the essay 'Atlas of Civilization', on the Polish poet Zbigniew Herbert, opens with the same story, in order to expand it into the generous conceit that what Herbert writes is the kind of 'ideal poetry of reality' which Socrates himself might have written, had he written poetry. Such correspondences mean that essays and poems form part of a single, even systematic effort of consciousness, an interior meditation which issues at once in acts of the imagination and constructions of the critical intelligence. The mutuality produces, sometimes, an almost unaccommodatingly chaste form of poetry, and a criticism tensely or even anxiously concerned with its own authority;[2] but the sharpened and unremitting scrutiny of the politics, ethics and aesthetics of writing to which it gives rise is an attempt to answer some of the most difficult questions of all.

2 Saying and Writing: 'Hailstones' and 'Alphabets'

The idea that we are written at least as much as we write, that language is a system in which human subjectivity is itself inscribed, results, in deconstructive or post-structuralist criticism, in a conception of the literary text as the site in which original experience is not so much re-created as replaced. Consequently, the word 'absence' is a significant one in this critical writing. It is also significant in Seamus Heaney, figuring in, for instance, 'Sunlight' in *North* ('There was a sunlit absence'), 'Gifts of Rain' in *Wintering Out* (where 'I cock my ear at an absence', that of the Irish language) and 'Station Island' in the ways I noted in the previous chapter (where, for instance, a meditation on the death of a child provokes the sense of an empty space, 'like an absence stationed in the swamp-fed air'). In 'Hailstones' the word occurs once more, but now probably more self-consciously in relation to the post-structuralist linguistic model, since in this poem a childhood experience – that of being hit by hailstones – is likened to the making of the poem itself, which replaces the experience:

> I made a small hard ball
> of burning water running from my hand

2 And I have criticisms to make of this procedure in *The Government of the Tongue* in Chapter 9.

> just as I make this now
> out of the melt of the real thing
> smarting into its absence.

The poem becomes the place where you are reminded of the essential unrecapturability of deeply meditated personal experience; and language, rather than acting as consolation for such loss, as it appears to do in *Death of a Naturalist*, becomes the poignant reminder of it.

Nevertheless, resisting this postmodern scepticism, there is an element of more Romantic-Modernist affirmation in 'Hailstones' too; and the poem holds both strains in tension. The Romanticism is present as, firstly, a ramification of the poem's originating image into various other significant experiences carried by the memory. The intense physical impact of being 'hit and hit' on the cheek by hailstones is emblematic of the way this child's classroom culture was itself sternly, even sado-masochistically, anti-permissive, 'like a ruler across the knuckles'. This subjection can be withstood only by the heroic achievement of a particular schoolboy, as the poem balances against 'the sting of hailstones' 'the unstingable hands of Eddie Diamond / foraging in the nettles'. 'Diamond' is a common enough Irish surname, but in 'Hailstones' it takes on an almost emblematic resonance. Like the 'diamond absolutes' of 'Exposure', the unstingability of these hands is a flourish of transcendence, an emphatic refusal of the customary forms of the culture offered in the classroom, an assertion of individualistic independence, a 'proof and wonder' to equal Thomas Traherne's visionary 'orient wheat' in his seventeenth-century *Centuries* (which is, relevantly, the first work in English convincingly to record the impact of childhood experience). In articulating such self-transcendence, and in placing such a premium on childhood, 'Hailstones' knowingly incorporates a history of visionary transcendence in English Romantic poetry; and, in so doing, it turns, in its final section, and, as it were, as an answer to the scepticism of its opening, to inquire into its own point and purpose:

> Nipple and hive, bite-lumps,
> small acorns of the almost pleasurable
> intimated and disallowed
>
> when the shower ended
> and everything said *wait*.
> For what? For forty years
>
> to say there, there you had
> the truest foretaste of your aftermath –
> in that dilation
>
> when the light opened in silence
> and a car with wipers going still
> laid perfect tracks in the slush.

This does, firstly, what so many other Heaney poems do so well too: it vividly locates sensation in language, identifying with lucid accuracy the feeling of suspension in the aftermath of a hailstorm. What it also does, however, is to associate that childhood sensation with others in the context of a later, mature emotional life. An 'aftermath' is literally the less successful crop of grass which springs up after an early summer mowing, and is therefore a word used figuratively for disappointment or enervation; here it may suggest the generalized disappointments of age, or it may have a more specifically sexual reference to do with post-coital *tristesse*. In either case, 'Hailstones' names the place where apparently discrete sensations surprise themselves by the suddenness of significant relationship, and where the poet surprises himself by finding this out (even if the discovery takes most of a lifetime); and the poem therefore justifies itself as the arena in which the healing or integrating powers of memory may be celebrated. In answering the question 'For what?', 'Hailstones' finds not only its own occasion but also its rationale: 'to say there' is to do what Rilke famously says we are here for in the ninth of his *Duino Elegies*: 'for such saying as never the things themselves / hoped so intensely to be'. Beginning in scepticism and ending in declaration, 'Hailstones' itself effects a 'light-filled dilation', the kind of amplification that does indeed turn lament into comprehension; and its final image is a submerged metaphor for this mobile act of writing, which lays its own perfect, printed tracks in the inevitably disintegrating slush of the actual. The ghostly origins of the poem, indeed, may well lie in Heaney's metaphor in his essay on Hopkins, 'The Fire i' the Flint' in *Preoccupations*, for the way language characteristically functions in a self-referential modern poem: 'The poem is a complex word, a linguistic exploration whose tracks melt as it maps its own progress.'

'Alphabets', written as the Phi Beta Kappa poem at Harvard University in 1984, is, appropriately, a poem about educational achievement. It opens with the young schoolchild learning to read and write in various classrooms, and it closes when the pupil has become the teacher (or celebrated international poet-professor) standing in the Shakespearian 'wooden O' of a lecture theatre. The emphatic plural of the title derives from the fact that this is a Northern Irish Catholic education in which the growing child assimilates, or is assimilated into, the different scripts of the English and Irish alphabets. The latter is prominently the one 'which felt like home', the one in which this poet, who writes now in the alphabet of English, first discovers 'the poet's dream'; which is the Irish language appearing like the figure of an *aisling*, a dream-vision, in an eighteenth-century Irish poem.

'Alphabets' is elaborate in its orchestration, moving through the stages of its alphabets with a confidently formal but also intimate address. This oxymoronic tone, at once private and podial, is exactly appropriate to the poem's commentary on 'writing'. Writing is what makes you 'other' or strange to yourself. It places, and publicizes, your privacies in the formality and form of the work; its 'letter' draws you up the 'ladder' of academic and critical esteem, as the pararhyme of the final stanza implies; it shapes pupil into teacher, child into poet. Despite this celebration of achievement and success, however,

'Alphabets' is also, in part, an elegy which focuses on a vanished child, a bulldozed school, a disappeared rural way of life, and a language in danger of extinction, the 'other writing' of Irish. The poem's opening imagines script in terms of nature (when a forked stick is a 'Y', for instance), but its final section figures nature in terms of print and script ('bales like printouts'; 'stooked sheaves' as 'lambdas on the stubble', and so on); and the success of the poet-professor is delicately, even precipitously balanced against the poem's strong sense that script and print may prevent, rather than disclose, an affective recognition of the world. Which is why 'Alphabets' begins its tremendous final cadenza – which culminates in the memory of what is virtually an ur-act of writing – on a conjunction of willed alternative, pushing itself out from lament into comprehension too:

> Yet shape-note language, absolute on air
> As Constantine's sky-lettered IN HOC SIGNO
> Can still command him; or the necromancer
>
> Who would hang from the domed ceiling of his house
> A figure of the world with colours in it
> So that the figure of the universe
> And 'not just single things' would meet his sight
>
> When he walked abroad. As from his small window
> The astronaut sees all he has sprung from,
> The risen, aqueous, singular, lucent O
> Like a magnified and buoyant ovum –
>
> Or like my own wide pre-reflective stare
> All agog at the plasterer on his ladder
> Skimming our gable and writing our name there
> With his trowel point, letter by strange letter.

The wonder with which the 'pre-reflective' child sees the family name elevated in writing on the gable of the house is an entirely appropriate place for this poem to end, since the idea of elevation by writing is of course its point. This writing is the first time the child has been made 'strange' to himself by the letters of the alphabet; and the idea of elevation is emphatically included in the almost vertiginous simile of the astronaut rising from the earth and looking back: 'all he has sprung from' richly puns on both derivation (the ovum) and departure (the globe of the Earth left behind in space-flight). The idea of such strange elevation is reinforced by two striking tropes: the 'shape-note language' as 'absolute' as the miraculous writing in the sky seen by the Emperor Constantine, who was converted to Christianity as a result; and the necromancer's 'figure of the universe'.[3] 'Shape-note language' appears to be Heaney's private metamorphosis of the 'shape-note music' of North Carolina, a kind of wordless singing. The concept acts, therefore, as a metaphor for the almost Platonic form of the perfect poem, that alphabet permanently sought, but never finally achieved, which will offer a proper, adequate and earned consolation for the depredations of time. Its 'absoluteness' is its power of command and its promise, since the writing seen by Constantine linked conversion to imperial expansion. The trope therefore proposes that writing is the always desirable, the always to be attained, and the promise of dominion.

This is given further intensification in the subsequent image of the necromancer's figure. The allusion here is to the Renaissance neo-Platonist Marsilio Ficino as he is described in Frances Yates's *Giordano Bruno and the Hermetic Tradition*. Ficino's 'figure of the world' is a magical talisman; and Heaney's lines stay close to Ficino himself as he is quoted by Yates. Ficino observes how someone might construct 'on the domed ceiling of the innermost cubicle of his house, where he mostly lives and sleeps, such a figure with the colours in it. And when he comes out of his house he will perceive, not so much the spectacle of individual things, but the figure of the universe and its colours.' Yates comments: 'By arranging the figure of the world with knowledge and skill, the Magus controls the influences of

3 A necromancer attempts to foretell the future by communing with the dead.

the stars ... The man who stares at the figure of the world on his bedroom ceiling, imprinting it and its dominating colours of the planets on memory, when he comes out of his house and sees innumerable individual things is able to unify these through the images of a higher reality which he has within.'[4] There is a strong sense in this hermetic allusion that this poem is rising rhetorically, and even Yeatsianly, to its occasion (particularly since many of Yeats's own arcane references are also to the neo-Platonic tradition) with a rhetoric perhaps not inappropriate for a poem written to be uttered from a professorial podium. Ficino's neo-Platonic, magical conception reinforces that sense of writing's dominion conveyed by the reference to Constantine. This figure of the world – like a work of art, like a poem – attempts to control the world by representing it, signifying it under another shape or form; and its function is one of unification, which may take on a particular and pointed aptness in a poem which begins in linguistic division, and specifically the division between the English and the Irish alphabets.

The rapturous intensity of the conclusion of 'Alphabets' also derives from the way the Ficino figure carefully brings to fulfilment the poem's previous imagery of the globe. The 'figure of the world' is a magical transformation of the schoolroom 'globe in the window' which 'tilts like a coloured O' in the poem's first part, of the globe which 'has spun' as an indication of both the passage of time and the revolution of individual destiny at the beginning of the third, and of the astronaut's globe of the Earth in the simile which follows. When 'the globe has spun' at the beginning of the poem's third section, Heaney refers also to the lecture theatre in terms of another theatre and another globe: the Globe theatre in which Shakespeare's plays were staged, which is called a 'wooden O' in the prologue to

4 Frances Yates, *Giordano Bruno and the Hermetic Tradition* (Routledge and Kegan Paul, 1964), 75. Poem xix of 'Squarings' in *Seeing Things* – 'Memory as a building or a city' – also derives from materials in this book and in Yates's other study of Bruno and neo-Platonic mnemonic techniques, *The Art of Memory* (1966).

THE POETRY OF SEAMUS HEANEY

Henry V. That figure is itself taken up again when the astronaut's globe becomes, in a rising, almost spiralling cadence, 'The risen, aqueous, singular, lucent O'. 'Alphabets', in a way befitting its title, is alert to the effectiveness of altered typeface; and these three upper-case Os – 'coloured', 'wooden', 'lucent' – are joined by others elsewhere in the poem: 'Book One of *Elementa Latina*' and Constantine's 'IN HOC SIGNO'. In the poem's opening section the young child is learning to make 'the letter some call *ah*, some call *ay*', the first letter of the alphabet; and in these upper-case Os, 'Alphabets' is uniting alpha and omega, the first and last letters of the Greek alphabet. It closes its own O, or circle, too, when the great globe of the Earth itself is compared to the ovum and to the poet's 'own wide pre-reflective stare'. The ovum is also shaped like an O, and being 'agog' is to make an O with your mouth, the expression of amazement. These are strange letters indeed, as strange at the end as at the beginning of an education; and still, there, the site of both self-recognition and self-transformation.

3 Parables

In *The Government of the Tongue* Heaney has a great deal to say about parable poems, whether the radically politicized kind of post-war Eastern Europe – notably those of the Czech Miroslav Holub, and the Poles Zbigniew Herbert and Czesław Miłosz – or the English kinds of Edwin Muir and W. H. Auden; and he also has much to say about translation itself. In 'The Impact of Translation' he discusses the significance of the Penguin *Modern European Poets* series of the 1960s and 1970s and praises Christopher Reid's *Katerina Brac* (1985), in which the author ventriloquizes through the 'sham persona' of his titular poet: Heaney is impressed by the book's way of 'echoing certain noises [Reid] could not naturally achieve in his own voice'. If these remarks ask to be read as ways of defining something of the aim of *The Haw Lantern* too, there are others in *The Government of the Tongue* equally suggestive and apposite. He finds in the Eastern bloc poets an analogous case for the Irish writer. There is, he says, 'an unsettled aspect to the different worlds they inhabit, and one of the challenges they face is to survive amphibiously, in the realm of "the times" and the realm of their moral and artistic self-respect, a challenge immediately recognizable to anyone who has lived with the awful and demeaning facts of Northern Ireland's history over the last couple of decades'.[5] He also refers to 'the dislocated geopolitical phantasmagorias of early Auden' and reflects on how, in poems such as 'The Interrogation', Edwin Muir is 'our representative ... stunned and ineffective at the centre of a menacing pageant'. This kind of poem is, he says, 'the road not taken' in English post-war poetry. It may also be the case, although *The Government of the Tongue* does not say this, that Polish parable is particularly relevant to Heaney in its combination of issues of territoriality and 'unsettlement' with an endemic Catholicism strongly associated with a subversive politics. Some of the parables of *The Haw Lantern* have, in particular, the quality of sober, although not sombre, judgemental poise to be found in certain poems by Czesław Miłosz.

The four poems whose titles begin with the word 'From' ('From the Frontier of Writing', 'From the Republic of Conscience', 'From the Land of the Unspoken', 'From the Canton of Expectation') in *The Haw Lantern* could be called strange letters too, letters here in the sense of fictional missives or messages from a foreign correspondent travelling in mysterious and dangerous places. That they appear scattered throughout the book, and not in a single sequence, disseminates their tonal influence and effect: their strict moralism seems very much the air this volume breathes. They are all, indeed, 'dislocated geopolitical phantasmagorias', even if the island of Ireland and the configuration of Northern Ireland seem within hailing distance of their political and topographical nowheres; and 'From the Frontier of Writing' takes as its setting a location

5 I discuss this proposed affinity further in Chapter 9.

common in early Auden: the frontier as the transitional zone where clearance involves scrutiny and inspection. The poem's interrogation, although it is not specifically located, clearly has its origin in that made of the driver of a car in Northern Ireland by a member of the security forces. The initial encounter might well recall that of 'The Toome Road' in *Field Work*, and the effect of gross intrusion is similar, conveyed here by a vocabulary of sexual violation (the 'quiver in the self' which leaves it 'emptier' and 'spent'). A poem of eight three-line stanzas, it elegantly pivots about its centre, where the actual 'pure interrogation', and the obedient subjugation it compels, turn into their own sensation or memory in the act of writing:

> So you drive on to the frontier of writing
> where it happens again. The guns on tripods;
> the sergeant with his on-off mike repeating
>
> data about you, waiting for the squawk
> of clearance; the marksman training down
> out of the sun upon you like a hawk.
>
> And suddenly you're through, arraigned yet freed
> as if you'd passed from behind a waterfall
> on the black current of a tarmac road
>
> past armour-plated vehicles, out between
> the posted soldiers flowing and receding
> like tree shadows into the polished windscreen.

In 'Alphabets' the act of writing carries, as we saw, a submerged political signification: the nearly vanished alphabet of the Irish language is a lost or destroyed 'home', an index of dispossession; and the plural of the poem's title is a refusal of single linguistic or cultural identity. Here, it carries another kind of political weight. Writing becomes the place or space in which you free yourself from repression or subjugation, the opportunity for disobedience, the frontier post at which you are ethically and aesthetically cleared. When the interrogation

'happens again' at the frontier of writing, the poem may be re-
calling Auden's insistence, in 'In Memory of W. B. Yeats', that
'Poetry makes nothing happen.' In Heaney, by making some-
thing nevertheless 'happen again', writing acts as the agency
of personal release. 'Writing', the rhyme of the first stanza
above suggests, is first an act of 'repeating', as the initial experi-
ence is remembered and re-presented; but then it becomes a way
of getting 'through'. That word is primarily the signal that
clearance has been effected: writing moves you across a frontier
to freedom; and this is the sense in which Heaney then subse-
quently uses the word 'frontier' in his next critical book, *The
Redress of Poetry*, which concludes with an essay on Northern
Ireland and its poetry actually entitled 'Frontiers of Writing'.
But the word also carries its other colloquial sense, that of
being finished with something once and for all. This feeling
of release is, in turn, powerfully carried by the cinematic,
quasi-surreal or dreamlike metaphor of the road as river,
which recalls some of the imagery of Louis MacNeice's late
parable poems: the place of static interrogation and intrusion
has suddenly become mobile and fluid. Finally, in its further
use of a modified Dantean *terza rima*, 'From the Frontier of
Writing' may also be urging at the formal level the conception
of writing as the place where you may move from an inferno of
political subjection to a paradiso of imaginative enablement.

When the poet-persona of 'From the Frontier of Writing' is, at
the last, 'arraigned yet freed', the implication is that, whatever
liberties are permitted by the act of writing, there must remain,
on the part of the writer himself or herself, a subjection to other
ethical obligations; and it is significant that in the organisation
of *The Haw Lantern* this poem faces the book's title poem with
its ethical scrutiny by Diogenes. It is as if the sullying interroga-
tion of 'From the Frontier of Writing' is countered by the
purifying haw and its 'blood-prick that you wish would test
and clear you'. The other 'missive' poems maintain and advance
this figure of the persona subject to the demands of ethical
responsibility. 'From the Republic of Conscience' sets the

international jet-traveller persona in a republic of filial and familial piety and figures the concept of a nation-state in which conscience and ethical probity inform public life as the demand that politicians at their inauguration must 'affirm their faith that all life sprang / from salt in tears which the sky-god wept / after he dreamt his solitude was endless'. If *The Haw Lantern* replaces the rich metaphorizing of Heaney's earlier work with a new plainness of diction and an almost transparent use of metonymy, sudden moments like this supply what might initially seem the lack with an equally arresting kind of poetic effect.[6] The inventive figure here proffers a metaphysic of conscience and sympathy as a genesis-myth to counter the various classical and Christian creation myths which involve divine anger, jealousy and retribution; and in doing so it offers the space of the poem as itself the arena in which a newly conscientious sensibility might be shaped.

'From the Republic of Conscience' ends with the persona returning to his own place as 'a representative / ... to speak on their behalf in my own tongue'. This concept of poetry as the place of conscientiously responsible speech is accompanied in 'From the Land of the Unspoken' by the testimony of implicit recognitions – where even the spoken word is unnecessary – among 'a dispersed people whose history / is a sensation of opaque fidelity'. This need not be limited to, but would certainly include, the members of the Irish diaspora, the Irish abroad. The poem regards them as in imminent danger of losing this kind of fidelity and solidarity by being dispersed irretrievably into the absorptive processes of 'a rich democracy', presumably the irresistible force of American money and power. 'From the Canton of Expectation', as we have already seen, encodes another view of Irish historical experience, now

6 Stan Smith writes very interestingly about the transparency of *The Haw Lantern* in 'The Distance Between: Seamus Heaney', in Neil Corcoran (ed.), *The Chosen Ground: Essays on the Contemporary Poetry of Northern Ireland* (Seren, 1992), 35–61, reprinted in Michael Allen's *New Casebook*.

specifically that of Northern Irish Catholics since the 1960s, as a grammar of verbal moods. Very much a poem that regards subjectivity as a construction of language, it reads recent Northern Irish history as a movement from the 'optative' of initial fatalistic resignation and desire, to the 'grammar of imperatives' of a generation newly empowered by education, which 'would banish the conditional for ever'. The final section views the progression from the one to the other – by way of 'intelligences / brightened and unmannerly as crowbars' – as a move from reprehensible Catholic-pietistic passivity to danger-ous or malevolent menace, and it culminates by picking up the marine imagery of 'From the Republic of Conscience', with a longing to know that:

> there is one among us who never swerved
> from all his instincts told him was right action,
> who stood his ground in the indicative,
> whose boat will lift when the cloudburst happens.

If a strict moralism inheres generally in these parable poems, then it culminates here in a view of what personal and historical heroism might be: an undeviating single-mindedness, the brav-ery of resolve, the trusting of disciplined instinct.

The perspective in which Ireland is viewed in these poems is markedly more detached than in Heaney's earlier work. Indeed, the view taken is, as in early Auden, an almost aerial one, 'as the hawk sees it or the helmeted airman'; the poet lifting off from his stationed island. This parabolic perspective is accompanied by new perspectives on the character of the poet-persona too. In 'Terminus' he is prominently placed in that prepositional location of negotiation and dialogue, 'in between', and is 'still parleying', where the participle activates a military metaphor even in the act of offering an orientation towards the pacific or reconciliatory.[7] 'A Peacock's Feather' is dedicated to Heaney's

---

7 Helen Vendler, in *The Breaking of Style: Hopkins, Heaney, Graham* (Harvard University Press, 1995), has an extended reading of this poem in

'English niece' on the occasion of her christening; and the poem
is prominently dated 1972, the year of Bloody Sunday and also of
Wintering Out, a book into which such a poem, despite the
anxiety with which it relates to this child of an English country
house, would have had great difficulty – ideological, as well as
formal – in fitting. In addition, the first of the 'Clearances'
sonnets commemorates 'the first stone / Aimed at a great-
grandmother's turncoat brow': at, that is, a maternal ancestor
of the poet's who has converted from Protestantism to Catholi-
cism. The poem's telling us that this story is inherited 'on my
mother's side' itself provides a new perspective on the poem
'The Other Side' in *Wintering Out*, since it reveals how the
'mother's side' was, once, 'the other side' too. These accidents
of personal history complicate what a certain kind of Irish
nationalism would wish to read as a single narrative of identity;
and in this they are at one with that strain in post-1960s Irish
historical writing known as 'revisionism', in which once deeply
cherished assumptions have been, at least to some degree, and
certainly still contestedly, modified or undermined. 'Parable
Island' and 'The Mud Vision' draw on a sense of the importance
of this kind of historical writing. In 'Parable Island' the fictional
island becomes a text which is differently interpreted depending
on the ideological preconceptions of those who study it; and
'island' of course is a near-homonym for 'Ireland'. The final
island interpretation, that of the elders, includes the fear that the
cutting of the Panama Canal, and its draining away of the ocean,
will make 'the island disappear by aggrandizement'. This absurd
fear offers a certain kind of Irish nationalist insularity or
economic and cultural protectionism an ultimate chastisement,

---

which she has illuminating things to say about it. Her belief, however, that it
mirrors her own anti-ideological bias accommodates it too readily to a
liberalism unaware of, or unwilling to declare, its own political assumptions.
The poem does not blandly accept an *a priori* position, but wins through to its
resolve by 'Suffering the limit of each claim', where the participle carries heavy
freight.

since it proposes that the anxiety that the island may no longer remain an island wins out over the more obvious terrors that would result if the ocean did indeed drain away. In this parabolic fiction an insular territoriality preposterously banishes the fear of geopolitical apocalypse.

The mutually conflicting narratives of 'Parable Island', and its tone of jaded wryness, suggest a disenchantment with the endless contentiousness of Irish historiography; and this mood persists into 'The Mud Vision', the strongest and strangest poem in *The Haw Lantern*. Heaney has observed in an essay that it took its inspiration from a work made in Dublin in 1986 by the English conceptual artist Richard Long: 'a huge display of concentric circles high on a whitewashed wall, each circle made up of hand prints and each hand print made with mud'.[8] Long's image supplies Heaney with the means for his own construction of a remarkable and inclusive phantasmagoria, in which the inhabitants of an anonymous country are the witnesses of the paradoxical vision of the poem's title, 'a rose window of mud / ... A gossamer wheel, concentric with its own hub / Of nebulous dirt, sullied yet lucent'. As the poem advances, the ambiguous vision is alternately honoured and wished away, rendered the object of religious veneration and resented; but it is always, nevertheless, in a way entirely in tune with this volume's consistent imagery of scrutiny, 'presumed ... a test / that would prove us beyond expectation'. The poem is, therefore, an allegory of optimisms and pessimisms, expectations and betrayals, moods of hope and despair, emotions of guilt and survival in modern Ireland. Possibly, and more specifically, it has application to the fate of the revolutionary nationalism which created the Irish Free State in the 1920s and subsequently corroded into reactionary Catholicism and, eventually, multinational capitulation; or to the Irish political

8 Seamus Heaney, 'The Frontier of Writing', in Jacqueline Genet and Wynne Hellegouarc'h (eds.), *Irish Writers and their Creative Process* (Colin Smythe, 1996), 3–16, 10.

moment of the late 1960s, when, in the Civil Rights movement in the North, there seemed the genuine stirrings of new possibilities and alignments, all too soon to be bitterly disappointed.[9] The mud vision itself, uniting the miraculous and the mundane, ends up recognized, bathetically, as 'folly', its original political or symbolic power become only the fodder of journalistic and academic inquiry:

Just like that, we forgot that the vision was ours,
Our one chance to know the incomparable
And dive to a future. What might have been origin
We dissipated in news. The clarified place
Had retrieved neither us nor itself – except
You could say we survived. So say that, and watch us
Who had our chance to be mud-men, convinced and estranged,
Figure in our own eyes for the eyes of the world.

'The Mud Vision' inherits a cadence and a grammatical con-struction from the greatest modern English parable poem, Edwin Muir's 'The Horses', which is set in a post-holocaustal world. Virtually once again primeval, the survivors of Muir's poem are met by the new companions of the poem's title: 'And then, that evening / Late in the summer the strange horses came.' Heaney's poem similarly introduces its moment of transcendence: 'And then in the foggy midlands it appeared, / Our mud vision.' The coincidence of cadence and construc-tion here allies these poems in seriousness of address and pur-

9 In the essay cited above, Heaney says that the poem grew out of the mix in his mind of a fascination with Long's artwork and a musing on 'de Valera's dream of transforming the local customs and folk Catholicism of rural Ireland in the middle of the twentieth century into something more self-conscious and purposeful, his dream of founding a culturally distinct and spiritually resistant Irish republic, a dream which has been gradually abandoned without ever being replaced by any alternative vision of the future, certainly not by anything as ardent or self-born.' This is fascinating as an index of Heaney's political emotions and admiration of de Valera, but also as a revelation of the obliquity with which, eventually, such straightforward and powerful feeling is displaced or deflected into a hauntingly unspecific and ramifying poetic allegory.

pose: Muir's large imaginative perspective on a historical termi-
nus is matched by Heaney's on a more local, geopolitical one.
They are also allied in a sense of the disappointed resilience
that might succeed a posthumous condition; if 'The Mud
Vision' cautiously celebrates the bitter knowledge of endurance
and survival, it also apportions the sting of rebuke. Survival is
made to seem a minimal achievement compared to the alterna-
tive promise held out by the disappeared vision; and when it
promotes only the narcissistically inward-turned theatrical dis-
play of the final line, it is almost ethically spurious. The rebuke
is, however, self-directed too, since the poet is prominently in-
cluded in the poem's first person plural; the condemnation of
satire is relieved by the self-recrimination of confession.

4 Clearances

The idea of 'clearance' figures prominently in *The Haw Lantern*
in addition to its use as the title of Heaney's short sonnet
sequence commemorating his mother. There is the 'squawk of
clearance' at the frontier of writing; 'the blood-prick that you
wish would test and clear you' in 'The Haw Lantern'; and the
'clarified place' in 'The Mud Vision'. In these instances,
'clearance' is both the freeing from an obstruction and the
giving of permission. In the title of the sequence, these senses
are allied to others: a clearance is the settlement of a debt or
claim, and it is a piece of cleared ground. The last two poems in
the sequence use the word in the second of these senses. In
sonnet 7 the moment of the mother's death is imagined like this:

> The space we stood around had been emptied
> Into us to keep, it penetrated
> Clearances that suddenly stood open.
> High cries were felled and a pure change happened.

The final sonnet, 8, elaborates this image of a double emptiness,
a space erupting into a space:

I thought of walking round and round a space
Utterly empty, utterly a source
Where the decked chestnut tree had lost its place
In our front hedge above the wallflower.
The white chips jumped and jumped and skited high.
I heard the hatchet's differentiated
Accurate cut, the crack, the sigh
And collapse of what luxuriated
Through the shocked tips and wreckage of it all.
Deep planted and long gone, my coeval
Chestnut from a jam jar in a hole,
Its heft and hush become a bright nowhere,
A soul ramifying and forever
Silent beyond silence listened for.

As I observed above, Heaney's figure here is glossed in the opening paragraphs of his essay on Patrick Kavanagh in *The Government of the Tongue*. He tells there of a chestnut tree planted in front of the family home by an aunt in 1939, the year of his birth, which he came to identify with his own life. When the Heaneys moved away from the house in his early teens the tree was cut down, and he forgot it:

Then, all of a sudden ... I began to think of the space where the tree had been or would have been. In my mind's eye I saw it as a kind of luminous emptiness, a warp and waver of light, and once again, in a way that I find hard to define, I began to identify with that space just as years before I had identified with the young tree.

Except that this time it was not so much a matter of attaching one-self to a living symbol of being rooted in the native ground; it was more a matter of preparing to be unrooted, to be spirited away into some transparent, yet indigenous afterlife. The new place was all idea, if you like; it was generated out of my experience of the old place but it was not a topographical location. It was and remains an imagined realm, even if it can be located at an earthly spot, a placeless heaven rather than a heavenly place.

In the essay this opposition is read as, also, that between the early and late poetry of Kavanagh, and in retrospect the reader will find the idea of a 'luminous emptiness' apposite to the 'Squarings' sequence in Heaney's next volume, *Seeing Things*. Manifestly, however, the idea or conceit illuminates, probably designedly, 'Clearances' too. In this conception of the 'clearance', the mother's death is translated deeply into the consciousnesses of the family she leaves grieving, but it is translated there not merely as grief. The 'clearances' in sonnet 7 are a sudden opening, the space of 'a pure change', and therefore another kind of dilation; and in sonnet 8 the space of absence, the place of grief, is, in an almost paradoxical single line, 'Utterly empty, utterly a source'. 'A pure change' and 'utterly a source' are ghosted by Yeats's 'Easter 1916', in which violent deaths bring about a state in which everything is 'changed, changed utterly', a revolution expressed in his famous oxymoronic line, 'A terrible beauty is born'; and the chestnut tree itself, however literally a feature of Heaney's childhood it was, must owe something of its symbolic associativeness here to Yeats's visionary chestnut tree in 'Among School Children'. In 'Clearances', the mother's death brings not a terrible beauty, but not only the terror of extinction either. The 'clearances' are those where grief is transformed into a new kind of outwardly directed energy. Death is luminous as well as negative, a 'bright nowhere' in which a soul 'ramifies', where the context reactivates the original meaning of the verb ('to branch out', used of the growth of a tree). It is a richly apt metaphor for the ways in which the death of parents may be understood, accommodated, contained and transformed as part of the inevitable process of a mature human existence.

When, nevertheless, the soul is 'forever / Silent, beyond silence listened for', this is a refusal of any traditional Catholic Christian consolation, where 'forever' would carry the assurance of an eternal afterlife; and the empty space of sonnet 8 is also very much a 'placeless heaven' rather than a 'heavenly place' too. This has a markedly corrective function as the conclusion of a sequence which prominently includes the mother's, the young son's, and the great-grandmother's Catholicism: in sonnet 1, the great-grandmother's sectarian victimization happens as she rides to Mass; in sonnet 3, mother and son peel potatoes for the family lunch while the others are at Mass; and in sonnet 6, their '*Sons and Lovers* phase' has its high point during the liturgy of Holy Week. This is reinforced by the way sonnet 8 originates in lines already published in 'Station Island' III, on the death of the child: 'I thought of walking round / and round a space utterly empty, / utterly a source, like the idea of sound', and the connection of that space with the 'ring of walked-down grass' where the rotten corpse of a family dog was once discovered. 'Clearances' therefore finds, in its concluding symbol, a way of moving beyond the sense of death as only absence and disintegration without returning to Christian orthodoxy. The reality and idea of death become an entirely undesired, but nevertheless necessary enlargement of imaginative capacity; and the conclusion of the sequence is, as a result, at once both desolating and consolatory.

In closing like this, 'Clearances' also appropriately resolves the relationship between mother and son in a way that suggests the applicability of the word 'clearance' to these sonnets in its sense of settling a debt or a claim: the mother's claim upon her son, the debt the son owes her. The sonnet sequence in English is characteristically the vehicle of love poems, not elegies; and, as the annotation of the '*Sons and Lovers* phase' in sonnet 6 makes plain, what is being recorded here is, to some degree, a love affair too. Heaney is delicate and understated here, and the evocation of the quasi-erotic ballet performed when mother and son fold sheets in sonnet 5 has the palpability only of hint and implication, defusing even while releasing the oedipal charge, making it a matter of noughts as well as crosses:

> So we'd stretch and fold and end up hand to hand
> For a split second as if nothing had happened

> For nothing had that had not always happened
> Beforehand, day by day, just touch and go,
> Coming close again by holding back
> In moves where I was x and she was o
> Inscribed in sheets she'd sewn from ripped-out flour sacks.

The rhyming of the word 'happened' with itself at the beginning of the sonnet's sestet, together with that slightly halting repetition of the word 'nothing' twice and 'had' three times across two lines (particularly when 'had' is also contained in both 'hand' and 'happened'), is the poem gulping as something sticks in its throat, but recovering too as it realizes that precisely such repetition is the truth about oedipal relationship. It is both what has always happened between mothers and sons, and it goes back for this mother and son as far as the relationship itself goes back. The poem, in finding this subtle figure for such a difficult thing, amply repays in imaginative terms what the oedipal debt demands.

In the line – a paradoxical one – 'Coming close again by holding back' there is, nevertheless, a balance maintained between affection and recoil; and the relationship we are shown in 'Clearances' is constrained as well as comforting. In sonnet 2, the polished domestic space is unrelaxingly forbidding to the child, who is the object of numerous prohibitions; in sonnet 3, the intimacy of the two as they peel the potatoes together is definitively sealed off by the sad portcullis of the final line ('Never closer the whole rest of our lives'); and in sonnet 4, education is what comes between them. This is the poem in which the phrase 'governed my tongue' appears; and it is, along with 'Making Strange' in *Station Island*, one of only two poems in Heaney's work (to date) to set clearly at its centre the issue of class mobility as a consequence of education. The mother's quoted speech splits the sonnet across octet and sestet, as her deliberate ungrammaticality splits her from her educated son:

> Fear of affectation made her affect
> Inadequacy whenever it came to

Pronouncing words 'beyond her'. *Bertold Brek*.
She'd manage something hampered and askew
Every time, as if she might betray
The hampered and inadequate by too
Well-adjusted a vocabulary.
With more challenge than pride, she'd tell me, 'You
Know all them things.' So I governed my tongue
In front of her, a genuinely well-
adjusted adequate betrayal
Of what I knew better. I'd *naw* and *aye*
And decently relapse into the wrong
Grammar which kept us allied and at bay.

This is virtually the territory of Tony Harrison's poems, with their figurings of the ways in which the scholarship boy from a working-class home pays for the privilege of his education by being set at odds with the culture of his parents. The poem, under the aegis of the mother, offers an altogether less stable and assured view of the difference made by education from that supplied, under the aegis of the father, in 'Digging', with its sympathetic and consolatory rhyming of pen and spade. Indeed, the son seems still bruised by, and even unforgiving of, the encounter it describes. Where we might expect the mother to accuse the educated son of affectation, in fact it is the son who accuses the mother of, as it were, inverted affectation. If this is read, excusingly, as her refusal to betray the 'hampered and inadequate' – those who, like her, have not had the benefit of education – it is also a manipulative domination of the son: 'So I governed my tongue / In front of her' is a rebukingly harsh index of obligation from the poet who, with his other hand, is writing the critical essays he will collect as *The Government of the Tongue*, a title in which the phrase is released from disablement into empowerment; and there is irony in the fact that it is Brecht, champion of the 'hampered', whose name she wilfully mispronounces.

His adjustment to this necessity is elegantly conveyed by the poem's own well-adjusted form, when the sonnet's, and son's, sestet picks up the vocabulary of, as it were, the mother's octet ('betray', 'inadequate', 'Well-adjusted') with a mirroring but desperate symmetry ('well- / adjusted adequate betrayal'). The difficulty and forlornness of this adjustment, which is capitulation to what would always keep one in one's place, rather than lead one out of it, is also tellingly figured in the way the mother's good adjustment is authoritatively positioned and capitalized at the beginning of a line, entirely sure of itself ('Well-adjusted'), whereas the son's humiliation breaks the word across a line and compels the only lower-case line-opening in the sequence ('well- / adjusted'). A well-adjusted adequate betrayal fractures itself with a sigh or a catch in the breath, and the poem displays, as it contains, the pain. And who is allied to whom when the alliance is 'at bay'? 'At bay', the OED tells us, relates to 'the position of a hunted animal when, unable to flee farther, it turns, faces the hounds, and defends itself at close quarters'. The sonnet, we might say, effects a clearance, repays a debt, by refusing to allow elegy to sentimentalize actual, even intractable human difficulty: the mother who, at the end of the sequence, is 'Silent, beyond silence listened for', is here in the immediacy of her spoken, wilful, domineering, affectedly ungrammatical presence: 'You / Know all them things.' Yet the mother who compels the son of 'Clearances' to 'relapse' from educated grammar is also the mother to whom he prays in the prefatory sonnet: 'Teach me now to listen, / To strike it rich behind the linear black.' She is, therefore, the educative muse of his poem, which is itself the product of, precisely, his having learned the right grammar. The 'clearances' of the sequence, which restore the figure of the mother to the afterlife of the poem, are, in the end, the spaces in which she can be both.

7

Breaking and Entering:
Seeing Things (1991)

1 Underworlds

The original poems of the bipartite *Seeing Things* are framed by two translations: one, 'The Golden Bough', drawn from Book VI of Virgil's *Aeneid*, and the other, 'The Crossing', from Dante's *Inferno*. The passages are related outside Heaney's joint use of them here, in that Dante's treatment of hell alludes to Virgil's account of the underworld in the *Aeneid*; which is one reason why Virgil acts as Dante's guide in the *Divine Comedy*. Heaney's use of these august texts is an audacious and extremely self-assured gesture, consonant with, but also exceeding, his earlier appropriations of Dante in *Field Work* and *Station Island* and also with John Kerrigan's sense of his poetic progress as itself a 'Virgilian' one (from the bucolics of *Death of a Naturalist* and succeeding volumes to the 'national epic' of *Sweeney Astray*); and it is difficult to think of any other contemporary poet who could carry off its implications with such panache.[1] Heaney is aware, no doubt, of T. S. Eliot as a mediating figure: Virgil and Dante feature centrally in Eliot's poetry and criticism; and 'The Golden Bough' uses, in the word 'foresuffered', the word Eliot uses of Tiresias at a crucial moment in *The Waste Land*. These translations ally Heaney, then, with the heritage of classicism endemic to Eliot's kind of Modernism, with its central

1 John Kerrigan, 'Ulster Ovids', in Neil Corcoran (ed.), *The Chosen Ground: Essays on the Contemporary Poetry of Northern Ireland* (Seren, 1992), 237–69.

awareness of what he calls, in his essay 'What is a Classic?', 'the predecessors'.[2]

Yet the establishment in these translations of a relation to the classical and Christian underworlds also supplies a framework for the book's preoccupation with other kinds of translation and transition too, of which the translation of the living into the dead is the crucial one. In 'The Golden Bough', Aeneas is told by the Sibyl how he, still living, may exceptionally penetrate hell in order to meet the ghost of his dead father; and in 'The Crossing' Charon, the boatman of the river Acheron, is unwilling to ferry the still living Dante across the river of hell. Virgil, however, advises the poet that this is because he is not himself damned: that is, he will remain uncontaminated by his descent. Both Virgil and Dante attest, therefore, from their classical and Christian perspectives, that, if a relationship with the dead induces anxiety, nevertheless poetry is the place where it becomes possible; in the space of the poem, what one of the 'Glanmore Revisited' sonnets in this volume calls 'breaking and entering' may occur. In Eliot, the relationship with Virgil and Dante has its Christian-metaphysical dimension, deriving from the belief finally expressed in *Four Quartets* that 'the communication of the dead is tongued with fire / Beyond the language of the living.' In Heaney, however, the metaphysical is only a spectral presence, even if the poems of *Seeing Things* notably retain a capacity for consolation inimical to a typical strain of melancholia and dejection in modern and contemporary elegy.[3] The balance between scepticism and yearning is signalled by the book's punning title which raises the possibility of delusion in the same phrase in which it declares the possibility of revelation. The result is a poetry of what we might call secular spirituality or displaced sacramentalism, in which satisfaction is expressed

2 T. S. Eliot, 'What is a Classic?', in *On Poetry and Poets* (Faber and Faber, 1957), 57.

3 See Jahan Ramazani, *Poetry of Mourning: The Modern Elegy from Hardy to Heaney* (University of Chicago Press, 1994), passim.

without complacency, desire without velleity, and a sense of the transcendent or the numinous without resort to traditional religious doctrine or language.

2 The Heartland of the Ordinary

Many of these things are implicit in the book's opening poem, 'The Journey Back', in which the poet Philip Larkin returns from the dead to quote Dante and to define himself as 'A nine-to-five-man who had seen poetry'. Larkin behaves remarkably unlike himself here, both in the high valuation he places on 'poetry' – he might have said that he had 'written' the stuff, but not that he had 'seen' it – and in the Dantean quotation itself, since he once notoriously said that he never read 'foreign' poetry. He does, however, behave in death in a way continuous with the critical reading of him in Heaney's essay 'The Main of Light' in *The Government of the Tongue* in which there is said to survive in him 'a repining for a more crystalline reality to which he might give allegiance', and which even envisages the kind of *Divine Comedy* he might have written. Just as Heaney makes James Joyce Heaney-like at the end of 'Station Island', he is here turning Larkin into a facet of his own poetic sensibility; and one implication of this might be that this is the way poets do survive death: by being transformed in the deferent but different work of others.[4]

The appropriation of Larkin here, which is both acknowledgement and deviation, is accompanied in *Seeing Things* by much naming of other poets and, to a lesser extent, painters. Heaney is always, as we have seen, a very allusive poet who embeds quotation and reference in his work; but this volume lucidly and explicitly engages with the work and reputations of

4 A similar point is made by R. J. C. Watt in his essay 'Seamus Heaney: Voices on Helicon' in *Essays in Criticism*, vol. xliv no. 3 (July 1994), 213–34, with a slightly different inflection: 'in putting words in the mouths of his shades Heaney sometimes tells us things about their kinship with others among the company of poets which they might not have admitted to themselves.'

other artists. This process begins prior to the Larkin poem in the book's dedication to the poet Derek Mahon, and continues through the naming, within individual poems and dedications, of such poets as Ted Hughes, John Hewitt, Sir John Davies, Dante, Virgil, Homer, Robert Lowell, Thomas Hardy, Yeats and Pasternak, of the painters Rembrandt, Matthew Lawless and Edward McGuire, and of the critic and biographer Richard Ellmann. In its explicit conversations with these figures, *Seeing Things* is a book which itself very much 'sees poetry' as its own generative and focusing centre. 'Incomprehensible / To him, my other life', the poem 'Casualty' in *Field Work* says of O'Neill's reaction to his work, and Heaney's responsive tact defines his poetry as, then, a 'tentative art'; in this volume the other life asserts its rights, and places itself in comprehending company.

'The Journey Back', however, also finds a resonant phrase for the origins of all such poetry: 'the heartland of the ordinary'. If this is not as dramatic, or as self-dramatizing, as Yeats's 'foul rag-and-bone shop of the heart' in his late poem about the loss of inspiration, 'The Circus Animals' Desertion', it is continuous with it, nevertheless, in its insistence on the usual, quotidian world that is always prelude to poetic transformation or translation. *Seeing Things* is a volume that sees things with the pellucid clarity which turns them into something other than themselves; and a large number of its poems define this process of translation itself. In the first part of the book the geography of the 'heartland of the ordinary' includes such features as a football match, fishing, a pitchfork, a settle bed, a basket of chestnuts, a honeymoon, a bicycle upended in mud, and a rainstorm. These are then meditated into revelation: the close act of attention, which is always firstly the manifestation of descriptive capacity, is extended beyond itself into an excess or superabundance in which the initial object or image becomes vision.

Many of these poems describe the process itself, individual texts becoming allegories of their own creation and performance. Football in childhood is 'fleetness, furtherance, untiredness / in time that was extra, unforeseen and free'; swinging a basket of chestnuts is to know what it is to be 'unburdened and dismayed'; the pitchfork is an instruction in how 'perfection' may be achieved by the following through of generous impulse; the flooding rain is discovered 'Biding and boding like a master-work / Or a named name that overbrims itself'; the honeymoon couple of 'A Royal Prospect', where the husband is a 'young dauphin in the once-upon-a-time', come through a violent history 'unscathed' but 'accountable'; two fishermen provoke what could be an image for Eliot's 'auditory imagination' itself, 'Each one absorbed, proofed by the sounds he's making', and therefore the opposite of sound-proofed. In both 'Markings' and 'Wheels within Wheels', this process of transformation is itself figured as an opening or entrance in the developing self, and indeed the verb 'enter' and its cognates recur throughout the book. In the former, 'All these things entered you / As if they were both the door and what came through it'; and in the latter, more expansively and definitively:

> all that entered me
> Like an access of free power, as if belief
> Caught up and spun the objects of belief
> In an orbit coterminous with longing.

Breaking and entering: the consciousness is intruded upon and disturbed by new experience, in an imagery having strong physical, even sexual connotations; but, the entry having been effected, the raw material of primary experience is raised above itself, displaced into spacial 'orbit', by the furtherance of desire. These lines rhyme the word 'belief' with itself, in a mode of repetition employed elsewhere in the volume too. Here, it prominently suggests the force of will involved in this process: as the word 'belief' repeats itself, the poem enacts the process by which furtherance is achieved; belief pushing beyond itself into the transformation of itself 'coterminous with longing'.

3 Face to Face

The volume's title poem focuses on the figure of the dead father in a way continuous with other poems in the book, which may all be regarded as shadowed by the figure of Anchises, Aeneas's father who is named in 'The Golden Bough', where the hero longs for 'one face-to-face meeting with my dear father'; 'Seeing Things' echoes this when it sees the father 'face to face'. The phrase is repeated elsewhere in the volume too, and it has biblical associations, notably to the first epistle of St Paul to the Corinthians, in the famous passage on charity which reads, 'For now we see, through a glass darkly; but then face to face: now I know in part; but then I shall know even as also I am known'; which is, of course, said of the way human beings may meet God after death, in a mutually self-revelatory encounter. In an act which displaces the metaphysical faith of St Paul's epistle into the humanism of revelatory memory, and which joins together Virgilian *pietas* – duty towards the father – with Christian charity, 'Seeing Things' concludes with an image of the father whose 'secular spirituality' may represent that of the volume as a whole. After recounting how, 'Once upon a time', the father narrowly avoided death by drowning, there comes a scene of mutual recognition and self-revelation between father and son, the father with 'his ghosthood immanent':

> That afternoon
> I saw him face to face, he came to me
> With his damp footprints out of the river,
> And there was nothing between us there
> That might not still be happily ever after.

Playing on the customary sense of the phrases 'nothing between us', which usually signals the denial of assumed intimacy between a couple, and 'happily ever after', which usually signals the way lovers exit from the end of fairy tales, the poem concludes with an image of eternal reciprocity, of redemptive and consolatory memory, which must now cope, in place of orthodox Catholicism, with the father's actual death. These are lines which restore to the beloved father the vivid reality of his presence in the only way now possible: in the texture and pressure of poetic language and form themselves, in the deliberate slow iambic progress and assonance of the line 'I saw him face to face, he came to me,' and in the uncertain, inconclusive wavering of those peculiar pararhymes of the last three lines, 'river/there/ever after', which make revelation still as much a matter of desire or longing as a matter of fact, and which therefore give subtle emotional and psychological credibility to the poem's whole conception of the way a dead father may be held as a permanent ghost in the memory of his son.

This conclusion is prepared for by the previous two sections of the poem in which actual experience is also transcended, in the one case by imaginative invention or fantasy, and in the other by art or artefacture. The poem's first section remembers a family boat-trip to Inishbofin, a small island off the coast of Donegal. The literal journey and its panic is matched first of all with the Dante translated in 'The Crossing', since the boatman here is, as Charon is there, a 'ferryman', and also with one of the 'Squarings' poems from the volume's second part. There, in 'Lightenings' viii, the old Irish annals recount an incident in which the monks of Clonmacnoise are disturbed at prayer in their oratory by a ship appearing above them in the air. A crewman shins down the anchor rope attempting to release it from the altar rails and the abbot helps him; upon which 'the freed ship sailed, and the man climbed back / Out of the marvellous as he had known it.' The little miracle-tale, then, is emblematic of the way two orders of being – those of imagination and reality, or of religious faith and experience, or of poetry and event – may coexist and interdepend, and may rely on each other in acts of mutually responsive generosity. The poem is the recommendation of a tolerant beneficence dependent on the recognition of, and fascination with, otherness.

In one of several interconnections between the first and second parts of the volume, this miracle-tale also shadows the conclusion of the first section of 'Seeing Things', when the poet remembers himself as a child, terrified on the dipping boat, and perceiving his family in a simile which places him in an else-where like that of the crewman of 'Lightenings':

> All the time
> As we went sailing evenly across
> The deep, still, seeable-down-into water,
> It was as if I looked from another boat
> Sailing through air, far up, and could see
> How riskily we fared into the morning,
> And loved in vain our bare, bowed, numbered heads.

These lines also bring two separate orders of being into congruence; not now, however, as aspects of 'the marvellous', but as elements in a consciousness developing in relation to the fear of death. The poem identifies here a very distinct and memorable phase of childhood perception and self-perception: the moment when the first knowledge that one's parents will die shadows everything in an almost vertiginous way. The emotional and psychological vertigo of the moment is brilliantly captured in the image adapted from the annals and in the desperation and pathos of the concluding line, whose heavily alliterated plosives bring, as it were, a lump to the poem's throat at the same moment at which they bring the resigned knowledge of inevitability.

The second part of 'Seeing Things' adds to the fictionalizing of the first the consolatory power of art itself, an art here directly inheriting the imagery of Christianity. Its opening word, *claritas* – 'the dry-eyed Latin word' – is the word taken from the medieval scholastic theology of St Thomas Aquinas by Stephen Dedalus in *A Portrait of the Artist as a Young Man*. There, Stephen translates it as 'radiance', using it as an element in his definition of the aesthetic: '*claritas* is the artistic discovery and representation of the divine purpose in anything or a force of generalisation which would make the esthetic image a universal one, make it outshine its proper conditions.'[5] Just as Joyce displaces the theological into the aesthetic here, so Heaney picks up the Joycean word for a similar displacement. The religious icon of the poem – a representation on the façade of a cathedral of the baptism of Christ – outshines its proper conditions by acting as an emblem not of doctrinal Christianity, but of the way an art – in this case, figures shown in sculptural relief – captures and manifests the otherwise unperceivable. In an image which alerts us to the fact that water is very much the symbol of *Seeing Things* – as earth is that of the early books and stone that of *The Haw Lantern* – the poem offers the transformation of water into stone as a quasi-religious act of magic or transcendence:

> ... in that utter visibility
> The stone's alive with what's invisible:
> Waterweed, stirred sand-grains hurrying off,
> The shadowy, unshadowed stream itself.
> All afternoon, heat wavered on the steps
> And the air we stood up to our eyes in wavered
> Like the zig-zag hieroglyph for life itself.

The stone alive with what's invisible here is a metaphor for the way the material of an art may radiate the inapprehensible. As such, the metaphor applies to the act of writing too, since the ziz-zag Egyptian hieroglyph for life is also inscribed on, and read off, stone. In these ways, the *claritas* of 'Seeing Things' itself is an utter visibility in which the memory of a family voyage to Inishbofin is re-presented and again made visible under the aspect of writing, and in which an invisible – because dead – father is re-presented with 'his ghosthood immanent' in more than one sense. It abides within him in life as the result of his brush with accidental death; but it also abides within this poem for as long as it survives, in the permanent residence of writing itself.

5 James Joyce, *A Portrait of the Artist as a Young Man*, ed. Seamus Deane (Penguin Books, 1992), 231.

4 Alleviations

'Seeing Things' works by a triptych-like juxtaposition and inter-relationship, in which each panel-poem comments on and interprets the others, around the central panel or poem that is the resonant declaration of its second section. It is itself complemented by other complex poems in Part One, notably 'The Settle Bed'. This takes to an ultimate point a characteristic grammatical feature of Heaney's later work: its adjectival and participial density. The adjectives, participles and participial phrases, as they accumulate, conjure an extraordinarily vivid sense of the 'in-placeness' of the settle bed, of its actuality, its solidity, its character as ' "an inheritance" '. It is almost as though the bed is being transformed into, or replaced by, a linguistic equivalent of itself; the poem too establishing itself on the page as 'an un-get-roundable weight'. In this, its language is coincident with its view of Ulster history, since the inheritance represented by the bed is that of Ulster itself, 'unwilling, unbeaten', its solidity and permanence a matter of both admiring attachment and sceptical disenchantment. This poem is one of only four in *Seeing Things* to refer with any specificity to the conflict in Northern Ireland, although the whole tone of 'lightening' – as alleviation, as the removal of a burden – may of course have a more than merely personal application in a volume from Seamus Heaney published in 1991, with something of the tentative optimism of the period leading up to the IRA's ceasefire in 1994. 'The Settle Bed' finds a radiantly dreamlike image for such a mood, both personal and political, when it suddenly sails free from its adjectival solidity into the directed, optimistic energy of imperative verb; the poem, as it were, rising above itself to erase itself, the bed unsettled:

But to conquer that weight,

Imagine a dower of settle beds tumbled from heaven
Like some nonsensical vengeance come on the people,
Then learn from that harmless barrage that whatever is given

Can always be reimagined, however four-square,
Plank-thick, hull-stupid and out of its time
It happens to be. You are free as the lookout,

That far-seeing joker posted high over the fog,
Who declared by the time that he had got himself down
The actual ship had been stolen away from beneath him.

Here political anachronism and the atavisms of immobile
attitudes are those of both 'sides', since the poem has earlier
defined 'the long bedtime / Anthems of Ulster' as, indis-
criminately and undiscriminatingly, 'Protestant, Catholic, the
Bible, the beads'. Now, they are lightened or loosened into a
surreal 'dower' created by the imagination: the inheritance of
the settle bed handed on, but with a difference. The word
'dower' proposes the settle bed as an inheritance which will
cement a marriage, which will be the agent of reconciliation;
and, in doing so, it transforms the in-placement of Ulster
historical and political experience into the imaginative else-
where of an alternative coexistence. That this remains an
option only in the surreal world of imagination, not in any
existing political actuality, is clear from the way the vision
is offered in, precisely, the terms of the conflict: if there is
'nonsensical vengeance' here, and a 'harmless barrage', the
nouns weigh as heavily as the adjectives in these oxymorons,
making this only a self-doubtingly optimistic poem. Yet its
final image – the lookout who loses his ship in the fog –
joins those images of the miraculous or visionary ships in
'Seeing Things' and 'Squarings' and does tentatively figure
an alternative future; the settle bed finally willed forward in
all its historical solidity, but as something entirely other than
itself.

The sonnet 'Fosterling' proposes a similar alleviation in the
poet himself as, in middle age, he returns to the original place of
his childhood, and of his earliest poems, to discover there an
alternative to the earlier work's 'in-placeness':

Heaviness of being. And poetry
Sluggish in the doldrums of what happens.
Me waiting until I was nearly fifty
To credit marvels. Like the tree-clock of tin cans
The tinkers made. So long for air to brighten,
Time to be dazzled and the heart to lighten.

These lines remember an earlier Heaney poem, 'Song' in *Field Work*, which ends with an allusion to a phrase from James Stephens's translation of a debate between Fionn and Oisin in an old Irish folk tale: 'the music of what happens' (' "The music of what happens," said great Fionn, "that is the greatest music in the world" ').[6] 'Fosterling' attests that, if 'what happens' has its music, it also has its 'doldrums', its dullness or depressions, and that there is a place of 'marvels' which may coexist with the hydraulics of these lowlands, just as the 'marvellous' coexists with the usual in the contingent worlds of the 'Lightenings' poem about the crewman. As such, 'Fosterling' is a deliberately transitional poem whose final word is already almost part of the sequence which follows in Part II, 'Squarings', which opens with the sequence-within-a-sequence that is 'Lightenings' itself.

5 Illuminations

'Squarings' carries to a further point the interest which earlier sequences in Heaney's work display in the possibilities of diversity-within-unity which the form offers. In this sequence, each poem has the same shape: all are twelve lines long and divided into four versets of three lines each, a form which obviously recalls the Dantean *terza rima*, without its interlinked rhyme scheme. This structure echoes the shape of the sonnet in briefer compass and perhaps owes something to Hopkins's

6 The translation appears in *The Faber Book of Irish Verse*, ed. John Montague (Faber and Faber, 1974), 79–80.

concept of the 'curtal-sonnet',[7] although there are so many
variations on sonnet form and the sonnet sequence in modern
poetry, which nevertheless keep traditional forms within ear-
shot, as to preclude Heaney's experiment from requiring any
direct precedent.[8] There are four shorter sequences within the
larger one: 'Lightenings', 'Settings', 'Crossings', and the con-
cluding sequence, 'Squarings' itself. Each of these contains
twelve poems: so that the shape of the sequence as a whole is
a kind of geometrical 'squaring': $4 \times 12 \times 12$. 'Squarings' is
opulent in its lexicon of luminosity: its individual poems have,
among other such usages, their brilliancies, radiance, blazing,
dawning, brightness, illumination, flaring, sealight, glitter,
shine, gleam, burnish, phosphorescence, beaming, shimmer,
flashing, fireflies, starlight and Henry Vaughan's 'world of
light'. This is also a Dantean inheritance: Eliot, for instance,
observes that 'The style of Dante has a peculiar lucidity – a
poetic as distinguished from an *intellectual* lucidity. The thought
may be obscure, but the word is lucid, or rather translucent.' He
also discusses Dante's 'masterly use of that imagery of *light*
which is the form of certain types of mystical experience'.[9]

One of the outstanding poems in 'Squarings', xv, combines a
further memory of the father with this imagery of light:

> And strike this scene in gold too, in relief,
> So that a greedy eye cannot exhaust it:
> Stable straw, Rembrandt-gleam and burnish
>
> Where my father bends to a tea-chest packed with salt,
> The hurricane lamp held up at eye-level
> In his bunched left fist, his right hand foraging

7 See Gerard Manley Hopkins, 'Author's Preface', in *The Poems of Gerard Manley Hopkins*, ed. W. H. Gardner and N. H. Mackenzie (fourth edn., Oxford University Press, 1967), 49.
8 Particularly notable examples are Robert Lowell's *Notebook, History, For Lizzie and Harriet* and *The Dolphin* and John Berryman's *The Dream Songs*.
9 T. S. Eliot, 'Dante', in *Selected Essays* (Faber and Faber, 1932; 1969 edn.), 239, 267.

For the unbleeding, vivid-fleshed bacon,
Home-cured hocks pulled up into the light
For pondering a while and putting back.

That night I owned the piled grain of Egypt.
I watched the sentry's torchlight on the hoard.
I stood in the door, unseen and blazed upon.

The self-communings of 'Squarings' are modulated partly in terms of their verbal moods: their vocatives, interrogatives and imperatives derive from some traditional elegiac modes.[10] Here, the imperative opening – 'And strike' – is a means partly of self-address, partly of addressing a reader, and partly a matter of suggesting some tertiary figure, a painter or sculptor, in the tradition of poetic 'instructions to painters'. The poem takes its place, therefore, in a long Western tradition of 'ekphrastic' poems, poems about paintings, of the kind Heaney has already written, to some extent, in the 'bog poems', as I observed in Chapter 2.[11] However, this is a poem not about an actual previous artwork but about an imagined one and, as such, it inherits a tradition which includes the earliest instance of ekphrasis, the shield of Achilles in Homer's *Iliad*. In 'Squarings' the imagined embossing is that of (we presume) a remembered event; and so the event, in the very act of being recounted, is transformed by becoming not merely one of the 'settings' of its sequence title, but already a 'scene', a moment transfigured into a frieze with something of Rembrandt's effects of lighting. In fact, of course, it is the son who is the poet-painter of this scene. Watching unknown to the father, he has been transformed by what he sees, since he will carry the memory of it for the rest of his life, and it will eventually give him the

10 For descriptions and analyses of such devices see Peter M. Sacks, *The English Elegy: Studies in the Genre from Spenser to Yeats* (Johns Hopkins University Press, 1985) and Jahan Ramazani, op. cit.
11 As I observed there, James A. Heffernan's *Museum of Words: The Poetics of Ekphrasis from Homer to Ashbery* (University of Chicago Press, 1993) is an excellent study of many poems of this tradition.

splendour of this poem. The poem has great filial affection in it, and in this it joins company with other poems of Heaney's, notably 'The Harvest Bow' in *Field Work*; but it 'overbrims' these too, in the word of 'The Sounds of Rain', as it pours light onto the scene, a light which permits the quasi-biblical enlargement of the final verset. The thing is extravagantly seen; and the image is one of entire beatitude, an unlooked-for grace in the actuality of the moment, transformative and enduring.

The theological dimension of 'grace' (the unmerited favour of God which operates in human life to guide people towards him) is, however, lacking in the sequence; and this is one of the several absences above which the structure of 'Squarings' raises its geometry. The opening poem conjures images of absence from the 'shifting brilliancies' of light: the image of a stone doorstep, a shivering beggar and an abandoned house with its hearth rained into, images which resolve themselves into a cumulative one – 'Bright puddle where the soul-free cloud-life roams'. Here, the compound adjective 'soul-free', which punningly suggests both 'free as' a soul and 'unencumbered by' one, erases the orthodox Christian concept of the soul as the principle in human beings which may survive death and gain immortality. The poem then reads out of that image an oblique question and statement about the absence of an afterlife:

> And after the commanded journey, what?
> Nothing magnificent, nothing unknown.
> A gazing out from far away, alone.

> And it is not particular at all.
> Just old truth dawning: there is no next-time round.
> Unroofed scope. Knowledge-freshening wind.

The sense of permanent absence here has its elegiac quality, and the sequence occasionally has something of the grand elegiac lament for the death of Christianity to be found in the poems of Wallace Stevens, notably his 'Sunday Morning', which culminates with an image of pigeons sinking 'Downward to darkness'. They do so, however, 'on extended wings'; and a similar 'ambiguous undulation' is tempered in Heaney's sequence into something resistant, even gratified. To be free of the old metaphysical assurances is to inherit instead an 'old truth'; and if this demands an isolating self-sufficiency, it also wakens the consciousness into a new 'scope', 'freshened' by the virtues of rationality and intellect. This is indeed, therefore, a 'lightening', as the title of this sequence has it: which, in poem xii, is defined as 'alleviation, / Illumination', and is therefore both the relief of a burden and a way of 'seeing things' clearly.

That poem is accompanied in the sequence by several others which similarly register the death of the old certainties. In poem xii, 'lightening' is further defined as 'A phenomenal instant when the spirit flares / With exhilaration before death'.[12] The poem makes of this a little parable of 'the good thief in us'; that is, the part of us that longs, like the thief in the gospel accounts of the Crucifixion, for the reality of eternal life. In fact, however, the poem figures him:

> Scanning empty space, so body-racked he seems
> Untranslatable into the bliss
>
> Ached for at the moon-rim of his forehead.

This remembers the image of the 'empty space' in 'Clearances', and implies a promise unfulfilled, a desire unaddressed. Other instances include poem xlii, which sees the afterlife of 'apparitions', caught uncomprehendingly on the territory of their previous lives. The poem's tone is one of awkward reverence: it displays an affection for the dead that is without any gloss of Christian consolation, and its 'shades' are kin, in the pathos of their incomprehension and abandonment, to those of the

12 Shakespeare uses the word in this sense, for instance, in *Romeo and Juliet*, 5. iii. 90, where he also defines it.

Virgilian underworld. In poem xliv, Henry Vaughan's seven-teenth-century metaphysical assurance that the dead are 'all gone into the world of light' is phrased instead as an opening question and then placed under sceptical agnostic scrutiny. This ultimately reduces the quotation to only its first two words, which are a reversal of its sense: not 'all gone into the world of light', but merely 'All gone'. That 'moment of admission' is married in this poem, as is often the case in 'Squarings', to a definitively revelatory image, here drawn from the art of fishing: the sudden moment when a line snaps:

> When the rod butt loses touch and the tip drools
> And eddies swirl a dead leaf past in silence
> Swifter (it seems) than the water's passage.

That has the homeliness and clarity of a Dantean simile – what poem xxxvi actually calls 'his head-clearing similes' – with its reserve of mysterious power; and it is the kind of imagistic lucidity which frequently accompanies the figuration of light itself in this volume. Its memorability is a matter of both the exactitude of physical evocation and the strangeness or impossibility of the perception being made: the leaf cannot be moving faster than the river, but only at the river's pace, and so the perception turns back on the consciousness of the perceiver, which is of course a consciousness meditating on death's permanence and life's brevity. The reflexiveness of the meditation is explicit in the wry or rueful parenthesis '(it seems)' which makes the lines melancholy, but alert too, and not about to give way to either self-pity or self-dramatization.

In the following poem, xlv, there is a further undermining of the orthodox metaphysic and a more complex adaptation of a Dantean motif:

> For certain ones what was written may come true:
> They shall live on in the distance
> At the mouths of rivers.

For our ones, no. They will re-enter
Dryness that was heaven on earth to them,
Happy to eat the scones baked out of clay.

For some, perhaps, the delta's reed-beds
And cold bright-footed seabirds always wheeling.
For our ones, snuff

And hob-soot and the heat off ashes.
And a judge who comes between them and the sun
In a pillar of radiant house-dust.

This proceeds in the way of many poems in the sequence: a speculative proposition gives rise to ruminative meditation which then modulates into the self-corrective production of an enduring image, emblem or figure. Here, the afterlife is rendered with absolute local specificity: the dead once more, as in xlii, are anchored in the ground of their previous dwelling. The phrase 'heaven on earth', that cliché of extravagant temporal fulfilment, serves now to define the only conceivable posthumous fulfilment too; that is, an intensification of the quotidian realities of their existences. The final lines replace the terrifying eschatology of Christian Judgement with a transformed image of domesticity and dutifulness which is both humorous in its metaphysical bathos and still magnificent in its metamorphic capacity. It seems, indeed, an appropriate final reward. As such, it acts as a benign form of what Dante, in the *Inferno* (xxviii.142), calls the 'contrapasso': a retribution for the sinner in hell which matches the sin committed on earth. Heaney's poem, that is to say, both absorbs the Dantean motif and deviates from it in a richly suggestive and revisionist way consonant with its witness to a secular, post-Christian consciousness. This makes it, like other poems in the sequence, a dazzlingly sensuous recreation of an intellectual or spiritual meditation in which the very terms of thought are themselves transformed into resolving image and figure.

In recreating, with a difference, the Dantean 'contrapasso', the poem is doing what several others in the sequence also do in more minor ways: they frequently reactivate traditional Christian and classical associations in ways that join together secular and spiritual significance or enlarge the apparently routine or trivial beyond its usual bounds. Poem xiv opens, audaciously, 'One afternoon I was seraph on gold leaf', where the studied casualness of the remembered temporal setting is crossed immediately with the exultation of the transformative experience, the 'I' as seraph carrying strong Miltonic resonance. In poem xxi, the unique experience of firing a rifle is figured in terms of Christian prayer and principle ('as it was in the beginning'; 'the sin against eternal life'; 'new light'). In xxv, the shock of an encounter with a fox at dawn is a revelatory moment imagined as a Christian baptism, a 'rebirth ... through water, through desire'. In xxix, the wonderfully particular recreation of the associations of the simple business of lifting a latch involves seeing it as 'a music of binding and loosing / Unheard in this generation' – where 'binding and loosing' activates sacramental associations; and in xxxii, 'stepping stones were stations of the soul', where the word 'stations' remembers Catholic 'stations of the cross', as Heaney's earlier sequence of prose-poems *Stations* (1975) did too. In poem xvi, rat-poison takes on a Homeric gloss, its phosphorescence as exciting as 'the anger of Achilles'. In xviii, a rope-seller is reinvented as 'a foul-mouthed god of hemp come down to rut'. In xxvi, being stuck behind a British Army lorry in Northern Ireland provokes the quasi-Dantean image of 'a speeded-up / Meltdown of souls from the straw-flecked ice of hell'. And in xxxvi, panic during the aftermath of a march in the North is also re-imagined in Dantean terms, with the car which the friends re-enter giving 'Like Charon's boat under the faring poets'.

These enlargements of the commonplace when it is brought into apposition with the Christian and classical are managed with tact and finesse in the sequence; there is a vibrantly authoritative assurance in Heaney's tone and address, created

by his now resourcefully dexterous use of this new approxima-
tion to Dantean *terza rima*, which commands assent to such a
richly idiosyncratic way of 'seeing things'. The form discovers a
way of modulating between various tones while still allowing
primacy to the oracular; and this is, as I observed earlier in
relation to *Field Work*, a very difficult art in a contemporary
poem. Nevertheless, the sequence includes within itself the sense
of how over-ambition always runs the risk of bathos. On two
occasions, in poems xxii and xxxviii, any tendency to self-
aggrandizement is undercut in the concluding verset. In the
former, very large metaphysical questions, initiated by 'Where
does spirit live?', climax in a parenthetical *moue* of embarrass-
ment: '(Set questions for the ghost of W.B.)'. The poem, that is,
suddenly sees itself as, reductively, an exam paper for the
spirit of Yeats; which carries the implication, presumably,
that Heaney is catching himself in a potentially magniloquent
Yeatsian mode. Alerting readers to the possibility, the poem of
course hopes to pre-empt it. In xxxviii, a moonlight visit to the
Capitol in Rome involves a knowing assurance about being
'privileged and belated', about being the social and cultural
inheritor of thousands of years of Western European culture.
This provokes an articulation from the poet of an inbuilt
resistance to what he calls 'form triumphant', which is the
marble form of the Roman monument itself, but which is also,
by implication, the form of these poems too, inheriting from
their Dantean sources. The poet's allegiance to 'Form mendicant
and convalescent' is, however, itself undercut by the voice of a
companion which challenges the self-dramatization of the
utterance itself, pulling the poet back from his vaguely ludicrous
ceremonious speech into the thumpingly ordinary heartland
with an inquiry about what he wants to drink. Although the
scruple with which Heaney includes these self-reducing mo-
ments in 'Squarings' makes for a certain corrective comedy in
the sequence, they run the risk of themselves appearing bathetic.
Emphasizing the degree to which an oracular tone has in fact
established itself as viable and reliable in the sequence, they

represent the final survival of uncertainty in an aesthetic which has in fact overcome it.

If the sequence inscribes its geometry over a metaphysical absence, however, replacing that with a sacramentality of the ordinary, it articulates other absences too, and also the restoration of possible presences. Wordsworth's conception of 'spots of time' and Joyce's of the 'epiphany' seem relevant to the reconstructions of many of these poems, in which memory acts both restoratively and definitively; but Heaney's vocabulary for modes similar to Wordsworth's and Joyce's is all his own, as the titles of the four sequences-within-a-sequence attest. 'Lightenings', as we have seen, is defined in one of the poems (xii), and so is the overall title 'Squarings', in poem iii, where the definition, drawn from the game of marbles in childhood, is a matter of:

> re-envisagings,
> All the ways in which your arms kept hoping towards
>
> Blind certainties that were going to prevail
> Beyond the one-off moment of the pitch.[13]

This title may also, of course, refer to the formal shape of the poems, which might – perhaps fancifully – be said to 'square' the sonnet. 'Settings' is not similarly defined, although the word does occur in several poems; but both its physical and psychological senses have relevance: a setting is 'the environment or surroundings in which a person or thing is "set"', and it is 'a person's disposition or cast of mind formed by experience and colouring his behaviour'. 'Crossings' is undefined too, although used in cognate form in poem xxxii, but it is clearly related to its use as the title of the concluding translation from Dante, and refers therefore to some form of movement across from one state to another (which is, in Dante, the passage from life to death).

13 This definition is not, however, known to the OED.

Lightenings, settings, crossings, squarings: all are ways of taking the measure of the self, of – it might be – squaring up to the self at a certain, possibly transitional stage of its development. The poems represent, as it were, the act of taking full possession of the self when it is in a new state of self-possession. Attempting to articulate the opaque, oblique, intangible, ineffable emotion, they display language in the act of negotiating with the barely remembered or the deeply recessed. The self is, 'Fosterling' tells us, that of a poet 'nearly fifty', and the losses are therefore those of common biographical experience; the absences sharpen individual poems into poignancy, resolve others into melancholy. Indeed, the losses extend beyond those of death and a traditional metaphysic of interpretation; they extend, in fact, to all of the remembered experiences themselves, and, as such, 'Squarings' may be thought to take off from the insights of 'Hailstones' in *The Haw Lantern*. In poem v, the marble-player 'vanished / Into Australia'; vi and vii make poems out of the poet's 'misremembering' an incident from the life of Thomas Hardy; in xiii, the space of childhood may be re-entered only 'as the adult of solitude', not in the cheering company of the original; and so on. Yet the sequence also celebrates the way memory may act restoratively within language and form. In poem xix, this becomes explicit, with its image of 'Memory as a building or a city' and its citation of the 'code of images' which was part of the disciplined 'art of memory' in the Renaissance: Heaney is referring to material similar to that adduced in 'Alphabets' in *The Haw Lantern*. Implicitly here, the lost art of memory is read into the poet's own memorial processes in one of his earliest childhood 'settings': 'You knew the portent / In each setting, you blinked and concentrated.' 'Squarings' is a series of hymns to portent and concentration, since to know portent in a setting is fully to appreciate the miraculousness of the ordinary, and to concentrate properly is to assimilate setting in a way that will eventually enable the reproduction of it in the new setting of the poem. The geometry of the sequence is, then, the plotting of a graph of the trajectory in which portent and

concentration become self-aware enough to articulate them-
selves; a process in which, as poem xi has it, 'accident got
tricked to accuracy', in which desire exceeds restraint, achieve-
ment catches up with intimation, reach coincides with grasp in
poems lucidly mobile with their own meanings. In this sense,
these poems are interestingly read in the light of Gaston
Bachelard's observation that 'it is not until late in life that we
really revere an image, when we discover that its roots plunge
well beyond the history that is fixed in our memories. In the
realm of absolute imagination, we remain young late in life.'[14]
Since many of the images of 'Squarings' are drawn from the first
home and hearth ('the bedrock of the threshold', poem ii calls
it), we might also understand them in terms of Bachelard's belief
that poets 'prove to us that the homes that were lost forever
continue to live on in us; that they insist in us in order to live
again, as though they expected us to give them a supplement of
living. . . . The old house, to those who know how to listen, is a
sort of geometry of echoes.'[15] Heaney's 'Squarings' are mature,
youthful poems of threshold and echo, disciplining loss and
absence into geometric linguistic form.

6 Une autre réalité

As I noted earlier, *Seeing Things* is dedicated to the poet Derek
Mahon who, in 1988, published his translations of the con-
temporary French poet Philippe Jaccottet. In his introduction to
that volume, Mahon tells us that Jaccottet wrote poems out of
his strong sense that 'Il y a une autre réalité mais elle est en celle-
ci', 'There is another reality, but it is in this one.' Jaccottet's own
poems are, in my view, thinner and less interesting than Mahon
finds them, and even he admits to certain lacks in them,
including those of humour, the demotic, 'the abrasive surfaces
of the modern world', and people (the poems are 'sparsely

14 Gaston Bachelard, *The Poetics of Space* (1958; Beacon Books edn., 1969), 33.
15 Ibid., 56, 60.

populated').[16] In 'Squarings' we have a sequence that also witnesses to the congruence between 'another reality' and 'this one' in a way itself congruent with some poems in the French tradition and perhaps, like them, dependent on the personal experience of Catholicism as belief first, and then the absence of belief. But 'Squarings' also offers the combination of that displaced religious or quasi-mystical feeling with, precisely, the substantiality and warmth of texture introduced by humour, modern surface abrasion, and human population. It is the most purely pleasurable and unexacerbated of Heaney's poems; the mind finding a fit for itself in a reality which is always at least half-imagined too:

> So let the ear attend like a farmhouse window
> In placid light, where the extravagant
> Passed once under full sail into the longed-for.

16 Philippe Jacottet, *Selected Poems*, selected and translated with an introduction by Derek Mahon (Penguin Books, 1988), 13.

8

Translating Freely:
The Spirit Level (1996)

1 Free Translations

Translation has figured in Heaney's work from an early stage. In *North* 'The Digging Skeleton', a version of Baudelaire's 'Le Squelette Laboureur', accords with the volume's many other images and metaphors of excavation; in *Field Work* Dante becomes the vehicle for emotions attached to contemporary Northern Irish political circumstance; in *Station Island* Dante goes on to supply other structural models and significant motifs, a version of a poem by St John of the Cross acts as a representation of Heaney's own developing attitudes to the Catholic faith of his origins, and the figure of Sweeney from the medieval Irish *Buile Suibhne* acts as a correspondence or correlative for authorial attitudes and moods; in *The Haw Lantern* a kind of parable poetry in English, with a strong Irish political inflection, is developed partly from a concentration on post-war Eastern European modes encountered in English translation; and *Seeing Things* bookends its original poems with translations from Virgil and, once again, Dante, whose *terza rima* supplies the ground for the versets of the 'Squarings' sequence. In addition, since he published his version of *Buile Suibhne* as *Sweeney Astray* in 1983, Heaney has produced other individual volumes of translation too: *The Cure at Troy*, a version of Sophocles's play *Philoctetes* (1990); *The Midnight Verdict* (1993), which combines into a single structure translations of the Orpheus and Eurydice story from Ovid's *Metamorphoses* and part of the long eighteenth-century Irish poem by Brian Merriman, *Cúirt an Mheán Oíche* (*The Midnight Court*); and a version of the Polish Renaissance poet Jan Kochanowski's *Laments* made with the Polish writer, Stanisław Barańczak.

If the translations included in volumes of his own have their clear personal reference and affinity, making them organically integral to the Heaney *oeuvre* and undertaking, these independent volumes have a fairly easily readable personal reference too. Kochanowski's *Laments*, a set of grief-stricken elegies for the poet's daughter who died aged two-and-a-half, have a tragic correspondence with Heaney's own poems on the accidental deaths of children: 'Mid-Term Break' in *Death of a Naturalist* and 'The Summer of Lost Rachel' in *The Haw Lantern*. *The Midnight Verdict* ingeniously reads Ovid into Merriman, or, in Heaney's own terms in a note to his translation, reads *The Midnight Court* 'within the acoustic of the classical myth',[1] in ways he explicates in the essay 'Orpheus in Ireland' in *The Redress of Poetry*; although a more proximate and pressing, if unstated, spur to that enterprise of translation may well have been the feminist critical onslaught on the extraordinarily unrepresentative *Field Day Anthology of Irish Writing* when it was published in 1990, an anthology to which Heaney contributed and in which, as a director of the Field Day company, he bore some executive, if not editorial responsibility.

Notably, though, *The Cure at Troy*, first performed at the Guildhall, Derry, in October 1990, seems intricated in personal and political preoccupations of Heaney's own. In its narrative, Philoctetes is abandoned on the island of Lemnos, lamed by a serpent bite which leaves him with a permanently suppurating foot. Odysseus and Neoptolemus require his bow in order to win the Trojan war, and they come to seek him out. Odysseus

---

1 Seamus Heaney, 'Translator's Note', *The Midnight Verdict* (Gallery Press, 1993), 11.

unscrupulously recommends to Neoptolemus the desirability of persuading Philoctetes, by deceitful means, to surrender his weapon. Neoptolemus, although he originally agrees, subsequently suffers guilt for his lack of integrity, and eventually persuades Philoctetes to return with him by telling the truth. In Sophocles's original, this is managed by the agency of a *deus ex machina*, the god Hercules. Heaney dispenses with this, internalizing the god as a function of Philoctetes' own consciousness and conscience, and therefore making the acts of persuasion and response seem more humanly generated than they are in the original. The play, apart from this, is a relatively straightforward and accurate version of the original, even though Heaney's translation prominently includes Northern Irish dialect. This encourages allegorical readings, of course, and although equivalences are not specified, they are implied. The lamed, self-obsessive wounded one on the island; the conflict between political expediency and personal integrity; the revision of fixed, antagonistic positions into mobile co-operation: all have their symbol continuity with the contemporary fate of Northern Ireland. And the position of Neoptolemus as go-between, as a man in two minds who is also independent-minded, is continuous with the view of the action of poetry both in Heaney's work elsewhere and also in this play's opening chorus, where poetry is a 'borderline', 'always in between / What you would like to happen and what will – / Whether you like it or not'. Further, Neoptolemus himself is continuous with Heaney's self-presentation in many poems throughout his work; and, at the point when he expresses to Philoctetes anguished guilt for his lack of integrity, he speaks in the voice of 'Exposure' in *North*. Neoptolemus self-exposed inhabits the self-interrogative mode and the imagery of that central poem: 'How did I end up here? Why did I go / Behind backs ever?' Given such correspondences, it is unsurprising that the play moves towards conclusion in a chorus entirely Heaney's, not Sophocles's, with its hortatory and affirmative lines:

> History says *Don't hope*
> *On this side of the grave*,
> But then, once in a lifetime
> The longed-for tidal wave
> Of justice can rise up,
> And hope and history rhyme.

In *The Cure at Troy* the desire for a rhyme between hope and history is expressed through the play's own rhyme between antiquity and contemporaneity, the rhyme that is the act of translation itself.

The Spirit Level moves the act of translation a stage further into Heaney's original poems by including it in various ways. 'To a Dutch Potter in Ireland' crosses the poet's own peaceful childhood in Northern Ireland with the dreadful one of its dedicatee, the potter Sonja Landweer, in wartime Holland, and the crossing culminates in Heaney's translation of 'After Liberation', a post-war poem of endurance, survival, constancy and renewal by the Dutch poet J. C. Bloem. 'Keeping Going', dedicated to Heaney's brother Hugh, who suffers from epilepsy (hence the reference to his 'turn', an epileptic attack, in the poem's concluding section) contains elements of terror and foreboding, and allies them, in its third section, with Macbeth's encounter with the witches in Shakespeare's play; a kind of 'translation', we might say, of the emotions of the poet's childhood into the heightened terms of the literary representation of such things which he discovered subsequently, but also a recollection of the process in which actual emotion prepares one for the emotions of literature ('I felt at home with that one all right', the poem says of the scene in *Macbeth*). In 'Damson' the childhood memory of a bricklayer's bloodied hand promotes him, in the literary present of the poem, to the status of Odysseus in the underworld in the *Odyssey*, a 'translation' continuous with Heaney's Virgilian and Dantean translations in *Seeing Things*, since Homer's Hades lies behind both Virgil's and Dante's depictions of hell.

In 'St Kevin and the Blackbird', one of the medieval legends developed around the figure of the sixth-century Irish saint of Glendalough is translated into a parable of self-sacrifice and self-forgetfulness which may also be read as a figure for the way the imagination can be totally possessed by its object. 'The Flight Path' is a summary of several of the topographical 'translations' of Heaney's own biography – Derry, Belfast, the United States, the Dordogne – which includes two explicit references to the writer as translator. At the end of section 3 the poet imagines himself in America as 'Sweeney astray in home truths out of Horace: / *Skies change, not cares, for those who cross the seas*'. Here, a memory of his own translation of *Buile Suibhne*, and of his translation of himself into the Sweeney figure in 'Sweeney Redivivus', is crossed with his translation now of that punning 'home truth' from Horace: a truth, that is, that one learns very early, at home, that is also a truth about home; that you take it with you when you leave. In section 4, Heaney pictures himself translating the 'Ugolino' passage from Dante which closed *Field Work* in 1979, and quotes several lines from the translation. He now makes explicit the political implications of that poem, its emotional entanglement in the circumstances of the 'dirty protest' begun by the internee Ciaran Nugent in Long Kesh internment camp in Northern Ireland in the late 1970s, which led eventually to the hunger strikes of 1980 and 1981. 'Ugolino', in its treatment of death by hunger, was, as it transpired, horribly prophetic of that later phase of Irish political history; but even at the time of the translation, Nugent's red eyes were, this poem says, 'Drilling their way through the rhymes and images'. Saying that, this poem now also offers an image of the poet as translator whose self-rebuke depends on what is in effect another pun: the rhymes and images are those 'where I too walked behind the righteous Virgil, / As safe as houses and translating freely'. This places the poet at a very 'safe' distance indeed from the prison-house in which the protest is happening; and it also presents the idea of a 'free translation' as one that is both unconfined by literal rendering, and also, simply, undertaken by an unconfined poet aware to the point of moral exacerbation and self-recrimination of those who are incarcerated.

'Whitby-sur-Moyola' presents, we might say, as its title implies, a light-hearted translation of the seventh-century Yorkshire poet-herdsman Caedmon into the form of a Co. Derry yardman from Heaney's childhood. In 'Remembered Columns' a legend about the Virgin Mary becomes a parable of the poet's 'Discovering what survives translation true', where 'translation' is displacement as well as linguistic re-creation. And in the lengthy sequence 'Mycenae Lookout', which is unpredictably quite unlike anything else in Heaney's work, the watchman who opens Aeschylus's *Agamemnon*, the first play in the trilogy of the *Oresteia*, meditates on episodes from the gruesome story of the house of Atreus and the ten-years Trojan war in a way that has manifest, if tangential, relevance to the history of Northern Ireland since 1969. In addition, the watchman himself, a kind of supernumerary chorus who in the original plays nothing like the large role Heaney assigns him here, has congruence with the figure of the poet himself at a time of violent inter-familial civil war. This is foregrounded when the watchman describes himself as 'the lookout / The queen's command had posted and forgotten', the very terms in which the Sweeney figure – that free translation of the poet – in 'Sweeney Redivivus' represents himself in the opening line of 'In the Beech': 'I was a lookout posted and forgotten.'[2] In both cases, the point is that the figure, posted and forgotten as he may have been by the significant actors in the political drama, is taking it all in and now, in the end, articulating it all for everyone's attention.

Many of these acts of translation may be regarded as what 'A Sofa in the Forties' defines as the entry into 'history and ignorance'. In that poem the children's pretence that their sofa is a railway train ('*chooka-chook*') is firstly dramatized fondly

---

2 In fact, the figure and part of the phrase have been with Heaney since 'Shoreline' in *Door into the Dark*, which ends with named sites which 'Stay, forgotten like sentries'.

and exuberantly, if also with an element of anti-parental recrimination (those long-remembered 'insufficient' Christmas toys which appear on it), but it then takes on much darker connotations as this train becomes, as it were, transparent to those others 'in the Forties' now known to the historically aware, mature consciousness of the poet: the 'ghost trains' and 'death-gondolas' which ferried their victims to the Nazi concentration camps of Germany and Poland during the Second World War. To enter history and ignorance, then, is to have a pristine childhood delight permanently shadowed by the knowledge first that you do not know, and then by the knowledge of atrocity. When the children's 'only job' is defined at the end of the poem as to 'be transported and make engine noise', the passive verb is a grimly punning one too: they are transported, taken out of themselves in the ecstasy of play, but millions have been 'transported' to their deaths by the actual trains of the time. The pun compacts the initial and the subsequent experience, the time of innocence or ignorance and the time of full historical and political awareness.

Elsewhere too, the translations of these poems compact the experience of an original childhood world with the later knowledge brought by history and literature. The density of the compaction is new in Heaney's work, and it returns it very vividly to those social, historical and political contingencies which it appeared a large part of the effort of *Seeing Things* to raise itself clear of. The self-corrective oscillation of mood and meaning between the two books is of course entirely in keeping with the movement of Heaney's whole career, which seems more than ever, with this book, a mode of 'keeping going' by virtue of its keeping going elsewhere. In *The Spirit Level* the return from 'lightening' to another kind of self-burdening is apparent also in the language and forms of many of the poems. Linguistically, they employ a newly forceful demotic ('fuck', 'cunt', 'shite', 'piss'); a more than customarily prominent use of Northern Irish dialect ('trindle', 'tally', 'motes', 'thrawn', 'cribs', 'plout', 'awn', 'grags', for instance, and the expressions 'in the halfpenny place' and 'not a bother on him'); and the sturdy, stubborn replacement of the oracular tone of 'Squarings' with what appears at times almost a deliberate brusqueness, off-handedness or reductively colloquial discursiveness ('Or words to that effect' in 'The Flight Path', 'Or something like that' in ' "Poet's Chair" ', and 'And so on' as one whole section, the final one, of 'The Thimble'). Altogether, these poems appear to want to inflict pain or damage once more on a previous lyric perfection, as Heaney long since, at the time of *North*, admired Robert Lowell for inflicting such damage in his 'sonnets'. 'So walk on air against your better judgement,' says 'The Gravel Walks'; and if 'Squarings' is the poet walking on air, *The Spirit Level* returns him robustly to the earth.[3] So much is this the case, indeed, that the analogue for the poet's pen in this volume may well be the brickie's trowel in 'Damson', 'Its edge and apex always coming clean / And brightening itself by mucking in'; a paradoxical implement, therefore, coming clean by telling the truth, but also by deliberately sullying itself.

These linguistic usages are, however, frequently combined with traditional forms and metres in poetic structures character-istically spacious, relaxed and varied, at the opposite end of the scale from the repeated twelve-line, five-stress forms of 'Squar-ings'. The volume includes many uses of the loose iambic rhyming quatrain in which the rhymes are sometimes full, sometimes almost ingeniously slant ('loved' / 'survived' in 'Mint', for example, and 'judgement' / 'cement' in 'The Gravel Walks') and contains also Heaney's first use of the sestina, one of the most complicated poetic forms, in 'Two Lorries'. This kind of formal complexity, combined with the new relaxedness of diction and manner, is very much the element in which *The Spirit Level* moves; and its effect is to

3 This may be a little intertextual quibble with Paul Muldoon who, in his book *The Prince of the Quotidian* (Gallery Press, 1994), 14, taking up a critical remark Heaney once made about him, says of the poet of *Seeing Things* that 'the great physician of the earth / is waxing metaphysical, has taken to "walking on air" '.

convey the impression of a poetry fully in possession of its own resources and means. This is a confident kind of writing mobile with purpose and intelligence, hungry for, seeking out and seizing its opportunities.

2 Mucking In

As my description of 'Mycenae Lookout' above indicates, the matter of Northern Ireland is again prominently to the fore in *The Spirit Level*, and this is one clear way in which the volume may be regarded as 'mucking in' once more. The poem in which that phrase occurs, 'Damson', begins by remembering from childhood a bricklayer's accident in which he bloodied his hand; this is the 'damson' stain which gives the poem its title. Through the transformations of memory, later experience and grief, the brickie is reinvented by the poem as an Odyssean figure in Hades encountering the local 'Ghosts with their tongues out for a lick of blood'; that is, the violently dead victims of Northern Irish political history. In this transformation or translation, the brickie's trowel becomes Odysseus's sword, in an identification which brings the gravity of classical literature to the interpretation of contemporary circumstance, in a mode initiated in poem xvi in 'Squarings', where, as I noted in the previous chapter, the phosphorescence of rat poison remembered from childhood takes on a Homeric gloss. The collocation in 'Damson' produces an extreme, wearied empathy which, in the end, undermines itself too. When the poem finally refuses the Homeric parallel, it also refuses the violence attendant on the conception. The negative rejection makes the same gesture as that made at the end of 'Sandstone Keepsake' in *Station Island*, where the Dantean analogue of Guy de Montfort is evoked in the same act in which it is dismissed ('but not really'); but here it translates itself out of the passive resignation of that poem into something tentatively regenerative, as the poet addresses and instructs the brickie:

But not like him –
Builder, not sacker, your shield the mortar board –
Drive them back to the wine-dark taste of home,
The smell of damsons simmering in a pot,
Jam ladled thick and steaming down the sunlight.

The violently dead are removed from the damson of their blood to the damson of their previous, pacific domestic lives; and the figure has grief, tenderness, longing and the desperate desire for reparation in it all at once.

In its inclusion of an element of the ominous or the uncanny, 'Damson' harmonizes with other poems in the volume which also return to the circumstances of the North. 'Keeping Going' remembers the superstitions of childhood, the 'foretime' when another kind of knowledge is learnt, 'a knowledge that might not translate beyond / Those wind-heaved midnights we still cannot be sure / Happened or not.' This confusion of imagination and reality, the evocation of an ominous element in the ordinary, is a kind of instinctive or intuitive translation, the child's inhabiting of two simultaneous worlds, where to piss at the gable is to summon a congregation of the dead, to cut down a thorn tree is to provoke the retaliation of a broken arm, and to see a strange bird perched on the roof, that classical emblem of evil omen, is to encounter 'dread'. This dread is itself translated into the grim and absolute reality of the poem's fifth section, which describes a killing on the home ground; here, the element of irrationality in childhood superstition becomes an altogether rational element of adult terror. The evocation is managed quite straight-forwardly, keeping its steady eye on the terrible object and attempting a physical representation of the literally unrepresent-able, the moment of violent death when the man 'just pushed with all his might / Against himself'. The straightforwardness, however, is made possible by the poem's elaborate structure, in which such things can get said as the acknowledgement of, and deference to, a brother's way of life and his persistence in it, his 'good stamina', his 'keeping going'. The familial affection, we might say, finally licenses Heaney's actual evocation of the circumstances of atrocity, just as certain of Michael Longley's poems of Northern Ireland, such as 'The Linen Workers', authenticate feeling about victims by being also feelings about the poet's own father. In 'Keeping Going', the stamina is up against a great deal, specifically the fact that the routine rural activity of whitewashing, which has been the source of the brother's innocently happy childhood play, must now forever bear the brunt of brutal sectarian killing: 'Grey matter like gruel flecked with blood / In spatters on the whitewash'. The poem also manages a tactful decorum in relation to the brother who must stay in his place, when the poet has of course himself long since found other places, 'keeping going' in quite a different sense: it has an empathetically ceremonious tributary quality, without a vestige of condescension.

The element of the ominous and the crossing of two worlds are both present also in 'Two Lorries', but operative now as a fundamental principle of structure. The sestina is an intricate form composed of six stanzas of six lines each, followed by an envoy of three lines, in all of which rhymes are replaced by end-words in a recurrent but shifting pattern; the envoy containing, in its three lines, all six end-words. Heaney himself has said in an account of one of Elizabeth Bishop's sestinas in *The Redress of Poetry* that the form is a system of 'inexorable formal recurrences'; in Bishop's poem simply called 'Sestina', these gradually promote a very dark 'second realization' behind the apparently comforting domesticities suggested initially by the end-words. The idea of doubleness, of at least two 'realizations', is operative in the very title of 'Two Lorries' which, we realize as we read on into its double narrative, refers to lorries widely separated in time: that of the coalman who flirts with the poet's mother, and that which, years later after the mother's death, carries the bomb which blows up the market of Magherafelt, the scene of his mother's projected, but never realized, dalliance with the coalman. In fact, there is another time in the poem too, the ghost time or visionary time in which the poet meets his mother again as a

'revenant', in Magherafelt after the bombing, where her inno-
cence is forced into confrontation with what happens 'In a time
beyond her time' – 'Her shopping bags full up with shovelled
ashes' – and where the coalman folds not coalbags but bodybags.
'Inexorable formal recurrences' therefore powerfully enforce the
poem's subject which is, precisely, the inexorability of the fact
that one lorry follows the other in this place; an inexorability
which is now formative of the consciousness, as it is of the formal
arrangements, of this poet from the place. Inexorability is further
enforced by the end-words themselves which, in a sestina, always
carry the drama and burden of the poem's meaning. Ashes, lorry,
coalman, mother, Magherafelt, load are the opening stanza's
words; and the first tale they tell is a tale of domestic routine, the
usual processes of supply and arrangement in a time before
central heating; even if this is a domestic routine cut across, to
some extent, by the coalman's flirtations and insinuations which
would, of course, if followed through, remove this mother from
the domestic sphere. They are not followed through, since this is
a 'nineteen-forties mother' who returns from her semi-flirtation
to the grinding 'business round her stove', which is displacement
and distraction but also, manifestly, confinement: so the recur-
ring end-words of the sestina lock her into her place too, her
place of ashes, lorry, coalman, mother, Magherafelt and load,
the script of her routine. Her son, however – here too a lookout
posted and forgotten, it may be – has noticed the extent of her
desire and unfulfilment and now, in the form of a sestina, gives
them their belated articulation.[4]

---

4 Heaney is alert here to the crossover of the social and the sexual in a previous
generation's domestic arrangements, where the regular contact between some
male suppliers of domestic services – coalmen, window-cleaners, butchers – and
women at home would of course lead to flirtation and sometimes, no doubt, to
what follows on flirtation. In relation to which, the sestina is also an
appropriate form, since it was initiated by the troubadours of medieval France
as one of the vehicles for the expression of courtly love, that elaborately
ritualized system which made casual contact between man and woman of great
erotic significance.

Writing about Bishop's sestina, Heaney also says that 'Like any successful sestina, this has a touch of virtuosity about it, but its virtuosity is not what engages one's attention.' The same holds good for his own in, precisely, the degree to which, as I have been suggesting, narrative, thematic and emotional meanings are coincident with formal means; even if one is alert to what was once called the fallacy of imitative form, a successful sestina makes a strong case for its viability and validity. Heaney's virtuosity, however, while it need not engage one's attention, exactly, nevertheless attracts it, particularly where he upsets usual sestina obligations. He does this when one original end-word, 'load', is not repeated but varied in homonym, rhyme and off-rhyme: 'lode', 'lead', 'payload', 'load', 'explode'. This foregrounded variation is, we might say, the structure which carries the poem's 'second realization', in which the coalman's lorry 'load' moves inexorably through its repetitions-with-variation until its transformation, in the poet's memory, into the lorry which will 'explode'; it is, indeed, as though the sestina form is carefully calculating the moment at which it will explode into alternative realization. This explosive, inexorable doubling is itself accompanied by another kind of doubling: that of image or motif, when the film which the coalman's flirtatiousness holds out as a seductive enticement to the mother, releases, in the second realization, a metaphor which makes memory itself – the memory which contains both of the poem's realizations, of course – a video film which 'fastforwards', and in which the second lorry 'groans into shot', a phrase in which both verb and noun also activate an anticipation of what this lorry's explosion will provoke. In addition, the idea and image of the 'film' are extended into what is virtually the pun of the last line, where the coalman's visionary reappearance after the explosion figures him as a 'Dreamboat coalman filmed in silk-white ashes', where 'dreamboat' suggests his Hollywood glamour for the mother, but 'filmed' makes him not the star of celluloid but the recipient of a membrane of dust from the explosion. The line thus dramatizes in a pun the coming-together of the poem's two worlds, its first and second realizations joining in an image at once oneiric and reductive: so that the poem terminates in a single lorry after all, held static inside, not at the end of, the envoy's second line. A further formal variation on strict sestina form, also functional, is the unorthodox order of the end-words in the envoy. Where the traditional sestina would have the pattern eca or ace (letting the letters a to f stand for the end-words as they occur in the opening stanza), Heaney has eda – Magherafelt, mother's, ashes – which reverses the order in which they appear in the opening stanza. The unorthodoxy makes these final end-words an ending in more than one sense: they are an insistence that Magherafelt and mother are both now ashes, given posthumous existence only by the ingenuity of a poem which follows the promptings of the poet's revivifying memory and imagination. Yet even the poem itself, reaching its ending, is inexorably trapped by its own powerless knowledge; which is, of course, the knowledge of death.

'Mycenae Lookout' is the poem in *The Spirit Level* which most clearly reveals the influence of translation on Heaney's recent original work. The poem's fiction has the watchman of the *Agamemnon* meditating on the action and circumstances of the play and, in its final section, the Yeatsianly entitled 'His Reverie of Water', envisaging an alternative to the relentlessness – the inexorability, indeed – of the cycle of internecine violence which is its plot. In that plot, Agamemnon, the king returned from victory in the Trojan war, is murdered, together with his Trojan lover Cassandra, by his wife Clytemnestra and her lover Aegisthus (partly because Agamemnon has previously sacrificed the child he had with Clytemnestra, Iphigeneia); and they are in turn murdered, in the second play of the trilogy, *The Libation Bearers*, by Orestes, the son of Agamemnon and Clytemnestra. In Aeschylus, the watchman opens the play, seeing the signal fires which announce the end of the Trojan war and the return of Agamemnon to Argos, but he plays no further part. However, he ends his introductory speech ominously, with a declaration of what he might say, if he had a mind to, about the house of Atreus. Aeschylus's metaphor for the watchman's governing of his tongue is the line Heaney takes as epigraph, 'The ox is on my tongue', which is also an image for the burden of the atrocity he would be expressing; and his final lines in the play put, as it were, a definitive finger to his lips: 'I speak to those who know; to those who don't / my mind's a blank. I never say a word.'[5]

Taking up these suggestions of secret knowledge, insider status and speaking a word to the wise, Heaney's sequence offers no narrative, but an interiorized reflection on the matter of the play, during which the watchman becomes expositor, commentator, judge, confidant and visionary, in all of which roles he is both involved and detached, an accessory to the crimes and guilts he evokes who is also their articulator and interpreter. The poem finds thereby Heaney's most unpredictable and original self-representation as a poet who has himself, throughout his career, been drawn to commentary on, and has withdrawn from propagandistic involvement in, a lengthy, on-going, local internecine war. The self-reference is, as I have said, made codedly in the phrase 'posted and forgotten'; otherwise, no specific analogy is drawn, and no contemporary reference is made. Indeed, 'Mycenae Lookout', in its obliquity, could be regarded as a firm poetic riposte to the interlocutor in section 4 of 'The Flight Path' who asks the poet, ' "When, for fuck's sake, are you going to write / Something for us?" '; to which the reply is, ' "If I do write something, / Whatever it is, I'll be writing for myself." ' 'Mycenae Lookout' is written for the self, and in the mode of meditative version-translation, a literary gloss; but its self-intrication makes it the clearest instance yet in Heaney's work of the way literary texts, and notably classical literary texts, operate for this poet as analogue and figurative projection, where the measuring of present and past brings emotions, impressions and attitudes into new clarity.

5 In the translation by Robert Fagles (Penguin Books, 1976), 104.

In 'The Watchman's War' the metaphor of the ox on the tongue is developed into what we may read as an analogy for the way a poet's tongue becomes burdened by the necessity to articulate atrocity; and the development crosses Aeschylean imagery with an imagery drawn from one of the ends of agricultural process which may also make oblique reference once more, as 'A Sofa in the Forties' does, to the deportations of the Second World War:

> And then the ox would lurch against the gong
> And deaden it and I would feel my tongue
> Like the dropped gangplank of a cattle truck,
> Trampled and rattled, running piss and muck,
> All swimmy-trembly as the lick of fire,
> A victory beacon in an abattoir ...

The relentless drive of these iambic couplets enforces the gravity and urgency of the watchman's situation, as he is compelled to stay awake to observe the fires which will signal the end of the Trojan war and the return of Agamemnon, while also hearing the 'love-shout' of Clytemnestra that heralds Agamemnon's death. Their intensity is equalled, but cut across too, by the 'Cassandra' section of the poem, where the abrupt, clipped, curt, headlong rhyming triplets have a savagery appropriate to the grimness of the episode of the *Agamemnon* which they evoke, while also giving vent to the self-implication of the watchman-poet in this outrage: 'No such thing / as innocent / bystanding'. The section makes of Cassandra, with her 'char-eyed // famine gawk', a figure reminiscent of the Windeby bog-girl in 'Punishment' in *North*; and the 'shock desire / in by-standers / to do it to her' registers the same herd emotions as those directed against the other adulteress of that poem. In this context, the watchman's knowledge of his own implication is a further version of the poet as bystander at the end of 'Punishment', with its ambivalent pull of both connivance and understanding. 'His Dawn Vision' reads across its vision of early morning Argos a vision of the North and its 'claques', for whom the watchman-poet feels 'disdain'. There is anger, impatience and desperation in this section of the poem, where it is, precisely, the refusal of translation that is read as the heart of the problem:

> No element that should have carried weight
> Out of the grievous distance would translate.
> Our war was stalled in the pre-articulate.

Translation here would be 'free' in yet another sense: it would release the present from the heaviness of the past, disturb the tenacity of fixed positions. The inability to translate freely in this sense results in stagnation; and the verse form, with its heavily insistent triple rhyme, is the imitation of stasis, the weariness of not moving forward.

The poem's fourth section, 'The Nights', presents the watchman as the unwilling repository of the sexual confidences of both Clytemnestra and Aegisthus. The resultant transfusion of the sexual into the violent, of carnality into war, picks up the image at the end of 'His Dawn Vision', when 'a man / Jumped a fresh earth-wall and another ran / Amorously, it seemed, to strike him down', and it once again returns to the characteristic imagery of the bog poems of *North*, which cross the sexual and the political. 'The Nights' is an almost priapic poem, recognizing the close kinship between sexual desire and the urge to violence; in it, lust of war and lust of the flesh are drawn into the darkest of collusions. The final section of 'Mycenae Lookout', 'His Reverie of Water', ends the poem with a vision of an alternative to war, and here its fiction of watchman and Argos becomes virtually transparent to this poet and his own writing, since the alternative is figured in an imagery of water, wells and pumps which Heaney's work has made its own, and frequently made into a symbol for the source of poetic inspiration, from 'The Diviner' and 'Personal Helicon' in *Death of a Naturalist*, through 'Rite of Spring' and 'Undine' in *Door into the Dark*, 'Anahorish' in *Wintering Out*, 'Sunlight' in *North*, 'Grotus and Conventina' in *The Haw Lantern*, the ending of *The Cure at*

Troy with its 'cures and healing wells', and 'At the Wellhead' in *The Spirit Level* itself.[6] The reverie of water contrasts with the fire of the poem's opening, where the signal beacons are awaited by the watchman; and its figuring of difference and release is continuous with the overall shape of the *Oresteia* itself, in which the final part of the trilogy, *The Eumenides*, returns chaos to order when the 'furies' of battle are transformed into the eponymous 'eumenides', the agents of peace. Similarly, the 'men puddling at the source // through tawny mud' in this poem end up 'like discharged soldiers testing the safe ground'. Clearly congruent, therefore, with soldiers who may lay down their arms after the long war of Northern Ireland, they too come clean, brightening themselves by mucking in:

> finders, keepers, seers of fresh water
> in the bountiful round mouths of iron pumps
> and gushing taps.

'Mycenae Lookout' is a brilliantly sustained phantasmagoria, running its contemporary insinuations freely through its 'translated' materials. Its form is an arrestingly novel one: the dramatic monologue taken to a further extreme, as the speaker or persona is both trapped within the circumstances of the original narrative, and also released from them by playing roles different from his minimal original role in Aeschylus, and also by his 'translation', as it were, into a version of the poet who writes 'His Reverie of Water'. The form perhaps takes a hint from such poems as Zbigniew Herbert's 'Elegy of Fortinbras', which has the minor character Fortinbras speaking at some length after the ending of *Hamlet*, in a way that shows how the character who is minor on the theatrical stage is

6 This imagery and symbolism is discussed as part of a rich argument about Heaney in R. J. C. Watt's 'Seamus Heaney: Voices on Helicon', *Essays in Criticism*, vol. xliv no. 3 (July 1994), 213–34. His pointing out 'the Celtic reverence for wells and spring water' is of course apposite to 'His Reverie of Water' too: in Ireland wells are still, in some rural areas, the scene of pilgrimage.

major on the political one; and it may also remember both Robert Lowell's moving in and out of monologues by historical and literary figures in his *Notebook* and *History* poems, and how W. H. Auden, in 'The Sea and the Mirror', presents characters from Shakespeare's *The Tempest* speaking differently from their assigned roles and language in the play, and prominently featuring a Caliban who speaks now in that most refined of all prose styles, a pastiche of the later Henry James. Both homage and opportunity, 'Mycenae Lookout' possesses and repossesses the ground of the *Agamemnon* with resourcefulness and with what, for all its gravity, we may think of as a kind of wit.

In envisaging an alternative, the ending of the poem chimes with the volume's other poem on the North, 'Tollund'. There are several returns to Heaney's earlier work in *The Spirit Level*, self-revisitings and re-situatings, some of which I have already noted. 'Tollund' of course revisits 'The Tollund Man' in *Wintering Out*. It is punctiliously dated 'September 1994' and dated, therefore, for the IRA ceasefire of the previous month which was followed shortly afterwards by that of the loyalist paramilitaries.[7] The poem has the poet and his companion returning to the countryside of 'Tollund Moss' from which the bog body was taken. Its opening reverses the future tense of the original poem ('Some day I will go to Aarhus' / 'I shall stand a long time'), substituting a perfect tense ('That Sunday morning we had travelled far') and a past ('We stood a long time'); and there are other reversals and realignments too. The ending of the original, with its poet almost oxymoronically 'lost, / Unhappy and at home', is matched now by a landscape 'Hallucinatory and familiar' which 'could have been Mulhollandstown or Scribe' in Northern Ireland. But the terrors unearthed from the bog in 'The Tollund Man', and the way they rhyme in that poem with the contemporary atrocities of Northern Ireland, are reversed in

---

7 The IRA ceasefire was since rescinded, although another is in force as I write in September 1997.

the new one, where the land seems 'Outside all contention', with its 'user-friendly outback'. The prominent use of the word 'home' in the original is picked up again here, to be shaken into new and different significance, as the companions are imagined 'footloose, at home beyond the tribe':

> More scouts than strangers, ghosts who'd walked abroad
> Unfazed by light, to make a new beginning
> And make a go of it, alive and sinning,
> Ourselves again, free-willed again, not bad.

Where 'The Tollund Man' makes its obeisances to tribal complicities, the new poem explicitly locates a 'home' beyond or outside such loyalties, and in doing so registers not condescension to past affinities and alignments, but a recognition that, in order to move beyond the stasis and stagnation evinced in 'Mycenae Lookout', such complicities must be transcended. Hence, 'Tollund' is a self-corrective poem and gesture, a revisiting of the old ground to possess it newly and differently, to turn it outwards from terror and 'man-killing' towards an alternative that is, in several senses, 'not bad'. In the original poem, the poet ends up lost and incapable of understanding the tongue of the locals, in an image of estrangement and alienation which has become perhaps the best-known 'emblem of adversity' in contemporary Irish writing. In 'Tollund', the companions of the poem are 'More scouts than strangers'; and the turning of estrangement into an act of reconnaissance keeps the poet on his toes, and within sound of military manoeuvres, while still oriented towards the conciliatory and the pacific. 'Tollund' becomes, thereby, a poem of cautious optimism, convinced in its attitude and gesture, but tentative in statement and assumption. In these ways, it may be thought to mark the mood of a constitutionally nationalist position in the Northern Ireland of the mid-1990s as indelibly as 'The Tollund Man' marked that of the early 1970s. As the poem says, 'Things had moved on'.

3 Lives of the Saints

The Spirit Level has its fair share of saints and divinities. There
is Kevin in 'St Kevin and the Blackbird', the Virgin of Loreto in
'Remembered Columns', Adaman in 'The Thimble', Brigid in 'A
Brigid's Girdle', Buddha in 'At Banagher', and Agatha in 'The
Butter-Print'. The poet Hugh MacDiarmid, that radical atheist,
is also turned into a kind of secular saint in 'An Invocation',
where the mode of address – 'Incline to me, MacDiarmid, out of
Shetland' – is a pastiche of Catholic intercessory prayer to the
saints: poetic form as a kind of posthumous ribbing, I assume.
Heaney's knowledge of the biographies and legends of these
saints is, I think, relatively arcane, even for someone born an
Irish Catholic in the 1930s; and in the poems, the arcane is
recovered by the ordinary. The power of the legendary and its
persistence as a means of imaginative analogy and instance
become the source of poems which themselves raise the usual
or the quotidian to a higher power. In 'The Butter-Print', the
finest of such poems in the volume, this happens when the boy's
life on the farm is transformed by, or translated into, a memory
of the legend of St Agatha:

> Who carved on the butter-print's round open face
> A cross-hatched head of rye, all jags and bristles?
> Why should soft butter bear that sharp device
> As if its breast were scored with slivered glass?
>
> When I was small I swallowed an awn of rye.
> My throat was like standing crop probed by a scythe.
> I felt the edge slide and the point stick deep
> Until, when I coughed and coughed and coughed it up,
>
> My breathing came dawn-cold, so clear and sudden
> I might have been inhaling airs from heaven
> Where healed and martyred Agatha stares down
> At the relic knife as I stared at the awn.

The legend of St Agatha is that she was tortured before her
martyrdom by having her breasts cut off; there are bizarre

and macabre representations of her carrying them on a dish by such painters as Cariani and Zurbarán. A memory of one of the curious consequences of such representations may lie dimly behind Heaney's poem: because the breasts in such paintings resembled round loaves, the custom developed in some Catholic countries of blessing bread in church on St Agatha's feast day. This complex of associations may source the way the poem's rye (which makes bread) is drawn into the radius of the saint's legend; and a representation of rye is carved on the butter-print because, of course, the butter will be spread on bread made from rye. The poem's second question is therefore answered on a literal level by this knowledge; but the fact that it is asked at all places the question back in the perceiving consciousness of the child who is astonished and appalled by this drawing together of the soft and sharp. It is an instance in the material world most closely to hand, perhaps the first such instance ever presented, of the way an 'open face', with its intimations of honesty and forthrightness, may be scarred unjustly and unnervingly. The child's-eye perspective is reinforced by the word 'awn', used twice in the poem – the second time as its final word – which is the Northern Irish dialect word, no longer in common use in England, for one of the bristles on an ear of barley or rye. That is the perspective in which the memory of the second stanza is set: the 'small' child suddenly, unpredictably subject to pain and physical danger is another instance of ingenuousness going unrewarded by reality, of the unforgettable confrontation with the shock of dangerous, potentially scarifying experience.

That, in turn, provokes the now mature recognitions made by the final stanza, in which the legend of St Agatha, who is martyred and in heaven, offers an imaginative analogy for the aftermath of such experience and a kind of salve for it, an understanding which relates hitherto separate areas of the self. The poem becomes an instance of the way the mind constructs its developing self-understandings by drawing together the rawness of primal experience, subsequent recall and deep meditation, and by discovering figures of permanent signifi-cance; in this case, one in which morbid and melodramatic martyrdom is transformed or translated into an image of curative beneficence. The result is as if the scene of the richly expressive 'Churning Day' in *Death of a Naturalist* – which is, in its own word, 'gravid' with implication for this poet's aesthetics – has been revisited to express, now, a metaphysics, but a metaphysics thoroughly embodied and sublunar. 'The Butter-Print' is a poem which, most appropriately in this punningly entitled volume, finds the spirit level, if unillusioned; and, for however brief a time, pacified.

9

The Activity of Listening:
Heaney's Literary Criticism

The physicality of his ear as well as the fastidiousness of its
discriminations, his example of a poet's intelligence exercis-
ing itself in the activity of listening ... confirmed a natural
inclination to make myself an echo chamber for the poem's
sounds. I was encouraged to seek for the contour of a
meaning within the pattern of a rhythm.

Heaney, 'Learning from Eliot'[1]

A man's theory of the place of poetry is not independent of
his view of life in general.

T. S. Eliot, 'Matthew Arnold'

1 Exemplars

In the foreword to his first critical book, *Preoccupations*, Seamus
Heaney tells us that the point of his critical writing is 'to come to
poetic terms with myself by considering the example of others'.
His is, consequently, a criticism self-consciously the product, or
offshoot, or even intellectual ambience, of his own poetry. As
several collocations of the criticism and the poetry in this study
have made plain, the degree of self-involvement in this writing is
at an exceptionally high and explicit level, even as poets' own
criticism goes. This is partly because Heaney's use of the word
'example' here has a more than merely aesthetic force. A word
frequently used, particularly in the earlier criticism, along with
its adjectival form 'exemplary', it indicates the extent to which
Heaney ponders not only the work but also the life of his chosen
subjects, as it is revealed in some of its most characteristic or

1 An essay published in *Agenda*, vol. 27 no. 1 (Spring 1989), 17–31.

problematic gestures, attitudes and alignments, with a view to making adequate or fitting gestures, attitudes and alignments of his own. It carries, that is to say, a strong ethical as well as aesthetic charge.[2]

This may well derive partly from Heaney's native Catholicism and its corrective confessionalism. The exemplary writer plays a role in Heaney's criticism which inherits both the requirement that the penitent make an 'examination of conscience' and that he or she consider the 'imitation' of the saints. In other ways too, the writing makes use of a Catholic Christian vocabulary. This is notably so when, for instance, an analogy between poetry and priesthood is made in relation to both Patrick Kavanagh and Nadezhda Mandelstam (she is 'a hunted priest in penal times'), or when Wilfred Owen is defined in terms of his 'sanctity'. A displaced Catholicism may also function more generally when the poem is regarded as a visitation to the poet, who acts as its transmitter; this is a version of creative intransitivity which no doubt draws on ideas of both Romantic inspiration and Modernist impersonality but it may also owe something to the concept of divine grace and its acting independently of the recipient's state of mind or being, or, indeed, to the Catholic concept of priesthood, in which, similarly, sacramentality operates independently of the state of grace of its agent. Such usages are bolstered occasionally by references in which the literary crosses with the theological or quasi-theological, when such writers as Jacques Maritain, Martin Buber, Simone Weil and Karl Barth are quoted; and central statements of the purpose and function of art give it an explicitly religious sanction, notably when Heaney maintains, with reference to Osip Mandelstam, that 'Art has a religious, a binding force for the artist',

---

2 Stanisław Barańczak, Heaney's collaborator on the translation of Kochanowski's *Laments*, memorably says that 'in this poet, aesthetics should perhaps rather be called "ethics of creativity".' See 'Polishing the sonnet sequence: Reflections of a Polish translator on Seamus Heaney's "Clearances"', in Hans-Christian Oeser (ed.), *Transverse II: Seamus Heaney in Translation* (Irish Translators' Association, 1994), 83–96, 85.

which draws on the etymology of the word 'religious' in exactly the way that the Catholic poet and painter David Jones does in his critical and aesthetic writings.[3] Although some have found in such usages a theory of poetry with an obscurantist or quasi-mystical element, the idea of the exemplary has a purely secular version too, and this is perhaps best expressed in Yeats's view of the poet's conducting an 'experiment in living', which Heaney cites admiringly in the essay entitled with the exemplary word itself, 'Yeats as an Example?' in *Preoccupations*.

Heaney's diagnostic essays on other poets, then, are more than usually forthright about the ways in which such diagnoses are also self-descriptive; and this leads to some of the most characteristic features of his criticism. It sometimes has an openly autobiographical element; notably where, at the beginning of an essay on Patrick Kavanagh in *The Government of the Tongue*, he relates the story of a chestnut tree planted in the year of his birth, which subsequently becomes a figure for different types of poetry – a story also incorporated into 'Clearances' in *The Haw Lantern*, as I observed in Chapter 6 – and when, in 'Frontiers of Writing', the essay concluding *The Redress of Poetry*, he describes his 'self-division' while staying in a Cabinet minister's room as the guest of an Oxford college during the IRA hunger strike in 1981. In addition to this element of autobiography, the criticism also includes a core of specifically biographical commentary on its chosen poets, in which letters and interviews, as well as poems, figure as text.[4] Yeats is admired for an arrogance or intransigence of behaviour which can be unexpectedly and slyly subversive, as well as for the finish and command of his poems; although the work is found most admirable when command is undermined by vulnerability. Robert Lowell is defined in relation to the 'caste' of Bostonian Brahmin into

3 See particularly Jones's essay 'Art and Sacrament' in *Epoch and Artist* (Faber and Faber, 1959). In fact, the OED tells us, the word is 'of doubtful etymology'.
4 This is of course in keeping with the fact that Heaney has himself given a large number of interviews, some of them of as much weight as the critical essays, containing remarks and *aperçus* of great eloquence and memorability.

which he was born, even as he is discovered apparently undermining the patriotism of his origins in the pacifism of admonitory public letters to two presidents of the United States. Elizabeth Bishop is revealed coping with the deprivations of her own early emotional life by 'outstripping' them in poems.

In *The Government of the Tongue*, the 'exemplary' quality of poetry and poets' lives is newly figured in relation to a number of poets regarded as 'witnesses' to political and historical catastrophe, notably the poets of Stalinist Russia, especially Mandelstam, and those of post-war Eastern Europe, and in particular Poland (especially Zbigniew Herbert and Czesław Miłosz). Some of these poets, through the agency of modern translation, constitute – again in markedly Catholic terms – a 'modern martyrology'. Making explicit the correlation of life and work which is his true subject in many of these essays – or even, we might say, the way the life is itself 'work' for a certain sort of poet, the work of living – Heaney says that 'In the case of the heroes, it is not so much their procedures on the page which are influential as the composite image which has been projected of their conduct.' When he writes about Mandelstam, he shows how the Russian poet's conduct in life and his conduct of the lyric are continuous, and how, therefore, the poem carries an ethical weight through the depredations of history, how it manifests an ideal of plenitude in the scene of loss. Heaney on Mandelstam is a poet-critic balancing reverence or awe with a spirited zeal of self-recognition. The sense that critical appreciation is coterminous with creative desire modulates obeisance into inheritance; and the critical writing, is, as a result, mobile with both definition and potential. In relation to the work of his East European contemporaries, however, Heaney is too abject. Their significance, he says, compels modern poets in English to recognize that 'the locus of greatness is shifting away from their language.' There is something too eagerly penitential in this, and also, in the context of exemplary witness to suffering, something almost vulgarly prone to think in terms of competitive 'greatness'; a proneness which may, of course, always constitute the obverse side to a poetics of the exemplary, in which emulation may be a response to envy as well as admiration. Where Heaney's essays in the exemplary can reveal a poet defining, as he makes or has them, the decisions, hesitations and scruples of one who, in Wordsworth's phrase in the preface to *Lyrical Ballads*, 'would presume the name of Poet', they can also appear, at times, hubristic. This is particularly problematic in *The Government of the Tongue*, where implied connections between contemporary Irish poetry and the poetry of post-war Eastern Europe (which I discuss further below), together with a certain podial tone, at times coarsen the spontaneity and instinct of *Preoccupations* into a self-approving *gravitas*.[5]

If in *The Government of the Tongue* Heaney seems sometimes on a slightly predatory hunt for figures of authority – a predation not really mitigated to any degree by an explicit, realistic acknowledgement that predation is an inevitable part of the poet-critic's confrontation with a fellow poet – *The Redress of Poetry* more relaxedly moves the idea of poetry as the tongue's 'government', with the various legalistic terms that conception draws along with it ('jurisdiction', for instance, as in 'the jurisdiction of achieved form'), towards a richer and, in the end, more humane conception. In one of the senses of the word 'redress' – poetry as the reparation for, or appeal against social and political wrongs – the word is continuous with the previous book's stern legalism; but in the sense primarily intended, it moves into what is virtually a metaphysical, rather than an ethical dimension. Citing George Seferis on how poetry may be 'strong enough to help', Heaney asserts that it may become so if it fits another, relatively arcane definition of the word 'redress', from the terminology of hunting: 'to bring back to the proper

5 Citing Edna Longley's acidic remark that, in these Eastern European references, Heaney's 'tentative approaches to an analogical minefield' are 'not quite tentative enough', Peter McDonald defends them, up to a point, by asserting that they form 'a statement of artistic predicament rather than a gesture of political aggrandizement'. See 'Seamus Heaney as a Critic' in Michael Kenneally (ed.), *Poetry in Contemporary Irish Literature* (Colin Smythe, 1995), 174–89, 186.

course'. The object of poetry, therefore, is to find 'a course for the breakaway of innate capacity, a course where something unhindered, yet directed, can sweep ahead into its full potential'. These terms, as they are used throughout the book, consistently imply a view of poetry as an overcoming, an outstripping, a transcending of contingent or corrupting circumstance. Such circumstance, indeed, is translated into something else at the place which Heaney's frequently-used conceit calls, as we have already seen, the 'frontier of writing', after the poem of that title in *The Haw Lantern*. The words 'excess' and 'excessive' figure in this critical terminology, and Heaney cites the Keatsian axiom that 'Poetry should surprise by a fine excess', which is undoubtedly influential on his concept of redress. It is a concept that, in these essays – originally all given as lectures in Oxford while Heaney was Professor of Poetry – enters into dialogue and sometimes combat with contemporary post-structuralist and post-colonial criticism. Where such criticism characteristically unmasks the discourses of power, Heaney, while recognizing the authority and accuracy of some instances of it, yet wishes to retain, under the rubric of 'redress', a space where the category of the aesthetic may continue to operate, even if it no longer names itself that. His theory of the function of poetry as excess demands that it exceed historical contingency rather than be merely collusive with, or subject to it.

At their finest, Heaney's essays in redress and in the virtues of a certain kind of excess are simply, self-justifyingly persuasive; they are themselves rapt exercises in the articulation of the pleasure given to a fine reader by what Wordsworth is quoted as naming 'the grand elementary principle of pleasure', that principle which meets, opposes and transcends the principle of unpleasure, the unavoidability of suffering, in history. Notable among these readings are those in which Elizabeth Bishop's work is discovered overcoming its own guardedness, and in which the opposition between two very different attitudes to death favours Yeats's over Philip Larkin's, with the former 'far more vital and undaunted'; where being 'vital' in the face of death is a kind of ultimate oxymoronic heroism, the introduction of the principle of pleasure into the scene of the deepest unpleasure of all. At times also, however, Heaney, as it were, himself exceeds his brief or his text. For instance, wishing to save something in Marlowe from contemporary accounts which regard his rhythms and plots as deeply collusive with the discourses of Elizabethan imperialist expansion (and the subjugation of local populations which accompanied it), Heaney reads 'Hero and Leander' as the answering poem of pleasuring excess. In doing so, however, for all the historical scholarship the essay manifests, he arguably underestimates the extent to which the poem's pleasure is in fact alloyed by another kind of discursive stress or distress, to do with its entanglement in issues of gender and sexuality. Where Heaney finds uncontaminated delight in Leander's pursuit of Hero and in her submission to his desire, other critics have discovered a more problematic tempering of deliciousness with suggestions of manipulative coercion and rapacity: the paintings in the temple of Venus where Leander first sees Hero depict scenes of rape.[6] And where Heaney discovers a similarly entirely pleasurable 'cruising' of Leander by the sea god Neptune, others may be more prone to see in that episode implications of stubborn importuning and harrassment; at the very least of it, the pleasure is all Neptune's. When the text even admits of such diverse or contradictory readings, and in relation to this most fraught of all areas of contention in contemporary critical discourse, Heaney may be thought unwise to instance it as an unruffled instance of pleasuring redress.[7]

6 See James A. W. Heffernan, *Museum of Words: The Poetics of Ekphrasis from Homer to Ashbery* (University of Chicago Press, 1993), Chapter 2.
7 It is of course precisely for such apparent blindness in his own poetry that feminist criticism censures Heaney. Patricia Coughlan's question when she deconstructs his poems, 'can poetry's implicit claim to universality of utterance and to utopian insight be upheld in the face of a reader's awareness of its gendered and therefore (perhaps unconsciously) partial perspective?', is one that the reader of this critical essay might ask too; or, to ask it more bluntly, does Heaney's reading of 'Hero and Leander' in fact suggest that one man's redress is another woman's distress? See ' "Bog Queens": The Representation

2 Unspoken Background

Although such a reading may not survive, then, as definitive of the text to hand here, it nevertheless takes its place in a powerful rhetoric of implicit self-definition. The Heaney lyric is itself, particularly as the career advances, manifestly an example of the 'recalcitrance' of the 'creative spirit', 'reminding the indicative mood of history that it has been written in by force and written in over the good optative mood of human potential'. The grammatical metaphor here is that of 'From the Canton of Expectation' in *The Haw Lantern* too; and Heaney is, in 'Frontiers of Writing', whose title also evokes a poem in that collection, explicit about the subtext of his theory of redress: 'The unspoken background', he says, 'has been a Northern Irish one.' In this context, the apparently aesthetic idea of excess, of realized potential, has, always, an implicitly or codedly political extension. The crossing of the frontier of writing, which is a crossing into the space made available by generous imagination, a space crossed over into – 'transgressed', it may be – from social and political constriction, is proleptic of the better political reality at least conceivable in Northern Ireland. The literal frontier here is the Irish border, 'a frontier which has entered the imagination definitively', but which may nevertheless be erased by the act of writing. The essay offers, consequently, what appears a definitive figuring of an alternative by Heaney himself; and the figuring, or metaphorizing, is conducted in terms of a literal geometrical figure, that of the 'quincunx' (which Heaney derives from Sir Thomas Browne's *The Garden of Cyrus*), a figure in which four objects occupy the corners, and the fifth the centre, of a square or rectangle.

---

of Women in the Poetry of John Montague and Seamus Heaney', in Toni O'Brien Johnson and David Cairns (eds.), *Gender in Irish Writing* (Open University Press, 1991), 99–111, reprinted in Michael Allen's *New Casebook*. The complicating homoeroticism of the poem is discussed, for instance, by Stephen Orgel in *Impersonations* (Cambridge University Press, 1996), 44–5.

This ingenious figure of the quincunx inherits the geometrical and architectural metaphors of Heaney's essays on modern Irish poetry published in the United States as *The Place of Writing*, but not otherwise collected, where he posits various conceptions of the way place is both constructed and deconstructed in modern Irish writing.[8] Now, in 'Frontiers of Writing', he offers in the figure of the quincunx an inclusive representation of an envisaged literary-geopolitical configuration of Ireland; and he offers this, of course, as the conclusion and summation of his lectures as Oxford Professor of Poetry, a post intimately associated with the study of English Literature in England. Heaney's figure hypothesizes five architectural points on the quincunx of Irish literary architecture: a 'pre-natal mountain' (the phrase is Louis MacNeice's) of 'prior Irelandness' at the centre of the figure; Edmund Spenser's colonizer's castle at Kilcolman in North Cork, where he wrote *The Faerie Queene*; Yeats's tower, Thoor Ballylee, in Sligo, the bastion of a latecomer's Protestant Anglo-Irish Ascendancy; Joyce's Martello tower in Sandymount in Dublin, built by the English as a defence against Napoleonic invasion, and now occupied by the ultimate subverter of both Irish nationalist and Anglo-Irish colonial pieties; and, finally, the keep of Carrickfergus Castle, the English fortress in the part of the North of Ireland in which Louis MacNeice grew up, and about which he wrote a well-known poem. MacNeice becomes, at this point in Heaney's criticism, an extremely significant figure. Inheriting the work of other Northern Irish critics, such as Edna Longley and Terence Brown, Heaney reads MacNeice as, decisively, a Northern Irish poet who also identifies with the West of Ireland, and in whose imagination, therefore, the Irish border does not figure. Heaney's conceit, then, is that the addition of Carrickfergus Castle to his geometry of modern Irish writing will allow access to the tradition of the literature of

8 Seamus Heaney, *The Place of Writing* (Scolars Press, n.d.), originally given as the Richard Ellmann Lectures in Modern Literature at Emory University in 1988.

the South to Northerners, and vice versa. The quincunx, he says, draws 'the shape of an integrated literary tradition'; it is an optimistic figuring by the imagination of a structure which has as yet no political equivalent.

The integrity of this figure, offered as a self-image to an Ireland which is not, of course, integral, but self-divided, asks to be read, then, as the political equivalent of Heaney's aesthetic celebration of imaginative plenitude or excess; the ultimate condition to be outstripped by this poetic imagination is the condition of fracture represented by the Irish border. This may go a long way towards explaining why Heaney places such a premium on excess in his critical writing, given that his own poetry, for all its sensuous celebration of realized potential, extravagance and exorbitance, is itself, perhaps almost to a fault, unexcessive. It is much to the point that the celebration of such things in the sequence 'Squarings' in *Seeing Things* is conducted in a perfectly shaped set of twelve-line poems; which is a geometry of restraint, not a graph of excess. Where there is danger and risk in some of the poets Heaney celebrates under the rubric of redress (Yeats, Hugh MacDiarmid, Dylan Thomas) who, the reader feels, are sometimes liable to veer altogether out of control formally, metaphorically or in the actual quality of thought or emotion, in Heaney there is always a discipline of continence, a deliberated sure-footedness which is absolutely certain where the next foot will fall. In this sense, therefore, there is a paradoxical element in the relationship between Heaney the poet and Heaney the critic. The former, in act, is more reticent, guarded and inhibited than the latter in recommendation; but Heaney's poetry makes virtue from such necessity, and the criticism makes capital from such directed energy and willed purpose.

3 Home

The attempt at inclusiveness in the figure and the liberality of its recognitions and invitations are, however, to some degree vitiated by the fact that the actual architecture of the quincunx is a military architecture: the towers, castles and keeps are the permanent reminders, in the Irish landscape and in the Irish literary tradition, that this is ground that has been fought over, and that the battles, still going on, have left permanent scars. If poems unwrite place even as they write it, in Heaney's deconstructive account in *The Place of Writing*, this figure of the quincunx too may unwrite its own generosity even as it attempts to inscribe itself on the Irish literary imagination. It may evince an attempt to manoeuvre into geometry and manageability what can hardly be so managed; and it has met with sophisticated demurral.[9] It is, however, the honest, well-intentioned hope of the constitutional nationalist figured in imaginative terms; and as such it is an epitome of the ways in which Seamus Heaney incorporates his Irishness into his literary criticism. Although he appears serene in his use of such concepts as 'the tradition' and 'the canon' at a time when they have been radically called into question by literary critics and theorists of various persuasions, Heaney in fact disturbs serenity in significant ways, sometimes reading the canonic writers in a very particular perspective, and sometimes introducing to the canon writers and works either previously not part of it at all or only very insecurely so; introducing them and stamping them there with his own authoritative and extremely influential critical utterance.

In an autobiographical piece in *Preoccupations*, written while he still lived in Belfast, Heaney insists that, although he teaches English Literature and publishes in London, 'the English tradition is not ultimately home'. The several autobiographical pieces

9 See, in particular, Peter McDonald in *Mistaken Identities: Poetry and Northern Ireland* (Oxford University Press, 1997), 15–16, where he says that 'the figure is ingenious as well as elegant, and might be seen as providing a satisfying instance of literature exercising its own imaginative capacities on a map to which the narrowest of politics had previously laid claim. Yet Heaney's imaginative instincts are perhaps reduced in scope as soon as he translates them into the language of politics and culture, where the available vocabulary sends the writer back to precisely those terms and definitions from which poetry repeatedly manages to escape.'

in that volume, and the autobiographical material elsewhere in the critical work too, all foreground his origins as a Catholic from Co. Derry, and he also emphasizes the degree to which he was initially encouraged by the discovery that his own local tongue could act as the linguistic vehicle for poems. In this respect, Patrick Kavanagh is the real liberator for Heaney; and he has offered his own redress to Kavanagh, who complained in the bitter first sentence of his 'Author's Note' to his *Collected Poems* that 'I have never been much considered by the English critics.' Heaney, as himself now one of the English critics – one who writes with the authority of English academic and publishing institutions behind him – has almost single-handedly brought Kavanagh to Anglo-American literary syllabuses and publishing houses. This act of redress or reclamation is of course the product of Heaney's high regard for Kavanagh as a poet, but the regard is provoked in part by the fact that Kavanagh, like other writers little known or appreciated by 'the English critics', such as William Carleton and Brian Merriman, brought into writing 'a hard, buried life', a life not unlike that of Heaney's own rural family and forebears. This making manifest of what has been hidden or disregarded is itself a politically charged act; and Kavanagh is exemplary for Heaney in 'raising the inhibited energies of a subculture to the power of a cultural resource'. The tenderness of empathy in his two essays on Kavanagh strongly suggests that Heaney regards him as what he himself might well have been, had he been born into a different generation and suffered the consequent lack of education and advancement. Heaney's establishing Kavanagh on the literary syllabus – his authorizing of him – is testimony to the kinds of revisionary jolt he has in fact administered to any serenely unitary conception of a 'tradition' or a 'canon'; and his subsequent inclusion of Carleton as well as Kavanagh as one of the ghosts of 'Station Island', along with his essay on Merriman's *The Midnight Court* in *The Redress of Poetry* (accompanied by his translation of part of the poem in *The Midnight Verdict*) have further credited inhibited subcultural energies from, now, a position of strength.

If Heaney was himself once enabled by the cultural resource supplied by Kavanagh, Carleton and Merriman, he has in turn made them newly visible and audible by virtue of his own cultural resourcefulness.

These revisionist gestures are consistent with the kinds of recognition Heaney makes when he offers, in 'Yeats as an Example?', an account of an interview in which Yeats presents an assertion that the power of England will not outlast the century under the guise of a prophecy by Madame Blavatsky: 'the calm surface of his speech,' Heaney says, is 'depth-charged with potential rebellion'. They are accompanied by the strong sense, in such essays as 'The Sense of Place' and 'The Poems of the Dispossessed Repossessed', of 'the peculiar fractures in our history' that make attitudes to both land and language so much more fraught and complex in Ireland than they are in England; and they are accompanied too, in the deconstructive essay 'Speranza in Reading', by an account of the way the flamboyant and dandyish Oscar Wilde (who was of course another Irishman in Oxford, as Heaney makes a point of noting) remains, in extremity, his Irish nationalist mother's son. In this reading, shadowed perhaps by Richard Ellmann's biography of Wilde, 'The Ballad of Reading Gaol', which Heaney first encountered, he tells us, in 'a book of ballads published during the 1930s with the intention of boosting British patriotism', is discovered to find its place more appropriately in a book of Irish ballads 'where it would appear as an example of that most disaffected of Irish genres, the gaol journal'. This is a prime instance of Heaney's focusing on a non-canonic and insecure text from a canonic writer's work with a lens formed from a quite different substance from those employed on Wilde by the generality of his critics. The focus turns, though it does not wrench, the poem into new, and newly unstable significance. Wildean disaffection, so often read as the product of the bruising humiliation of the wounded aesthete, surfaces here as consistent with other kinds of bruisings and humiliations too: those of Irish political prisoners incarcerated for their antagonism to English colonial power, an antagonism shared – and shared in her poems – by Speranza, Wilde's mother.

Some of these revisionist gestures and realignments are in tune with contemporary post-colonial and new historicist readings and models; but they are subtly, or stealthily, reinforced in the essay 'Englands of the Mind' in *Preoccupations* and throughout *The Government of the Tongue* by what we might regard as a specifically Irish attitude to, or take on, the English canon and tradition to which Heaney elsewhere seems at some pains to appear obedient. In 'Englands of the Mind' he offers a version of the work of three of the most highly regarded, or 'central', post-war English poets – Philip Larkin, Ted Hughes and Geoffrey Hill – in which all reveal a 'defensive love of their territory' akin to that displayed by poets from post-colonial nations: 'England' becomes a 'region' rather than a national or, to an even greater degree, an imperial idea. In the act of generously celebrating the achievement of these poets, then, defining them with an exceptionally inward technical empathy, Heaney is at the same time displacing them from the serenity of a unified English poetic tradition; and this is actually a powerful putting of them in their place by this English-speaking and English-writing, but not nationally English poet. The essay, which was originally a lecture delivered at the University of California, Berkeley – and therefore in a location topographically but not linguistically displaced from both England and Ireland – concludes by foregrounding its own linguistic medium as that 'which England has, for better or worse, impressed upon us all, the English language itself'. 'Impressed' is an impressively ambivalent verb in such a context; varying in meaning, as it does, from the relative neutrality of leaving a mark upon something to the more politically loaded sense of exerting force on something by pressure.[10]

10 John Wilson Foster in *The Achievement of Seamus Heaney* (Lilliput Press, 1995), 56, makes a similar point when he says that this essay evinces 'a subtle shrinking of England to imaginative versions and mental regions of itself of the kind Irish writers have been driven in compensation and colonial divison to create and inhabit'.

In *The Government of the Tongue*, the post-colonial region-
ality of contemporary English poetry is viewed in perspectives of
even deeper insecurity and marginality. In 'The Impact of
Translation', Heaney offers Christopher Reid's *Katerina Brac*,
a book which ventriloquizes on behalf of a fictional East
European poet, as an instance of the way in which 'many
contemporaries writing in English' have been 'displaced from
an old at-homeness in their mother tongue and its world-
defining poetic heritage'. It is in this context that Heaney
reads the work of the post-war poets of Eastern Europe available
in English translation; and here he appears to include himself in
the first person plurals which acknowledge the sense of limita-
tion and disablement: 'because we have not lived the tragic
scenario which such imaginations presented to us as the life
appropriate to our times, our capacity to make a complete act of
faith in our vernacular poetic possessions has been undermined.'
However, the same essay refers specifically to 'the insular and
eccentric nature of English experience in all the literal and
extended meanings of those adjectives', which contemporary
English poets are assumed to feel as a result of England's 'history
of non-defeat and non-invasion since 1066'. Here, there is
manifestly a move away from the sense of a shared fate to one
which is exclusively that of English (not Irish) nationals; and the
movement is phrased in an even slightly melodramatic way
which appears to forget how close both defeat and invasion have
come in recent English history, how a 'tragic scenario' was
indeed 'lived' both by those who suffered Nazi bombs in
England (and the rest of Britain) and by those English nationals
who fought in Europe and elsewhere between 1939 and 1945,
and how adequately this is defined in the English (and Welsh)
poetry of, for instance, Alun Lewis and Keith Douglas, and how
frequently it is returned to in the poems of the next generation.

Heaney exaggerates the extent of England's political and
poetic insularity, however, because he wants to suggest a correla-
tion between recent Irish historical experience and the more
'appropriate' recognitions made by the poets of Eastern Europe:

... there is something in their situation that makes them attractive to a reader whose formative experience has been largely Irish. There is an unsettled aspect to the different worlds they inhabit, and one of the challenges they face is to survive amphibiously, in the realm of 'the times' and the realm of their moral and artistic self-respect, a challenge immediately recognizable to anyone who has lived with the awful and demeaning facts of Northern Ireland's history over the last couple of decades.

This clearly separates out the experience and condition of Irish poets, and therefore of Heaney himself, from the condition of 'contemporary poets writing in English' diagnosed elsewhere in *The Government of the Tongue*; indeed, it proposes a near-identity or equivalence of interest and address. If this runs the risk of a very selective reading of modern literary history, and of an implicitly self-important alignment of Irish work with an appropriate and adequate modern poetry elsewhere, it also suggests how, at a very deep level, Heaney's criticism is fuelled both by the post-colonial desire to redress a literary-political wrong, and also by the desperation of the need for 'amphibious' survival, a need that presses vibrantly everywhere in Seamus Heaney, in the poetry as well as the critical prose.

4 Listening

In the citation from his essay on Eliot which I use as an epigraph to this chapter, Heaney speaks of 'the example of a poet's intelligence exercising itself in the activity of listening'; and this arresting phrase – which takes its edge of course from the fact that we casually assume listening to be not an active but a passive function – is also used in relation to Wordsworth in *Preoccupations*. It might be said that without this kind of example no other exemplary instance in Heaney's criticism would matter much, and no theory or principle of poetry and its motive power and effect would have the necessary sanction. What distinguishes Heaney as a critic is the physicality of his ear too, the way, precisely, in which the contour of a meaning is traced within the pattern of a rhythm, or, sometimes, a rhyme or even, indeed, an etymology. Poetic authority is sought within poetic music; an ethics of interpretation is grounded in the description of a technique. In the echo chamber of the critic's own head, certain key passages from previous critics have, in this regard, played a central role in the construction of the procedure of attentive listening or 'sounding'. Cited or alluded to frequently, these passages act almost as Arnoldian touch-stones of memorable authority, providing the basis for the sometimes intense physicality of Heaney's own creatively oriented criticism. The passages most prominent in this forma-tion are Eliot's concept of the 'auditory imagination', evolved in an essay on Matthew Arnold in *The Use of Poetry and the Use of Criticism* (1933); Robert Frost's idea of 'sentence sounds', which he offers in relatively oblique form in a letter, together with several formulations in his short essay 'The Figure a Poem Makes' published with his *Complete Poems* (notably 'Like a piece of ice on a hot stove the poem must ride on its own melting'); several almost numinous observations of Wallace Stevens's, particularly the principle enunciated in his 'Adagia' that 'Poetry creates a fictitious existence on an exquisite plane', together with the general influence of his essay 'The Noble Rider and the Sound of Words' in his book *The Necessary Angel* (1951); such passages from Yeats's critical and autobiographical writings as that from 'Samhain: 1905' in *Explorations* which gives *Preoccupations* its title and which Heaney uses as epigraph ('Coventry Patmore has said "The end of art is peace," and the following of art is little different from the following of religion in the intense preoccupation it demands'); and, above all and throughout the work, the criticism and poetry of Wordsworth. This figures outstandingly when a lengthy passage from the Preface to *Lyrical Ballads* is quoted in summation at the end of *The Government of the Tongue*; when Heaney refers to his own earlier uncollected essay 'Place and Displacement' in 'Frontiers of Writing', in which Wordsworth in 1791, after England's declaration of war on revolutionary France, is read as an analogous case with poets of the Catholic minority in Ulster; and perhaps most remarkably when, discussing Sylvia Plath, he allegorizes the famous passage from the *Prelude*, 'There was a Boy', as an account of the three stages of a poetic career.

Watching, or listening in to Heaney interiorize such passages and transform them into the characteristic gestures and figures of his own criticism is to witness high powers of absorption and response, and an unerring sense of what, as Ezra Pound said in another context, is 'of present use', or may be made so. Many other instances could be cited, but the opening paragraph of 'Englands of the Mind' offers a clear case of the process, as Heaney generates himself, as it were, out of Eliot:

One of the most precise and suggestive of T. S. Eliot's critical formulations was his notion of what he called 'the auditory imagination', 'the feeling for syllable and rhythm, penetrating far below the conscious levels of thought and feeling, invigorating every word; sinking to the most primitive and forgotten, returning to the origin and bringing something back', fusing 'the most ancient and the most civilized mentality'. I presume Eliot was thinking here about the natural depth-charges latent in certain words and rhythms, that binding secret between words in poetry that delights not just the ear but the whole backward and abysm of mind and body; thinking of the energies beating in and between words that the poet brings into half-deliberate play; thinking of the relationship between the word as pure vocable, as articulate noise, and the word as etymological occurrence, as symptom of human history, memory and attachments.

In fact, one could be forgiven for finding Eliot's formulation far more suggestive than it is precise, particularly since the context in which it is originally made is the negative one of his not discovering any such imagination in Arnold's poetry. Still, Heaney vigorously pursues the suggestions here. To 'presume' what Eliot was thinking may have its presumptuousness, and it is certainly a rhetorical device for insinuating Heaney's own sense of what a poem at its best might be or do. The passage generated from Eliot is a characteristic metaphorical and allusive run in which Heaney's own most recognizable lexicon is brought into play. 'Depth-charges' as a metaphor and 'vocable' as a phonetic term recur elsewhere in the criticism ('depth-charged with potential rebellion' above, for instance) and, in the latter case, in the poetry. The use of 'his notion', 'the whole' and the prefix 'half-' to modify a strong adjective, here 'deliberate' (which thereby promotes a vivid sense of the unconscious at play in the making of a poem), are all frequent in the criticism and have a certain Irish inflection. The 'backward and abysm' is a casually thrown-off Shakespearean allusion of a kind which, again in a characteristic way, serves similarly elsewhere also to heighten the literary charge of a critical passage.[11] And, perhaps above all, the stealthy qualifications, hesitations and even slight prissiness of the original Eliot passage (not all of which Heaney quotes: he omits, for instance, 'It works through meanings, certainly, or not without meanings in the ordinary sense ...') is wholeheartedly assumed into, or subsumed by, the much more robust physicality and playfulness of Heaney's prose, which contains, not at all atypically, a submerged amatory or sexual metaphor (a 'binding secret' and 'energies beating in and between') and, possibly, a hidden allusion to the notable touchstone from Frost that 'a poem begins in delight and ends in wisdom.'[12] If

11 The allusion is to 'the dark backward and abysm of time' in *The Tempest*, I.ii.50.

12 The original source of the Eliot passage is 'Matthew Arnold' in *The Use of Poetry and the Use of Criticism: Studies in the Relation of Criticism to Poetry in England* (Faber and Faber, 1933). The passage also appears as a gobbet, on its own, in John Hayward's edition of Eliot's *Selected Prose* (Penguin, 1953); and, since Heaney nowhere refers to its original context in the Arnold essay, it could be that he first encountered it here. If so, it would only add to my sense of the usefulness of Arnold's term 'touchstones' in relation to Heaney's use of these critical passages, since when Arnold employs the term in his essay 'The Study of Poetry' – where he is of course talking about passages of poetry, not criticism – he makes a point of the usefulness of 'short passages, even single lines'.

Similarly, it may be apposite to note that some of the other significant passages for Heaney are contained in James Scully's selection, *Modern Poets on Modern Poetry* (Fontana, 1965).

this procedure has, inevitably, like the search for exemplars, a slightly predatory element – and Heaney refers to 'the slightly predatory curiosity of a poet interested in the creative processes of another poet' when he discusses Hopkins reading Keats – the transformative absorption of the original into a mode all Heaney's own turns predation away from pillage towards recovery. In the act of careful attention, authority is being asserted while a tradition is being powerfully forwarded and renewed.

The characteristic signatures of Heaney's own critical discourse, as they are written into this passage, are accompanied by others in the prose which make it immediately recognizable, even in a sentence or two. Terms such as 'assuage', 'appease', 'somnambulist' (as an adjective), 'buoyant', 'incubate', 'opulence', 'voluptuous', 'ratified', 'profiled' achieve such patented signature as to make it a little dispiriting to find, occasionally in the later criticism, their unique identity embarrassed a little by the much more professional, even modish, academic discourse of terms such as 'empowered', 'heuristic' and 'transgressive'. If such epithets indicate an admirable readiness on Heaney's part to take stock, as a critic, of the contemporary discourses of post-modernism – and the essay on Wilde, in particular, makes use of some procedures characteristic of New Historicism – the individuality of Heaney's essential critical lexicon, and its development of the critical 'touchstones' I have identified here, anchors him as still, in many ways, an exponent of a brand of the New Criticism, or New Criticisms, which developed in response to the poetry of Modernism. And, as that, Heaney is manifestly drawn to those elements of Modernism and New Criticism which most clearly inherit the paradigms of Romanticism. When he writes on Eliot, for instance, he appreciates the way C. K. Stead's reading of him in *The New Poetic* (1964) emphasizes his Romantic heritage, focusing on the 'dark embryo' of poetic origin and composition, rather than presenting the magisterially self-annotating, controlled neo-classicist of an earlier generation of critics and expositors.[13] Yeats, of course, classified himself as one of 'the last Romantics', and Stevens has been so identified by his critics too; both are, as we have seen, woven into the texture of Heaney's own prose. Above all, however, the permeability of Heaney's critical consciousness to Wordsworth makes his basic conceptions of poetry essentially late Romantic ones, however much they may have been put through a Modernist or, in some respects, a post-modernist filter.[14] Approbation, celebration and self-identification, rather than irony, temper and measure, are the characteristic motives and moods of his criticism. Even where he does criticize 'the autocracy of ... romantic presumption', as he does in *The Government of the Tongue*, it is in a context which makes clear his attachment to precisely such self-justifying autocracy: 'I do not ... see how poetry can survive as a category of human consciousness if it does not put poetic considerations first – expressive considerations, that is, based upon its own genetic laws which spring into operation at the moment of lyric conception.'

If this is an autocracy which inheres in the poem and the moment of its composition rather than in the figure of the poet himself or herself, Heaney's biographical readings make manifest the closeness of the two in his understanding of the activity of reading; and 'the government of the tongue' is a phrase which, although Heaney never cites it or discusses the poet, inevitably calls to mind Shelley's ur-Romantic conception of poets in his

13 Chapter 6 of Stead's book is called 'Eliot's "Dark Embryo" ' and its subtitle is also relevant to the Heaney I have been describing in this chapter: 'The merger of morals and aesthetics'. See C. K. Stead, *The New Poetic: Yeats to Eliot* (Hutchinson, 1964).

14 Notable among critics who define Heaney in terms of postmodernism are Richard Brown in 'Bog Poems and Book Poems: Doubleness, Self-Translation and Pun in Seamus Heaney and Paul Muldoon', in Neil Corcoran (ed.), *The Chosen Ground: Essays on the Contemporary Poetry of Northern Ireland* (Seren, 1992), 153–67, and Thomas Docherty in 'Ana-; or Postmodernism, Landscape, Seamus Heaney' in *Alterities: Criticism, History, Representation* (Clarendon Press, 1996). The essay is reprinted in Michael Allen's *New Casebook*.

Defence of Poetry as 'the unacknowledged legislators of the world'. The most fundamental element of his criticism is, consequently, an anxious, scrupulous, hesitant and principled defence of the possibility of Romantic persistence in a period understandably hostile to many of the attitudes and stances such a thing might assume. In this sense, indeed, it might be said that Heaney the critic is the sometimes almost embarrassed protector or custodian of the secret knowledge acquired by Heaney the poet. That knowledge, which makes for creativity, is not to be denied or gainsaid, but the words in which it may be affirmed or publicized are now much scarcer than they were for the Romantics themselves. The characteristic rhythm of Heaney's strongest critical prose is, consequently, a delighted moving towards, and a sceptical veering away from a cry of approbation or ecstasy; just as the figure at its centre is that of the poet blaming himself for his own poetry: which is a figure scandalous in several senses.

Where Heaney's urge towards the celebratory is insufficiently grounded in the text itself, he can be prone to over-writing and a rhetoric of hyperbole or orotundity, his metaphors self-generatingly unreined. This can result in prose in which critical admiration lapses into something more like the admiration of its own admiration. This occurs, for instance, in an otherwise excellent account of Hopkins, when he describes the image in symbolist poetry as 'the unburdening of the indefinable through pangs that are indescribable, where the poem survives as the hieroglyph of a numinous nativity'; where the criticism, despite the fact that there may be irony in it, does not survive the aggregation of the ineffable. There is too, in the earlier criticism particularly, a tendency to over-schematic or even specious binary thinking, particularly in relation to gender, where 'masculine' and 'feminine' are used as categories of both linguistic and political differentiation in ways altogether too closely allied to, or derived from, stereotype ('masculine will and intelligence and feminine clusters of image and emotion' in *Preoccupations*, for instance).[15] In a related way, and in a way consonant with his too euphoric reading of *Hero and Leander*, as I have described it above, his lexicon of the amatory in relation to poetry, while it can wonderfully summon a sense of physical delight and sympathetic perception, a Barthesian *jouissance* in the creative act and in readerly response, can also appear presumptuously masculinist in its categories. It is surely not too puritanical, for instance, to find the word 'philandering' oddly used, as it is several times in Heaney, as a neutral term of aesthetic approbation, whereas, in the world of human behaviour from which it derives, it is hardly that.

The finest moments in Heaney's criticism come when the pressure of a patiently attentive, slowly cumulative close reading – in which inwardness with the work combines with a sense of empathetic delight at creative difficulties overcome – prompts, or permits itself, an entirely appropriate act of celebration or rapture. An outstanding example is his reading of Geoffrey Hill's *Mercian Hymns* in 'Englands of the Mind', where etymology is raised to a very high critical power as, for instance, Heaney pesters the verb 'pester' in one of the hymns until it releases a meaning congruent with the method of the poem itself; and where paraphrase is much less what it usually is in criticism – a thin dilution of the original – and much more a rendering of the separate elements of the poem into the compound of Heaney's own learnedly intertextual prose. Another is the evocation of the *Ariel* poems in 'The Indefatigable Hoof-taps: Sylvia Plath', which names their 'irresistible given-ness', their 'sense of surprised arrival, of astonished being', the way they are 'the vehicles of their own impulses', and – the poem's illuminating literary-historical point – the fact that this represents a Poundian imagism taken to an extreme point. Here, the brilliant, concentrated, accurate and memorable impressionism of Heaney's phrases does not rest content with itself in any self-

---

15 These figures have of course been subjected to a great deal of scrutiny and derogation; notably, but not exclusively, by feminist critics.

approving manner (it is not 'phrase-making'), but pushes beyond itself into persuasive literary history, a literary history congruent with a personal biography since, in relation to Plath, the idea of extremity always points both inward to the conception of the poem and outward towards a psychology of distress and suicidal orientation.

A third such instance is the reading of Elizabeth Bishop's 'Sestina' in 'Counting to a Hundred', to which I referred in the last chapter. Here, an exploration of formal obligation and necessity releases an almost surprised, and certainly surprising, sense of the way technique produces meaning and emotion:

Like any successful sestina, this has a touch of virtuosity about it, but its virtuosity is not what engages one's attention. Its immediate effect is as emotionally direct as a fairytale. Just as Dylan Thomas's villanelle 'Do Not Go Gentle into That Good Night' comes across as a dramatic cry rather than a formal set-piece, so the narrative and dramatic interest of Bishop's sestina very quickly deflects attention from its master-class excellence as a technical performance. The poem circles unspoken sorrows, and as it circles them, it manages to mesmerize them and make them obedient to creative will.

Here the criticism also, self-forgetfully, deflects attention from its own perceptiveness and redirects it towards what may properly be called the mystery of the poem, its capacity to mobilize technique in the interests of assuaging suffering; for poet herself, first, and then for reader. Heaney's activity of listening here – of listening to the way a successful sestina operates its intricate end-word scheme – hears, or overhears, something not actually in the poem, exactly, 'unspoken sorrows'; and by holding these in fine balance with the recognition of achieved form and its alleviating powers, it becomes itself an altogether exemplary critical act. If a poet curious about the creative processes of another poet is always 'slightly predatory' – and Heaney's own sestina 'Two Lorries' is, as I showed in the last chapter, also illuminated by this essay on Bishop – here is a prime instance of predation overtaken by delighted appreciation, which is then a phase in its own transformation into new imaginative and creative power. At such moments, Heaney's criticism takes on a dialogic or even dramatic quality, itself circling but not mesmerized by its subject, until the prose seems to steady itself for the new poem that will flower from the encounter.

APPENDIX

In Between:
On Seamus Heaney's Life*

Two buckets were easier carried than one.
I grew up in between.

My left hand placed the standard iron weight.
My right tilted a last grain in the balance.

Baronies, parishes met where I was born.
When I stood on the central stepping stone

I was the last earl on horseback in midstream
Still parleying, in earshot of his peers.

'Terminus' (from *The Haw Lantern*)

One definition of 'Irish' that I liked a lot was Samuel Beckett's. When he was interviewed by a French journalist, the journalist said: 'Vous êtes Anglais, Monsieur Beckett?' To which Beckett replied: 'Au contraire'.

Seamus Heaney in interview, 1982

Seamus Heaney was born on 13 April 1939, to Patrick and Margaret Kathleen (née McCann) Heaney, on a farm called Mossbawn, in the townland of Tamniarn, Co. Derry, Northern Ireland. He was the eldest of nine children, two girls and seven boys. His father, in addition to farming the fifty-acre Mossbawn, also worked as a cattle dealer. From 1945 to 1951 Heaney attended the local Anahorish School, and from 1951 to 1957 he went as a boarder to St Columb's College in Derry city, about forty miles from his home. When he was fourteen, the family moved from the Mossbawn farm to one at the other end of the

---

* Uncited references in this appendix are taken from conversations I had with Seamus Heaney in Dublin on 5 and 6 July 1985.

parish called The Wood, on which Heaney's father had been brought up, and which he had now inherited from an uncle. Heaney believes that a contributory factor in the decision to move when they did was probably the death at the time, in a road accident close to the house, of one of his brothers, Christopher – the incident commemorated in one of his earliest poems, 'Mid-Term Break'.

The move to The Wood seems definitively to have sealed off the world of Heaney's childhood: in his prose recollections, it is the 'kindly' name of Mossbawn which stands guardian over the world to which he instinctively returned for the material of most of his earliest poems. 'Mossbawn' is also the title of two poems which dedicate his fourth book, *North*, to his aunt, Mary Heaney, who lived with the family. Her position in Heaney's early life was clearly a very significant one:

She was the affectionate centre. I'm not saying in any way that my mother was distant, she was just always so busy with children; but Mary's function was almost entirely benign. She was the heart of the house in some ways, and as a child I was 'petted' on her, as they say. There were two women, as it were, in my life – happily there. Mary was always there as a kind of second mother, really.

Everything Heaney has himself written about his childhood re-inforces the sense of intimate domestic warmth and affection as its prevailing atmosphere. It is a quality which Heaney's wife, Marie, envied when she first came across it:

His family life was utterly together, like an egg contained within the shell, without any quality of otherness, without the sense of loss that this otherness brings. They had confidence in the way they lived, a lovely impeccable confidence in their own style.[1]

This 'togetherness' inside the walls of the home was not re-flected, however, in the world beyond those walls, where every-thing spoke, on the contrary, of division. This was, first of all, a matter of the accident of local topography:

1 Quoted in Polly Devlin, *All Of Us There* (Pan, 1983), 17.

From the beginning I was very conscious of boundaries. There was a drain or stream, the Sluggan drain, an old division that ran very close to our house. It divided the townland of Tamniarn from the townland of Anahorish and those two townlands belonged in two different parishes, Bellaghy and Newbridge, which are also in two different dioceses: the diocese of Derry ended at the Sluggan drain and the diocese of Armagh began. I was always going backwards and forwards. I went to school in Anahorish School, so I learnt the Armagh catechism; but I belonged, by birth and enrolment, to Bellaghy parish. So I didn't go with the rest of the school to make my first communion in Newbridge. And when I was confirmed in Bellaghy, the bishop had to ask us these ritual questions and I didn't know the Derry catechism. When we moved to the other end of the parish when I was fourteen, I still played football for Castledawson, though I was living in the Bellaghy team's district. I seemed always to be a little displaced; being in between was a kind of condition, from the start.

What begins there as a description of topographical division shades inevitably into the greater divisions of Heaney's childhood in Northern Ireland, the interwoven divisions of religion and culture, since Heaney's 'football' is Gaelic football, played exclusively by the Catholic minority. In the essay 'Belfast' written in 1972 and collected in *Preoccupations*, this consciousness of division leads him to derive from the name 'Mossbawn' itself, with its Scots and possibly Gaelic etymology, 'a metaphor of the split culture of Ulster'. The farm was located between Toomebridge, where the rebel Rody McCorley was hanged in 1798, during the rebellion against English rule in Ireland, and Castledawson, the estate of the Chichester-Clarkes, a leading Unionist family; and Heaney regards this as placing him, symbolically for a Northern Catholic, between the site of nationalist local sentiment and the site of colonial and British presence, between the 'bog' and the 'demesne' (the Anglo-French word for 'estate' or 'landed property' still current in Northern Ireland, though not in England). Although his first school, Anahorish, was attended, exceptionally, by both Catholics and Protestants, and although religious differences in this small rural community were usually submerged pragmatically in the interests of the business of agriculture, everything in Heaney's childhood bore the imprint of the fact that he was born a Catholic in the North of Ireland.

There were, firstly, the liturgical and popular forms of the religion itself, which all figure at times in the poetry: the Mass, confessions, the family rosary, the recitation of the catechism, and those numerous small pieties of a now virtually extinct phase of Irish Catholicism, which supplied almost the whole context for an ordinary life. There was the customary, routine veneration of the Blessed Virgin Mary which offered the vivid sense of an intercessory female presence in human affairs. There was that 'sacramental' sense of the landscape described in 'The Sense of Place' in *Preoccupations*, the vestigial presence of an older 'magical' or 'marvellous' view of the world which survived in rituals such as the plaiting of Brigid's crosses, the gathering of flowers for May altars, the turnip-candles of Hallowe'en. It was a disappearing world in which, Heaney has said in his essay 'The Poet as a Christian', 'we never felt ourselves alone in the universe for a second.'[2] Perhaps of most significance for his own future work were the rituals attendant on death:

My childhood was full of death – only the first couple of times scary and strange. Two of my grandparents, and lots of granduncles and aunts died when I was quite young and I went to the wakes and funerals. Then, since I was the eldest, in my early teens I used to represent the family at some funerals and the sight of a corpse and the whole ritual were quite common to me. It's a big social engagement, everyone comes to the house. Neighbours would sit up all night, and one or two of the family. This business of sitting all night in the wake-house, it's inscrutable as the Red Indians, an inner system of courtesy and honour and obligement. So I took all that as just an ordinary fact of life. I'm certain all those funerals and corpses had some definite effect, and I remember after writing 'The Tollund Man' I began to think if I were to go to an analyst, he would certainly link the outlined

2 'The Poet as a Christian', *The Furrow*, vol. 29 no. 10 (1978), 603–6, 606.

and pacified and *rigor mortis* face of the Tollund man with all that submerged life and memory.

But being a Catholic in Northern Ireland extended, and extends, far beyond the forms of the religion itself: as Heaney defined it in an interview, 'It's almost a racist term, a label for a set of cultural suppositions.'[3] It meant that the reading matter of his childhood included, along with English comics and adventure stories, such Irish nationalist publications as the *Wolfe Tone Annual*, with its celebrations of the 1798 rebellion and its contemporary significance. Such material, and the singing of Irish patriotic songs within the family, created for Heaney, as for most members of the Catholic minority, a set of cultural assumptions and practices profoundly at odds with the dominant Unionist culture of the North. Fostered by an early reading of Celtic heroic stories and by his study of the Irish language for six years at school, this instilled in Heaney a radical sense of being Irish in a state which considered itself British. Although his own family was pacifically nationalist rather than more aggressively republican, there were, of course, real and bitter political grievances inherent in these 'cultural suppositions'. Even prior to the late 1960s the silent awarenesses of religious and cultural division became all too audible every so often: when, for instance, the drums of the twelfth of July – the Loyalist celebration of the battle of the Boyne – filled the air with a noise designed to intimidate Catholics; when one of Heaney's brothers was beaten up after attending a republican meeting; and when Heaney himself experienced the usual aggravations of the minority, being stopped regularly at roadblocks by RUC patrols and by his armed and uniformed neighbours acting in their capacity as the B-Special Constabulary (incidents which lie behind 'The Ministry of Fear' in *North*).

The social forms of Heaney's early life were exclusively

3 'The Irish quest', with Raymond Gardner, *The Guardian*, 2 November 1974, 8.

Catholic: the church, the Gaelic football team and the Catholic village hall were the sole congregating places for a small rural community. His secondary education, at St Columb's College, in Derry city, a Catholic boarding school which also served as the diocesan seminary, powerfully reinforced the religious and cultural context:

There was the sense of a common culture about the place; we were largely Catholic farmers' sons being taught by farmers' sons. The idea of a religious vocation was in the air all the time; not a coercion by any means, but you would have to be stupid or insensitive not to feel the invitation to ponder the priesthood as a destiny. However, in the first year, the way people separated themselves was that those who came with notions of the priesthood would choose Greek and the others chose French. So I chose French.

In attending St Columb's, Heaney was one of the earliest beneficiaries of the 1947 Northern Ireland Education Act, which made a proper secondary education a possibility for the rural farming class Heaney came from, and for the urban working classes of Northern Ireland. In eventually supplying, for the first time, a broad-based professional Catholic middle class in the North, this act of legislation may be considered largely responsible for the release of cultural and political energy there in the 1960s. In addition to Heaney, St Columb's produced a number of other leading figures in the public life of modern Ireland, including the critic Seamus Deane, the dramatist Brian Friel, the politician and leader of the SDLP, John Hume, and the journalist and broadcaster Eamonn McCann, who was one of the organizers of the Civil Rights march in Derry in 1968. Heaney says of the school:

We certainly had some sense of capacity about us. The school was very much geared to getting you through the exams, very academically pitched, and very good at that. Some of the teachers were terrifically dedicated people. We were tuned like violins to play the tune of the exams.

Having successfully played his own tune, Heaney went to Queen's University, Belfast in 1957 to read English Language and Literature, and graduated with a First Class honours degree in 1961. His awareness of a 'split culture' took on a new meaning at the university, as he attempted to hold in the balance the sophistications of a modern literary education and the received ideas and impressions of his childhood. Unlike many university students who have found themselves, for one reason or another, in a broadly comparable position, including those British writers who were the working-class, ambivalent beneficiaries of the 1944 Education Act, Heaney did retain a loyalty to the original culture. In a lecture delivered at Queen's University in 1983 and published as *Among School-children* he tells us that, as well as attending university sherry parties on the Malone Road in Belfast (where he presumably did not drink sherry), he also joined the Bellaghy Pioneer Total Abstinence Association; as well as reading Shakespeare and Oscar Wilde, he was also a member of the Bellaghy Dramatic Society, 'playing Robert Emmet in a one-act melodrama and having my performance hailed in the crowded columns of the *Mid-Ulster Mail*'; as well as discussing loss of faith in Victorian literature, he was driving his mother to Catholic 'evening devotions' and attending at the exposition of the Blessed Sacrament.[4] This gap between parish and academy was to be bridged eventually by his reading of Daniel Corkery's study of eighteenth-century Gaelic poetry, *The Hidden Ireland* (1924), a book which defines, in a nationalist perspective, the achievements of members of an oppressed majority who, in the face of oppression, celebrated and lamented, in the Irish language, their own native culture. The gap was further bridged for Heaney by his discovery of the mixture of Irish Catholic affiliation and alienation in the writings of James Joyce, that exemplary presence who appears at the end of the 'Station Island' sequence.

4 See *Among Schoolchildren* (John Malone Memorial Committee, 1983).

Appendix: On Seamus Heaney's Life

Of the English literature he read at the university, Heaney was most drawn to the densely textured and highly wrought poetry of Webster, Keats and Hopkins. The last is certainly an obtrusive presence behind a stanza from a poem written at university which he prints in the essay 'Feeling into Words' in *Preoccupations*:

Starling thatch-watches, and sudden swallow
Straight breaks to mud-nest, home-rest rafter
Up past dry dust-drunk cobwebs, like laughter
Ghosting the roof of bog-oak, turf-sod and rods of willow.

It is worth noting, nevertheless, that this is not constructed only of what Heaney disparages in that essay as 'frail bucolic images', but that it already contains those much sturdier substances, re-dolent of a real landscape and a real history, the 'turf-sod' which makes its next appearance in 'Digging', the opening poem of Heaney's first book, *Death of a Naturalist*, and the 'bog-oak' which has a poem named after it in his third collec-tion, *Wintering Out*. Although Heaney published one or two such poems in the university magazines *Gorgon* and *Q*, under the pseudonym 'Incertus' ('uncertain, a shy soul fretting and all that', as 'Feeling into Words' has it), he had no sense of con-temporary poetry while he was a student; and indeed it is possi-ble to read the pseudonym as the camouflage of a young male writer conscious that, even in an English department, his own signature may have made him vulnerable to certain kinds of macho Belfast hostility to poetic preciosity or pretension.

In the year after leaving Queen's, Heaney studied for a postgraduate teachers' training diploma at St Joseph's College of Education in Andersonstown, Belfast. This may seem a relatively unambitious course, in those days of opportunity and a reasonable level of funding in British universities, for someone who has just taken a First in English; and, indeed, other possibilities were canvassed:

I always had this notion that I was going to be a secondary school teacher, living the generic life of the newly upwardly mobile eleven-plus Catholic; it was a very passive, conveyor-belt sense of things. But Peter Butter, who was chairman of the English Department then, suggested a studentship at Balliol, or certainly some graduate work at Oxford, and I remember just being bewildered, and my father and mother had absolutely no sense of that. They wouldn't have stopped me, I'm not saying that, but the world I was moving in didn't have any direction for them, the compass needle just *wobbled*. Butter was very encouraging and urged me to do it, but I suppose there was just some lack of confidence, and lack of *nous*, and lack of precedent. I suppose, too, that there was *some* expectation that I would earn, just because of that traditional shape of life – pay something back to the home, you know. So that moment passed.

During his year at St Joseph's, Heaney did write, as one of the requirements of his diploma, an extended essay on literary magazines in the North of Ireland since 1900. This introduced him to some of the important literary and cultural holdings of the Linen Hall Library in Belfast and to the work of the elder Ulster poet, John Hewitt. Heaney considers this 'the glimmering of link-in, the glimmering that writing could occur on your own doorstep'. He also bought Robin Skelton's anthology *Six Irish Poets* in which he encountered, for the first time, some contemporary Irish poetry, notably the poems of Thomas Kinsella, John Montague and Richard Murphy; and he began to read Ted Hughes. These poets, Heaney writes in the preface to a limited edition of his work, were 'more in tune with the actual voices of my own first world than the ironies and elegances of MacNeice and Eliot ever could have been. At last I had discovered sounds in print that connected with the world below and beyond print I had known early on in Co. Derry.'[5] In 1962 he started teaching at St Thomas's Intermediate School in Ballymurphy, Belfast; an 'intermediate school' was

5 *Poems and a Memoir*, selected and illustrated by Henry Pearson with an introduction by Barry Flanagan and a preface by Seamus Heaney (Limited Editions Club, 1982), xviii.

the Ulster name for what, in England, was then known as a 'secondary modern school' – that is, the kind of school attended by less achieving and therefore usually socially disadvantaged children. The headmaster there was Michael McLaverty, the short-story writer, and he introduced Heaney to the poetry of Patrick Kavanagh, lending him *The Great Hunger* (1942) and *A Soul for Sale* (1947). With their rural setting in Co. Monaghan (one of the counties of the historic province of Ulster, though not of the post-Partition province of Northern Ireland), these books reflected an experience very close to Heaney's own, and Kavanagh was to become one of the major points of literary reference for him; he has said in an interview that Kavanagh's great achievement was 'to make our subculture – the rural outback – a cultural resource for us all; to give us images of ourselves'.[6] At this time too Heaney's persistent interest in the academic life led him to register, for a year, for a part-time postgraduate degree in Queen's. He had a thesis on Wordsworth's educational ideas in mind:

I was just floundering really, but there was the kind of neediness and that little sense of destiny which comes with getting a First: that was certainly taken in. And I suppose then the poetry came rushing in as a kind of gap-filler: I felt, well, I didn't do this, and I didn't do that, but maybe I can do this.

Under the compulsion of this 'neediness', and under the direction of these new influences and exemplars, Heaney began to write in earnest in 1962. In November of that year his first poem, 'Tractors', which he disparages now as 'an anxious piece about tractors "gargling sadly astride furrows"', was published in the *Belfast Telegraph*, and shortly afterwards poems were taken by other Irish journals. Especially encouraging was the *Kilkenny Magazine* which, from 'down in the great unknown in the South', took 'Mid-Term Break' early in 1963:

I was kind of eager and wide-eyed. Everything's so inchoate at that time, you're just wanting; there's some bleep calling. The *Kilkenny*

6 Interview, with Caroline Walsh, *Irish Times*, 6 December 1975, 5.

Magazine was a wonderful thing for me because they did 'Mid-Term Break', which was written very quickly one evening in early February, when Christopher's anniversary was coming up. I sent it off and they took it almost by return of post. So that was a terrific sense of confirmation.

During this period, Heaney retained links with Queen's, and in particular with Alan Gabbey, a lecturer there who edited a magazine called *Interest*, in which Heaney published some poems in 1962–3. It was Gabbey who first told Heaney about Philip Hobsbaum, a lecturer who had recently joined the English Department. Hobsbaum, who had read English under Leavis at Cambridge, was a poet himself and an admirer of Ted Hughes. He had organized regular sessions among poets, known as the 'Group', in London since the mid-1950s, in which poems by participants would be read and discussed. Heaney met him when he was initiating similar sessions in Belfast in the autumn of 1963, at about the time Heaney left schoolteaching and returned to St Joseph's as a lecturer in English. Although Hobsbaum's influence has been much disputed by other writers with whom he has been associated, the meetings of the Belfast Group undoubtedly deepened the sense of confirmation Heaney had gained from his earliest publications. In the article 'The Group', written for the Belfast review, *The Honest Ulsterman*, in 1978, and reprinted in *Preoccupations*, Heaney describes Hobsbaum as 'one of the strongest agents of change' in an otherwise apparently moribund literary culture:

When Hobsbaum arrived in Belfast, he moved disparate elements into a single action. He emanated energy, generosity, belief in the community, trust in the parochial, the inept, the unprinted. He was impatient, dogmatic, relentlessly literary: yet he was patient with those he trusted, unpredictably susceptible to a wide variety of poems and personalities and urgent that the social and political exacerbations of our place should disrupt the decorums of literature.

The Group, which at different times included Michael Longley, Derek Mahon, Stewart Parker and James Simmons, met regularly in Hobsbaum's flat until he moved to Glasgow in 1966; and after that the sessions continued in Heaney's own house until 1970, attended in this later period by younger poets such as Paul Muldoon and Frank Ormsby.

In addition to nurturing creative talent, Philip Hobsbaum was also a practised entrepreneur, and he ensured that the work of the Belfast Group was brought to public attention. The poets were given some exposure in the Belfast Festival of 1965 which the journalist Mary Holland wrote up for the *Observer* in London, describing what she considered a cultural flowering in the city. The Festival produced a series of poetry pamphlets which, in addition to titles by Longley and Mahon, included, in November, Heaney's first slim collection, *Eleven Poems*. Heaney is, however, resistant to the idea of a Belfast 'renaissance' in the mid-1960s, considering it 'a media event': 'There was something there, but then there was something everywhere at that time: Liverpool, Newcastle – it was all the buoyancies.' It is notable that when, in July 1966, he was given the opportunity to write at some length about Belfast in the 'Out of London' column in the *New Statesman*, he chose to use most of his space to analyse the deteriorating political situation and the ominous emergence of Ian Paisley, writing powerfully and resentfully for the Catholic position. Confining his description of the artistic scene to his concluding paragraphs, he nevertheless observed, with what optimism he could muster, that 'the possibility of a cultural life here is the possibility of salvation.'[7]

By the time *Eleven Poems* was published, Heaney's own literary career was well under way. Hobsbaum had sent 'Group-sheets' – versions of poems xeroxed for discussion – to the poet and critic Edward Lucie-Smith, an associate from the days of the London Group, who forwarded them to various literary editors. Karl Miller of the *New Statesman* took three of Heaney's poems – 'Digging', 'Storm on the Island' and 'Scaffolding' – which he published together on 4 December 1964:

7 'Out of London: Ulster's Troubles', *New Statesman*, 1 July 1966, 23–4.

Then inside six weeks or so I had a letter from Fabers. I just couldn't believe it, it was like getting a letter from God the Father. I had a collection of poems at that time with Dolmen Press in Dublin. I left it with them for about a month after I got the Faber letter and wrote and asked them had they taken any decision. I didn't say anything about Fabers, I felt that I could play *some* cards. Liam Miller sent the manuscript back to me and said they weren't quite sure. So I felt I acted honourably enough at Dolmen. If they'd said they were going to accept it, I might have been in a different position.

This was not, however, the manuscript that became *Death of a Naturalist*:

Charles Monteith of Fabers asked me in January [1965] did I have a manuscript. I sent them what I had and they didn't think there was a book there but they would like first refusal if ever I thought I had a book. So in about four months I wrote a hell of a lot, and I think I sent them another thing in about May or June. I got married in August and we went to London for our honeymoon, and by then they said they were going to take it. So it all happened very quickly.

Heaney had married Marie Devlin, whom he first met in October 1962. From a large family in Ardboe, Co. Tyrone, she had done a course in English and Speech and Drama at St Mary's College of Education in Belfast, and was teaching in intermediate school at the time of her marriage. The Heaneys had a son, Michael, in July 1966. Another son, Christopher, was born in February 1968, and a daughter, Catherine Ann, in April 1973.

In May 1966, when Heaney was twenty-seven, Fabers published his first full-length collection, *Death of a Naturalist*. It received, for a first volume, extraordinary critical acclaim. In England, Christopher Ricks in the *New Statesman* thought it 'outstanding'; C. B. Cox in the *Spectator* called it 'the best first book of poems I've read for some time', and Alan Ross in the *London Magazine* considered it 'a book of enormous promise'. In Ireland, John Hewitt in the *Belfast Telegraph* said that 'we confidently expect him to broaden his range and our imaginative estate'; Michael Longley in the *Irish Times* believed that 'his childhood landscape has acquired the validity of myth'; and the senior poet in the Republic, Austin Clarke, reviewing it on Radio Eireann, said that 'unlike most first books, this one is mature and certain in its touch.' Heaney received a Gregory Award for young writers, and subsequently *Death of a Naturalist* earned him the Somerset Maugham Award and the Geoffrey Faber Prize, the first of numerous literary awards which Heaney has collected, culminating in the Nobel Prize for Literature in 1995. The critical reception was obviously an enormous stimulus and encouragement to Heaney. It was also practically useful to him in being, no doubt, one of the factors which secured him a lectureship in English at Queen's on Philip Hobsbaum's departure for Glasgow in 1966.

Prior to that, in 1965, Heaney had begun to publish articles and reviews in various journals in England: he wrote an account of producing a mystery play in St Joseph's College, for instance, called 'A Chester Pageant' which he published in the teachers' journal, *The Use of English* in Autumn 1965, and he reviewed educational books for the *New Statesman*. In 1966 this kind of work broadened to include more comprehensive topical articles for the *New Statesman* and the *Listener*, and broadcasts for BBC radio and television: he became a well-known communicator, on both cultural and political matters, in the late 1960s and early 1970s. This may be regarded as a translation into other areas of the educational career he had always imagined for himself, and it still persists in a more than usual accessibility for a poet held in high regard.

In Heaney's first years as a lecturer at Queen's, the situation in Northern Ireland became more dangerous and tense, as the Civil Rights movement among Catholics gathered momentum and was met with fierce opposition from Protestant Loyalists and from the Royal Ulster Constabulary. On Saturday 5 October 1968, in Derry city, one of the most economically depressed areas even in Northern Ireland, the first major violent clash of the present 'Troubles' occurred when 2000 civil rights marchers, protesting mainly against gerrymandering (vote-rigging) and discriminatory housing allocations, defied a ban by the Home Affairs Minister, William Craig. Eighty-eight were injured in police baton charges, and television coverage of the march that evening was greeted with international outrage. Rioting followed in the Catholic Bogside area of Derry, and a few days later a large student protest march in Belfast city centre was organized from Queen's. Violence continued throughout Northern Ireland in the following months, and on 12 August 1969 there occurred the sectarian clashes in Derry which became known as the 'Battle of the Bogside'. On 14 August the British Army entered the city; and in January 1970 the Provisional IRA was officially formed in Dublin.

Heaney was himself involved in the Civil Rights movement, and after the 5 October 1968 march in Derry he wrote a piece in the *Listener*, 'Old Derry's Walls' (24 October 1968), on 'the indignation and determination of the civil rights marchers' and on Craig's 'bland indifference'. 'It seems now,' he said, 'that the Catholic minority, if it is to retain any self-respect, will have to risk the charge of wrecking the new moderation and seeking justice more vociferously.' The composer Sean O'Riada (for whom Heaney was later to write an elegy in *Field Work*) presented a programme on Radio Eireann and asked Heaney for a contribution. He provided a bitterly satirical song called 'Craig's Dragoons', to be sung to the Loyalist tune, 'Dolly's Brae':

Come all ye Ulster loyalists and in full chorus join,
Think on the deeds of Craig's Dragoons who strike below the groin,
And drink a toast to the truncheon and the armoured water-hose
That mowed a swathe through Civil Rights and spat on Papish clothes.

We've gerrymandered Derry but Croppy won't lie down,
He calls himself a citizen and wants votes in the town.
But that Saturday in Duke Street we slipped the velvet glove –

The iron hand of Craig's Dragoons soon crunched a croppy
   dove...

O William Craig, you are our love, our lily and our sash,
You have the boys who fear no noise, who'll batter and
   who'll bash.
They'll cordon and they'll baton-charge, they'll silence
   protest tunes,
They are the hounds of Ulster, boys, sweet William Craig's
   dragoons.

Heaney only once subsequently wrote such a directly political
song – a lamentation for the dead of Bloody Sunday, 30 January
1972, when thirteen civilians were killed by the British Army in
Derry, the event also commemorated in 'Casualty' in *Field
Work*. Written for the late Luke Kelly of the Dubliners folk
group, the song, called 'The Road to Derry', which Heaney
wanted Kelly to sing to the tune of the nationalist song 'The
Boys of Mullaghbawn', was withheld from publication, but
eventually published in part in the *Derry Journal* and reprinted
in the London *Sunday Times* to commemorate the twenty-fifth
anniversary of the event in 1997. Its final verse reads:

My heart besieged by anger, my mind a gap of danger,
I walked among their old haunts, the home ground where
   they bled;
And in the dirt lay justice like an acorn in the winter
Till its oak would sprout in Derry where the thirteen men
   lay dead.[8]

The image of resurgence or resurrection in the final line – which
is also a reference to the 'oakwood' that is 'doire', and then
'Derry', in Irish – is very similar to that of the final line of 'Re-
quiem for the Croppies' in *Door into the Dark* in 1969; and the
continuity of Heaney's Irish nationalist sympathies in that

8 'Nobel poet discloses his despair at Bloody Sunday', *The Sunday Times*,
2 February 1997, 3.

period – to which he presumably still gives some allegiance in 1997, when any inquiry beyond the bland exculpations of the Widgery tribunal has still been lacking – is manifest. This makes the title of the article in the London *Sunday Times* which reprinted the poem from the *Derry Journal* – 'Nobel poet discloses his despair at Bloody Sunday' – something of an obfuscation of the quality of the song's actual feeling, which is not so much 'despair' as an abiding anger, resentment and desire for prosecution and reparation.

Heaney's second volume, *Door into the Dark*, was published in June 1969. Although it was made a Choice of the Poetry Book Society, a number of reviewers, while appreciative, thought they sensed something transitional in the book – 'a formidable talent', as the poet Norman Nicholson put it, 'biding his time before the bigger gesture'. In the summer of 1969 Heaney was actually in Madrid during a visit to France and Spain with money from the Somerset Maugham Award of the previous year: he watched the events in the North on Spanish television, somewhat guiltily, as he remembers in 'Summer 1969' in the 'Singing School' sequence of *North*. It was immediately clear to him that the experience of 1969 must put its pressure on his own work, as he explains in 'Feeling into Words' in *Preoccupations*:

From that moment the problems of poetry moved from being simply a matter of achieving the satisfactory verbal icon to being a search for images and symbols adequate to our predicament ... I felt it imperative to discover a field of force in which ... it would be possible to encompass the perspectives of a humane reason and at the same time to grant the religious intensity of the violence its deplorable authenticity and complexity.

When he read P. V. Glob's *The Bog People*, published in the same year, Heaney realized that his search for such 'images and symbols' had made one of its major discoveries. With its account of propitiatory Iron Age ritual killings in Jutland, and its extraordinarily compelling photographs of the bodies of the victims – preserved for two thousand years by the chemical properties of the peat bogs in which they had been buried – Glob's book seemed to offer an imaginative parallel for the Irish present. Heaney's meditation on it was eventually to produce his sequence of 'bog poems'. He also, however, began to publish, in literary journals and reviews, some poems more straightforwardly addressed to the situation in the North – among them the poem 'Intimidation', which appeared in the Canadian journal *The Malahat Review* (no. 17, 1970). It angrily bites out its resentment against the threatening Loyalist bonfires of the twelfth of July:

> Each year this reek
> Of their midsummer madness
> Troubles him, a nest of pismires
> At his drystone walls.
>
> Ghetto rats! Are they the ones
> To do the smoking out?
> They'll come streaming past
> To taste their ashes yet.

Several reviewers of Heaney's next collection, *Wintering Out* (1972) were disappointed that such poems as this did not appear in the book; and *North* (1975), which did reprint some of them (but not 'Intimidation'), was perhaps, at least in part, a response to these reviews. The more oblique strategy of the poems Heaney did collect in *Wintering Out* may be regarded, among other things, as an aspect of his response to the developing 'complexity' of the violence after the eruption into Northern affairs of the Provisional IRA in 1970, and particularly after the stepping-up of their bombing campaign in 1971. After that, this kind of pugnacity would have been liable to misconstruction, to too casual an assimilation to positions with which Heaney would not be identified.

Heaney spent the academic year of 1970–71 in America, at the University of California at Berkeley, where he read William

Carlos Williams properly for the first time, later remarking in an interview that 'in the poems of *Wintering Out*, in the little quatrain shapes, there are signs of that loosening, the California spirit.'[9] He also encountered the poetry of Gary Snyder, Robert Bly and Robert Duncan, and its engagement with protest against the war in Vietnam. He learnt from it a lesson he could apply to his own work in a different political context – the 'awareness' that poetry is 'a force, almost a mode of power, certainly a mode of resistance'.[10] The year in America was also, however, 'a very Irish year too': Heaney got to know Tom Flanagan, the author of a book called *The Irish Novelists 1800–1850* (1959), and 'his concern with Irish history and literature, and his learning in it, were somehow fortifying, and gave me a conviction about the Irish theme, as it were.' Heaney's poem 'Traditions', in *Wintering Out*, is dedicated to Flanagan; and Flanagan was later to publish his novel about the 1798 rebellion, *The Year of the French* (1979), in which, it has been said, the poet MacCarthy is partly based on Heaney.

Even in California, then, Heaney's mind was never far from Ireland: one of his pieces in the *Listener* that year noted grimly that 'while Berkeley shouts, Belfast burns'; and he began there a series of prose-poems which return once more to the world of his childhood in Co. Derry. Heaney did not complete the sequence in America, and was put off doing so by the appearance, in 1971, of Geoffrey Hill's volume of prose-poems, *Mercian Hymns*. 'What I had regarded as stolen marches in a form new to me had been headed off by a work of complete authority,' he says in his preface to the eventual publication of the sequence, as a pamphlet called *Stations*, from the *Honest Ulsterman* press in Belfast in 1975, after he had completed it in May and June 1974. The sequence is of great interest, marking that vital moment in Heaney's career when – again as he has it in his preface, and as opposed to his first two books – 'the sectarian dimension of that

9 With James Randall, *Ploughshares*, vol. 5 no. 3 (1979), 7–22, 20.
10 Ibid.

pre-reflective experience presented itself as something asking to be uttered also.' He acknowledges the significance of these poems when he reprints seven of them in his *Selected Poems 1966–1987* (1990).

When Heaney returned to Northern Ireland in September 1971, the situation had further deteriorated. Internment without trial had been introduced the previous month, and, as he wrote in the piece collected in *Preoccupations* as 'Christmas, 1971' – an article fraught with the anxiety, depression and tension of its moment – 'It hasn't been named martial law, but that's what it feels like.' By the time *Wintering Out* was published, however, in November 1972, Heaney had left the North for the Republic. He had resigned from his job at Queen's and moved, in August 1972, to a cottage in Glanmore, near Ashford, a very beautiful, secluded area in Co. Wicklow, about twenty miles from Dublin, where he began to work as a freelance writer. Heaney has offered various explanations for the move, and it seems clear that there were artistic, practical and political reasons for it. Afraid of becoming locked into familiar patterns of working in Belfast, he wanted, as he says in the foreword to *Preoccupations*, 'to put the practice of poetry more deliberately at the centre of my life. It was a kind of test.' In practical terms, he had been offered the Glanmore cottage at an extremely low rent by the Canadian academic, Ann Saddlemeyer; this, together with the fact that in the Republic writers' incomes are untaxed, was obviously an attraction for a man with a family giving up a salaried job. But the move also, as Heaney of course realized, had an 'emblematic' significance. It was read as a decisive political alignment: literally *read*, since Ian Paisley's paper, the *Protestant Telegraph*, bade farewell to 'the well-known papist propagandist' on his return to 'his spiritual home in the popish republic', and the *Irish Times* in Dublin welcomed him with an editorial headlined 'Ulster Poet Moves South'. Heaney's most revealing interpretation of the 'emblem' of his move occurs in an interview with his close friend Seamus Deane in the *New York Times Book Review* in 1979, where he offers his opinion that, whereas for the Northern Protestant writer, the Troubles could be regarded as a mere 'interruption' of the status quo:

For the Catholic writer, I think the Troubles were a critical moment, a turning point, possibly a vision of some kind of fulfilment. The blueprint in the Catholic writer's head predicted that a history would fulfil itself in a United Ireland or in something ... In the late '60s and early '70s the world was changing for the Catholic imagination. I felt I was compromising some part of myself by staying in a situation where socially and, indeed, imaginatively, there were pressures 'against' regarding the moment as critical. Going to the South was perhaps emblematic for me and was certainly so for some of the people I knew. To the Unionists it looked like a betrayal of the Northern thing.[11]

The move nevertheless inevitably occasioned anxieties – about missing a major historical moment and being thought to have abandoned a responsibility. Such self-doubt, together with the media attention the move received, fuels one of Heaney's finest poems, 'Exposure', which concludes *North*.

In Glanmore Heaney immediately set to work on a version of the long medieval Irish poem, *Buile Suibhne* (literally, *The Madness of Sweeney*):

I was going to be free and I wanted to make sure I had tasks to fill my life. I was thinking of myself as a professional writer for the first time, and I thought of it as a kind of freelance writer's enterprise, among other things: I had a half-notion that I might get a children's story out of it, and a radio programme. I'd spoken to an actor, Jacky Mac-Gowran, a wonderful man, whom I thought of as a Sweeney, perhaps, and he expressed an interest. Then when he died in 1973 a little bit of the steam went out of it for me. But the prose sections were written with the notion of a radio link, almost: that's why they were chastened down from their rather euphuistic shape in the original.

A first version of the whole text was completed very quickly, by April 1973, done with 'a strong sense of bending the text to my

11 'Talk', with Seamus Deane, *New York Times Book Review*, 2 December 1979, 47–8.

purposes' (St Ronan, for instance, was referred to as 'the bully boy', when the Unionists were accused of using 'bully boy tactics' in the North; and Sweeney was given such lines as 'My relief was a pivot of history'). Deciding that this version was too 'infected with the idiom of the moment', Heaney put it aside for as long as seven years (apart from the section he called 'Sweeney Praises the Trees', which he recited occasionally at readings). Then, after a semester in Harvard in 1979, he 'just jumped on it' again while staying with his family in a house on Long Island lent to him by Tom Flanagan. This time he knew he wanted it to be 'bare and fairly obedient and plain and strict in some way'; and, returning to Ireland, he completed it over the next year or so and first published it, as *Sweeney Astray*, in 1983.

It is hardly surprising that the first version was so attuned to the contemporary moment, since Heaney was working simultaneously on those poems of his which most directly confront Northern sectarianism, the poems of *North* itself, which eventually appeared in June 1975. Keeping the promise made in the opening line of 'The Tollund Man', he had in fact visited Denmark, in October 1973, and had seen in the museum at Silkeborg there the preserved bodies described in *The Bog People*.[12] His growing belief in the relevance and usefulness of this material to his own work was confirmed when Ted Hughes enthusiastically greeted the earliest bog poems and encouraged him to go on with them. Hughes's sister, Olwyn, published a limited edition of the whole series, as *Bog Poems*, from her Rainbow Press in 1975.[13]

---

12 In the line 'Some day I will go to Aarhus' Heaney is more concerned with euphony than actuality, knowing, of course, that the bodies are in Silkeborg, not Aarhus.

13 An excellent account of the affinities between Hughes and Heaney in this regard is provided by Neil Rhodes in '"Bridegroom to the Goddess": Hughes, Heaney and the Elizabethans', in Mark Thornton Burnett and Ramona Wray (eds.), *Shakespeare and Ireland: History, Politics, Culture* (Macmillan, 1997), 152–72.

The archaeologizing appetite of Heaney's imagination was also being fed at this time by events in Dublin itself:

Irish archaeology was on the move in the late sixties and early seventies. When I came down here [to Co. Wicklow] there were excavations going on, and the revisionism about the Vikings was in the air. I had a sympathetic interest in it – not very systematically reading up on it, but I knew Tom Delaney [the archaeologist recalled in 'Station Island VIII'] and through him I got some little flicker of intimacy with it. I remember going to the *Viking Dublin* exhibition in the National Museum and seeing the child's drawing and the combs, the little scale-pans and so on. I was terrifically awakened to all the Bronze Age stuff; I used to love the gold. It was just that my receiving stations were open for it for a couple of years.

It was during this period too that Heaney began, or deepened, his study of three poets who have profoundly affected his subsequent work: Dante, Yeats, and the modern Russian poet Osip Mandelstam.

North was greeted with great critical acclaim in the English press, most reviewers delighted that Northern Ireland had finally found what they considered appropriate expression in poetry. Martin Dodsworth's review in the *Guardian*, which declared the book 'unequalled in our contemporary poetry as a testimony to the patience, persistence and power of the imagination under duress', may be considered representative, if more enthusiastic than some. Of particular note was Conor Cruise O'Brien's account in the *Listener*: 'I had the uncanny feeling, reading these poems,' he wrote, 'of listening to the thing itself, the actual substance of historical agony and dissolution, the tragedy of a people in a place: the Catholics of Northern Ireland.' The book's reception in Northern Ireland itself was markedly less warm: in *The Honest Ulsterman* the poet Ciaran Carson castigated Heaney as 'the laureate of violence – a mythmaker, an anthropologist of ritual killing', and Edna Longley thought that 'a poet who has already articulated so much of the experience of his people and country in oblique terms has no need to prove his credentials.'

Appendix: On Seamus Heaney's Life

In a 'Books of the Year' column for the *Observer* the Christmas after *North* was published, however, the eminent American poet Robert Lowell described it as 'a new kind of political poetry by the best Irish poet since W. B. Yeats'. When Heaney was awarded the Duff Cooper Memorial Prize for the volume the following year, it was Lowell who presented it to him. Many critics have discerned the influence of Lowell on Heaney's work, particularly on the poems in his next book, *Field Work* (1979), which included an elegy for Lowell, who died in 1977. Heaney also gave the address at his memorial service in London, and clearly the relationship, though brief, was an important one for him:

The first time I met him was in 1972 in London. The night he got married to Caroline [Blackwood], there was a party in Sonia Orwell's, and Karl Miller, whom I was staying with, took me over to it. We talked a bit then, but I was extremely shy of him, because he had this aura of a great classic: when I was an undergraduate we were reading 'The Quaker Graveyard' in that old Geoffrey Moore anthology of American poetry. Then when *History* and *For Lizzie and Harriet* and *The Dolphin* came out together in 1973 I did a thing on *Imprint* on the radio, and he got a copy of it and wrote and thanked me. I never thought much about it, but later I wrote and asked him would he do a reading in Kilkenny [at an arts festival Heaney was involved in there in 1975]. He spent a week in Kilkenny and stayed on afterwards and came to see us in Wicklow. That was a wonderful, happy time. Then he used to come here with Caroline; they had a flat out in the big house, Castletown, and we went out for meals and so on. I find that in the matter of relationships with writers and confirmations from writers, it's not necessary always to talk about poetry; it's a sensation that you have, and an instinct you have, that the other person regards you somehow, and that's a kind of fortification of your own confidence. In a sense, that's more important than any technical thing that can be said. I felt I got that from Lowell a bit. But I must also say that when I read those *Lizzie and Harriet* books, I loved the ignorance, I loved the destruction he had practised upon the lyric. It may have been an error in the end but, at that particular moment, the bull-headedness, the rage and uncharmingness of the writing attracted me enormously. I mean, it may have been an error, but there was some kind of morality about it, I thought. But I love *Near the Ocean* too, those Marvellian stanzas; I think that 'Waking Early Sunday Morning' is a terrific poem, it's a great, public, noble piece of work. And then *Life Studies* is a kind of necessary book, you know, it's *the* book, in some ways.

The radio programme Heaney refers to there, *Imprint*, was one he hosted himself on Radio Eireann intermittently between 1973 and 1977. This was done 'as journeywork, to make money'; but he came to feel, by 1975, that he would have to return to a full-time job in order to buy a house in Dublin itself. He joined the English Department at Carysfort, a tea-chers' training college in Dublin, in October 1975, and the family eventually moved into Dublin in November 1976, to the Edwardian house in Sandymount which they still occupy. Heaney was appointed Head of Department in Carysfort in 1976 and stayed in that post until 1981. He regards the decision to take the original job as, in some ways, a 'caving-in':

I felt there was something terrifically enabling and freeing about the risks and exposure of living in Wicklow in that way, and you had to prove yourself. In order to prove yourself, you had to feel you had achieved something in your art, that you had verified your life. Somehow when you get onto the cushions of a salaried position, that neediness and sense of danger disappears. It's a different kind of engagement with the world, of course, but I'm ever grateful for that little moment of 'exposure'.

What he did initially like about the job, however – its offering him a less public role than he felt he would have had in a uni-versity in the Republic, 'a little lean-to that would shelter me with a salary and leave me alone' – came to have its drawbacks too. In addition to feeling himself 'crumbling down into an ad-ministrator again', the Irish Catholic forms and presuppositions of the institution seemed to be demanding from him a degree of ratification which he felt increasingly unable to give.

From the early 1970s, Heaney's reputation had been growing

in America and, in 1979, the year he published *Field Work* – a book whose character derives largely from his 'pastoral' years in Glanmore – he had spent a term in Harvard as one of several temporary successors to Robert Lowell, who had taught a poetry workshop there. At the end of 1980, he was offered a five-year contract by Harvard, to teach there for one term a year; and, having decided in 1981 to resign from his job at Carysfort, he started at Harvard in January 1982. In 1984 he was elected to the Boylston Chair of Rhetoric and Oratory there. Since he began teaching at Harvard, Heaney has divided his time between America and Dublin, spending four months a year in Harvard, where he conducts poetry workshops with students he has himself selected:

It's the sort of thing that went on in the Group in Belfast, except that it's a bit more ritualized, and the system permits it in America. It's actually quite exhausting, because you are like the centre of a target, and there are twenty-eight human arrows coming at you all the time flighted with manuscripts, and each time you meet one of them there's a judgement to be made, and there's a *tactful* judgement to be made.

Heaney is delighted with, and grateful for, the audience his work has attracted in the States, but still surprised by it:

Their noise isn't my noise, their concerns aren't my concerns. Luckily, the English language and the art of verse sometimes link us but I'm puzzled, in a way, that they can actually *read* some of the stuff. It's the texture and the inner dynamics of a poem that interest them, and of course poems have to be able to live in that way. My impatience with a lot of American poetry is that that's the *only* way it can live. In one way, of course, that's all there is: there's just a form, and there's a form housing a set of harmonies and balances. But I think that in the culture and situation I come from, you want to punish the form with some relationship to the actual. It seems to me that in a lot of contemporary American poetry the words have less specific gravity than they have within the language in Ireland and Britain. They are on a kind of bouncy moonwalk, the language just *floats*. There's a kind of wafting garrulousness about it. Our difficulty here is something opposite; it's a kind of cross-legged, prim-mouthed thing.

Much as Heaney admires, then, some American poets who are more or less his contemporaries – Robert Pinsky, Robert Hass and Frank Bidart, for instance – he feels most affinity, in the States, with three expatriate poets: Derek Walcott from the Caribbean; Joseph Brodsky from Russia; and Czesław Miłosz from Poland:[14]

Walcott didn't divest himself of what are, in one way, the marks of the conqueror, in another way the resources of English tradition. His negotiation between poles, the exterior pole of literature, London and the world out there, and the inner pole of the Caribbean – it kind of interested me, that balance. I first met Brodsky at the time when I had just started out in Wicklow, and I liked his sense of exile and his intensity – someone absolutely a poet, you know. The three of us have a language which involves English literature, in a way, and involves a different sense of the world of literature from most American poetry. Miłosz I just find enormously close: the wonderful sense of loss of what is most cherished, and the way he can turn what, in lesser hands or with a lesser writer, would be a poem of personal nostalgia into a symptom of great cultural and historical change, without portentousness. That move from personal lyric lament to visionary, tragic lamentation: I just love the note. And he's so stern too, he's both stern and tender, and I like that very much. And I guess somewhere in it all is a closeness because of the kind of Catholic subculture into which his sensibility pays, and out of which it springs. It's not a note that you hear in English language poetry very much because, both in America and in England, the religious sensibility has been bred out of the poetry.

1980 was a stocktaking year for Heaney, with the simultaneous publication of his *Selected Poems 1965–1975* and his collection of prose pieces, *Preoccupations*, in October. In 1982 he co-edited with Ted Hughes a poetry anthology for older children, *The Rattle Bag* (which includes his translation of a Middle English poem, 'The Names of the Hare'), and in 1983 he published *Sweeney Astray* in Ireland. It was published in England simultaneously with *Station Island* in October 1984.

14 Joseph Brodsky died in January 1996.

Appendix: On Seamus Heaney's Life

The decision to publish *Sweeney Astray* first in Ireland was made as the result of Heaney's directorship, along with several others, including Tom Paulin and Seamus Deane, of the Field Day company. This was initially a theatre company formed in Derry in 1980 by Heaney's close friend the playwright Brian Friel, and the actor Stephen Rea, to produce Friel's play *Translations* outside the commercial theatre. The play, set in 1833, locates a crucial moment in the death of the Irish language, making of it an implicit parable for the Irish present. Its examination of Irish history, and its directed effort to address the relationship between Ireland and England, thereby making an intervention in the cultural politics of the North, may be seen as the essential signatures of Field Day. It is in this context that Heaney viewed the initial publication of *Sweeney Astray*:

The act of publishing is a sign, a gesture, a form of solidarity; and I always thought that when *Sweeney* came out I would publish it in Ireland. When we started Field Day, I liked the idea of it being published in Derry. It's a kind of all-Ireland event situated just within the North, and there's a little bit of submerged political naughtiness in that. This was one of the reasons I translated the placenames into their modern equivalents: I hoped that gradually the Northern Unionist or Northern Protestant readership might, in some minuscule way, feel free to identify with the Gaelic tradition.

In 1983 Heaney also published with Field Day a fairly lengthy pamphlet poem, *An Open Letter*. This received considerable media attention, since in it he dissociates himself from the adjective 'British' under which he was classified by Blake Morrison and Andrew Motion, the editors of the *Penguin Book of Contemporary British Poetry* (1982):

> Caesar's Britain, its *partes tres*,
> United England, Scotland, Wales,
> *Britannia* in the old tales,
> Is common ground.
> *Hibernia* is where the Gaels
> Made a last stand

And long ago were stood upon –
End of simple history lesson.
As empire rings its curtain down
This 'British' word
Sticks deep in native and *colon*
Like Arthur's sword.

Heaney's subsequent doubts about the advisability of publishing that poem are one measure of his characteristic hesitation between declaration and withdrawal:

I advance and retire from any conscious or deliberate entry into that public life. I've got so much attention that my impulse is to retreat rather than to go forward at this stage. I don't know whether that's an irresponsibility or a salutary piece of survival. I just don't know; these are questions that I'm not too clear about myself.

The 'attention' is not in any doubt: Seamus Heaney is enormously popular. His books sell exceptionally well for a contemporary poet; he has received a large number of honorary doctorates from universities throughout the world; from 1989 to 1994 he was Professor of Poetry at Oxford; and he was the recipient of the ultimate accolade, the Nobel Prize for Literature, in 1995. He has indeed been what he has one of his ghosts in 'Station Island' call him, a 'poet, lucky poet'.

It is significant, however, that that remark is made in a context which turns recognition into something very like rebuke; and the self-accusations of his later work define an uncomplacent refusal to stay still, to rest secure in any fixed position – particularly, perhaps, the fixed position of his own reputation. If being 'in between' was a *donnée* of his birth, his exemplary quality derives from his disciplined, resourceful and subtle negotiation of boundaries which he has chosen, as well as been chosen by; and his work may be admiringly characterized in the terms of approbation he has on occasion offered others, citing a remark of Marina Tsvetaeva's: it is inscribed with 'the good force of creative mind at work in the light of conscience'.

Select Bibliography

Books by Seamus Heaney

(all published by Faber and Faber unless otherwise stated)

Death of a Naturalist (1966)
Door into the Dark (1969)
Wintering Out (1972)
North (1975)
Stations (Ulsterman Publications, 1975)
Field Work (1979)
Preoccupations: Selected Prose 1968–1978 (1980)
Selected Poems 1965–1975 (1980)
The Rattle Bag: An Anthology of Poetry, selected by Seamus Heaney
   and Ted Hughes (1982)
Sweeney Astray (Field Day Theatre Company, 1983; Faber and Faber,
   1984)
An Open Letter (Field Day Theatre Company, 1983)
Station Island (1984)
The Haw Lantern (1987)
*The Government of the Tongue: The 1986 T. S. Eliot Memorial Lec-
   tures and Other Critical Writings* (1988)
The Place of Writing (Scolars Press, n.d.; lectures delivered in 1988)
The Cure at Troy: A Version of Sophocles's 'Philoctetes' (1990)
New Selected Poems 1966–1987 (1990)
Seeing Things (1991)
The Midnight Verdict (Gallery Press, 1993)
The Redress of Poetry: Oxford Lectures (1995)
Jan Kochanowski, *Laments*, translated by Seamus Heaney and
   Stanisław Barańczak (1995)

Crediting Poetry: The Nobel Lecture 1995 (Gallery Press, 1995)
The Spirit Level (1996)
The School Bag, ed. Seamus Heaney and Ted Hughes (1997)
Homage to Robert Frost [with Joseph Brodsky and Derek Walcott] (1997)

Books on Seamus Heaney

Allen, Michael (ed.), *Seamus Heaney* (Macmillan New Casebooks, 1997)

Andrews, Elmer, *The Poetry of Seamus Heaney: All the Realms of Whisper* (Macmillan, 1988)

– (ed.), *Seamus Heaney: A Collection of Critical Essays* (Macmillan, 1992)

Bloom, Harold (ed.), *Seamus Heaney: Modern Critical Views* (Chelsea House, 1986)

Byron, Catherine, *Out of Step: Pursuing Seamus Heaney to Purgatory* (Loxwood Stoneleigh, 1992)

Curtis, Tony (ed.), *The Art of Seamus Heaney* (Seren, 1982; third ed., 1994)

Foster, John Wilson, *The Achievement of Seamus Heaney* (Lilliput Press, 1995)

Foster, T. C., *Seamus Heaney* (O'Brien Press, 1989)

Garratt, Robert F. (ed.), *Critical Essays on Seamus Heaney* (G. K. Hall, 1995)

Hart, Henry, *Seamus Heaney: Poet of Contrary Progressions* (Syracuse University Press, 1992)

Molino, Michael R., *Questioning Tradition, Language, and Myth: The Poetry of Seamus Heaney* (Catholic University of America Press, 1994)

Morrison, Blake, *Seamus Heaney* (Methuen, 1982)

Murphy, Andrew, *Seamus Heaney* (Northcote House in association with the British Council, 1996)

O'Donoghue, Bernard, *Seamus Heaney and the Language of Poetry* (Harvester Wheatsheaf, 1994)

Parker, Michael, *Seamus Heaney: The Making of the Poet* (Macmillan, 1993)

Tamplin, Ronald, *Seamus Heaney* (Open University Press, 1989)

Select Bibliography

Vendler, Helen, *The Breaking of Style: Hopkins, Heaney, Graham*
(Harvard University Press, 1995)

Other Texts Cited

Aeschylus, *The Oresteia*, trs. Robert Fagles (Penguin Books, 1976)

Allen, Michael, 'The Parish and the Dream: Heaney and America,
1969–1987', *The Southern Review*, vol. 31 no. 3 (July 1995), 726–38

Auden, W. H., *The Dyer's Hand and other essays* (Faber and Faber,
1963; 1975 edn.)

Bachelard, Gaston, *The Poetics of Space* (1958; Beacon Books edn.,
1969)

Barańczak, Stanisław, 'Polishing the sonnet sequence: Reflections of a
Polish translator on Seamus Heaney's "Clearances"', in Hans-
Christian Oeser (ed.), *Transverse* II: *Seamus Heaney in Translation*
(Irish Translators' Association, 1994), 83–96

Benjamin, Walter, *Illuminations* (1970; Fontana edn., 1973)

Bloom, Harold, *The Anxiety of Influence* (Oxford University Press,
1973)

Brown, Richard, 'Bog Poems and Book Poems: Doubleness, Self-
Translation and Pun in Seamus Heaney and Paul Muldoon', in Neil
Corcoran (ed.), *The Chosen Ground: Essays on the Contemporary
Poetry of Northern Ireland* (Seren, 1992), 153–67

Corcoran, Neil, 'Heaney's Joyce, Eliot's Yeats', *Agenda*, vol. 27 no. 1
(Spring 1989), 37–47

– *English Poetry Since* 1940 (Longman, 1993)

– *After Yeats and Joyce: Reading Modern Irish Literature* (Oxford
University Press, 1997)

Coughlan, Patricia, '"Bog Queens": The Representation of Women in
the Poetry of John Montague and Seamus Heaney', in Toni O'Brien
Johnson and David Cairns (eds.), *Gender in Irish Writing* (Open
University Press, 1991), 99–111

Cronin, Michael, *Translating Ireland: Translation, Languages, Cul-
tures* (Cork University Press, 1996)

Cullingford, Elizabeth Butler, '"Thinking of Her ... as ... Ireland":
Yeats, Pearse and Heaney', *Textual Practice*, vol. 4 no. 1 (1990),
1–21

– 'Seamus and Sinéad: From "Limbo" to *Saturday Night Live* by way
of *Hush-a-Bye Baby*', *Colby Quarterly*, vol. xxx no. 1 (March 1994)

Deane, Seamus, *Celtic Revivals* (Faber and Faber, 1985)

Devlin, Polly, *All Of Us There* (Pan, 1983)

Docherty, Thomas, *Alterities: Criticism, History, Representation* (Clarendon Press, 1996)

Dunn, Douglas (ed.), *Two Decades of Irish Writing* (Carcanet, 1975)

Eliot, T. S., 'Critical Note', in *The Collected Poems of Harold Monro*, ed. Alida Monro (Cobden-Sanderson, 1933), xiii–xvi

– *The Use of Poetry and the Use of Criticism: Studies in the Relation of Criticism to Poetry in England* (Faber and Faber, 1933)

– *Selected Prose*, ed. John Hayward (Penguin, 1953)

– *On Poetry and Poets* (Faber and Faber, 1957)

– *Selected Essays* (Faber and Faber, 1932; 1969 edn.)

Fennell, Desmond, 'Whatever You Say, Say Nothing: Why Seamus Heaney is No. 1', *Stand*, vol. 32 no. 4 (Autumn 1991), 38–65

Graves, Robert, *The White Goddess* (Faber and Faber, 1961)

Haffenden, John, *Viewpoints: Poets in Conversation* (Faber and Faber, 1981)

Heaney, Seamus, 'Out of London: Ulster's Troubles', *New Statesman*, 1 July 1966, 23–4

– 'Deep as England', *Hibernia*, 1 December 1972

– 'The Irish quest', interview with Raymond Gardner, *The Guardian*, 2 November 1974, 8

– *Stations* (Ulsterman Publications, 1975)

– interview, with Caroline Walsh, *Irish Times*, 6 December 1975, 5

– 'Unhappy and at Home', interview with Seamus Deane, *The Crane Bag*, vol. 1 no. 1 (1977), 61–7

– 'The Poet as a Christian', *The Furrow*, vol. 29 no. 10 (1978), 603–6

– 'A Raindrop on a Thorn', interview with Robert Druce, *Dutch Quarterly Review*, vol. 9 (1978), 24–37

– and Noel Connor, *Gravities: A Collection of Poems and Drawings* (Charlotte Press, 1979)

– 'In the mid-course of his life', interview with Dennis O'Driscoll, *Hibernia*, 11 October 1979, 13

– interview with James Randall, *Ploughshares*, vol. 5 no. 3 (1979), 7–22

– 'A tale of two islands: reflections on the Irish Literary Revival', in P. J. Drudy (ed.), *Irish Studies* 1 (Cambridge University Press, 1980), 1–20

– *Poems and a Memoir* (Limited Editions Club, 1982)

Select Bibliography

- interview with Frank Kinahan, *Critical Inquiry*, vol. 8 no. 3 (Spring 1982), 405–14
- *Among Schoolchildren* (John Malone Memorial Committee, 1983)
- 'Envies and Identifications: Dante and the Modern Poet', *Irish University Review*, vol. 15 no. 1 (Spring 1985), 5–19
- 'Learning from Eliot', *Agenda*, vol. 27 no. 1 (Spring 1989), 17–31
- 'The Frontier of Writing', in Jacqueline Genet and Wynne Helle-gouarc'h (eds.), *Irish Writers and Their Creative Process* (Colin Smythe, 1996), 3–16

Heffernan, James A. W., *Museum of Words: The Poetics of Ekphrasis from Homer to Ashbery* (University of Chicago Press, 1993)

Hopkins, Gerard Manley, *The Poems of Gerard Manley Hopkins*, ed. W. H. Gardner and N. H. Mackenzie (fourth edn., Oxford University Press, 1967)

Hunter, Jefferson, *Image and Word: The Interaction of Twentieth-Century Photographs and Texts* (Harvard University Press, 1987)

Jaccottet, Philippe, *Selected Poems*, selected and translated with an introduction by Derek Mahon (Penguin Books, 1988)

Jarrell, Randall, *Poetry and the Age* (1955; Faber and Faber edn., 1973)

Jones, David, *Epoch and Artist: Selected Writings* (Faber and Faber, 1959)

- *The Dying Gaul and Other Writings* (Faber and Faber, 1978)

Joyce, James, *A Portrait of the Artist as a Young Man*, ed. Seamus Deane (Penguin, 1992)

Kerrigan, John, 'Ulster Ovids', in Neil Corcoran (ed.), *The Chosen Ground: Essays on the Contemporary Poetry of Northern Ireland* (Seren, 1992), 237–69

Lloyd, David, *Anomalous States: Irish Writing and the Post-Colonial Moment* (Lilliput, 1993)

Longley, Edna, *Poetry in the Wars* (Bloodaxe, 1986)

Macafee, C. I., *A Concise Ulster Dictionary* (Oxford University Press, 1996)

McDonald, Peter, *Mistaken Identities: Poetry and Northern Ireland* (Clarendon Press, 1997)

- 'Seamus Heaney as a Critic', in Michael Kenneally (ed.), *Poetry in Contemporary Irish Literature* (Colin Smythe, 1995), 174–89

Montague, John (ed.), *The Faber Book of Irish Verse* (Faber and Faber, 1974)

Muldoon, Paul, *Knowing My Place* (Ulsterman Publications, 1971)

– *The Prince of the Quotidian* (Gallery Press, 1994)

O'Brien, Conor Cruise, 'A Slow North-east Wind', *The Listener*, 25 September 1975, 204–5

Oeser, Hans-Christian, *Transverse II: Seamus Heaney in Translation* (Irish Translators' Association, 1994)

Paulin, Tom, and Graham Martin, 'Seamus Heaney's "Broagh"', *The English Review*, vol. 2 no. 3 (1992), 28–9

Peacock, Alan, 'Mediations: Poet as Translator, Poet as Seer', in Elmer Andrews (ed.), *Seamus Heaney: A Collection of Critical Essays* (Macmillan, 1992), 233–55

Ramazani, Jahan, *Poetry of Mourning: The Modern Elegy from Hardy to Heaney* (University of Chicago Press, 1994)

Rhodes, Neil, ' "Bridegroom to the Goddess": Hughes, Heaney and the Elizabethans', in Mark Thornton Burnett and Ramona Wray (eds.), *Shakespeare and Ireland: History, Politics, Culture* (Macmillan, 1997), 152–72

Ricks, Christopher, *The Force of Poetry* (Clarendon Press, 1984)

Sacks, Peter M., *The English Elegy: Studies in the Genre from Spenser to Yeats* (Johns Hopkins University Press, 1985)

Scully, James, *Modern Poets on Modern Poetry* (Fontana, 1965)

Smith, Stan, 'The Distance Between: Seamus Heaney', in Neil Corcoran (ed.), *The Chosen Ground: Essays on the Contemporary Poetry of Northern Ireland* (Seren, 1992), 35–61

Stead, C. K., *The New Poetic: Yeats to Eliot* (Hutchinson, 1964)

Trotter, David, *The Making of the Reader: Language and Subjectivity in Modern American, English and Irish Poetry* (Macmillan, 1984)

Watt, R. J. C., 'Seamus Heaney: Voices on Helicon', *Essays in Criticism*, vol. xliv no. 3 (July 1994), 213–34

Yates, Frances, *Giordano Bruno and the Hermetic Tradition* (Routledge and Kegan Paul, 1964)

– *The Art of Memory* (Routledge and Kegan Paul, 1966)

Index

Index

Index

Index